A Commentary on
GALATIANS

UNLOCKING THE NEW TESTAMENT

A Commentary on
GALATIANS

David Pawson

Anchor Recordings

First published in ebook format 2011
Revised edition published in volume form 2012
under the title *Come with me through Galatians*.

This edition published in Great Britain in 2013 by
Anchor Recordings Ltd
72 The Street, Kennington, Ashford TN24 9HS

For more of David Pawson's teaching, including MP3s, DVDs and CDs:
www.davidpawson.com
For further information, email info@davidpawsonministry.com

Editor: Martin Manser www.martinmanser.com

www.davidpawson.org

ISBN 978-0-9575290-5-2

Printed by Createspace and
Printed in Great Britain by Imprint Digital, Exeter

Contents

This book is based on a series of talks. Originating as it does from the spoken word, its style will be found by many readers to be somewhat different from my usual written style. It is hoped that this will not detract from the substance of the biblical teaching found here.

As always, I ask the reader to compare everything I say or write with what is written in the Bible and, if at any point a conflict is found, always to rely upon the clear teaching of scripture.

David Pawson

INTRODUCTION

A significant letter

Paul's letter to the Galatians tends to divide people into two camps: those who think highly of it and those who do not. Some notable Christians in the past have been very positive about Galatians. Luther said it was the best book in the Bible. He said, "This is my epistle. I am married to it." John Bunyan, the author of *Pilgrim's Progress*, said, "I do prefer Luther's commentary on Galatians, except the Holy Bible, before all the books that I have ever seen as most fit for a wounded conscience." Clearly, Galatians had a profound effect on Bunyan. The letter has had a deep influence on Christian history, and many Christians love it.

However, some people dislike Galatians intensely. It has been called "a crucifixion epistle" and "a thorny jungle." Some say that every sentence contains a thunderbolt. Here are five reasons why people dislike it so much:

"It's too emotional"

It is a highly charged letter. It is written in white heat, perhaps on asbestos papyrus! It is full of emotion, and this makes some people uncomfortable. Many people, particularly in Britain, have tried to keep emotion out of religion, but when they read Galatians they find a man burning with anger, and this disturbs them.

"It's too personal"

Some people argue that Galatians is too personal. Certainly, Paul has put more about himself into this letter than into any other. He talks about his physical handicaps at one point, pleading with his readers on the basis of his own weakness. He mentions a public argument that he had with the apostle Peter, where he had to stand up to Peter in front of a whole congregation and tell him that he was wrong – a reminder that even in the early Church the apostles had their public differences. We are sometimes too anxious to agree rather than differ, too anxious to avoid confrontation. When truth was at stake, even Peter and Paul would face up to each other and fight for it.

"It's too intellectual"

In Galatians, Paul is using all his rabbinical background and training to argue the case he is making, and it is a very tight intellectual argument. None of the translations that I have ever read has really got to grips with the thread of the argument, so I confess that I have actually translated it myself (the translation appears at the beginning of each chapter). The argument is quite subtle and there are some very fine points in it, requiring some hard thinking. Do not let this deter you. We are to love God with all our mind. One of the most frequent comments I get after preaching is a kind of mild rebuke that says, "Well, you gave us something to think about today." It is said in a tone of "I didn't come to church to think, you know." Well, I make no apologies for stretching minds, and Paul stretches your mind too. We need to study Galatians very carefully and go through it again and again to see what Paul is saying.

"It's too spiritual"

Galatians strips off spiritual veneers and strikes at an individual's pride. If you have got any pride left, then don't read Galatians, because you will have none left by the time you have finished. It really does go to the root of the matter, beyond your mind and your heart, through to the marrow. It is the sharp, two-edged word of God that penetrates deeply.

"It's too controversial"

Above all, people have found Galatians too argumentative. The modern mood is that we do not want to argue about religion. We do not want to quarrel, but to be comfortable with each other. Galatians is not that kind of a letter. Paul argues with other Christians, not with unbelievers, and his message in the letter has in turn caused many arguments.

Arguments can be good. If Luther had not been willing to get into an argument, the Reformation would not have occurred. So argument has benefited us greatly. The reason why it is not popular today is that we fear that differences will lead to division. The two prime virtues considered today are tolerance and tact, though neither is a virtue in the Bible. Jesus was neither tolerant nor tactful.

Is this unwillingness to face our differences a good thing or a bad thing? I believe it depends on whether the issues are primary or secondary. The trouble is that we tend to get so heated over secondary issues that we are not really confronting people over primary things. Does it really matter whether we use alcoholic or non-alcoholic wine for the Lord's Supper? Yet people get so upset about this.

Take the Sabbath issue, for example. I do not believe this is an issue that Christians should be making too much of. Paul says that each should be fully persuaded in his own mind. If one wants to regard Sunday as special, that is his privilege. If another wants to regard every day as the Lord's day, that is his privilege. We do not have the right to impose Sunday on each other as believers, never mind on unbelievers.

But when we come to Galatians, we are handling some of the biggest issues of all. There are fundamental issues without which you lose the Christian gospel, so, I am afraid, fighting is involved. Many of the biggest battles that Christians have to face are inside the church, not outside it. That is painful. Who likes a family that is arguing? Whenever the devil attacks the church from the outside, the church gets stronger and bigger. His attacks are much more successful when they come from the inside, and one of the quickest ways to do that is to pervert or corrupt or erode the gospel. If he can do that, he knows that he has destroyed the church from the inside.

In Galatians we see two leading men, Peter and Paul, involved in a public confrontation on a fundamental issue. I believe that God has given to Christian men the responsibility of fighting for and protecting the doctrine of the Church, and it is a tragedy that we don't have more strong men of conviction who will fight to protect the gospel. There are many women who want to and who try to, but I believe there are not enough men who are prepared to stick their necks out and confront error when they hear it or see it.

Peter and Paul did fight it out. Peter was in the wrong and Paul was in the right, and the Bible has been honest enough to share that with us. Clearly, God wanted us to know about that confrontation.

Reading New Testament letters

It is important to read a New Testament letter all the way through, especially if it is addressing one particular issue, which is the case with Philemon and Hebrews, for example. Only then can you get the sense of what the writer is saying. You must remember that you are only hearing one side of a conversation. It is rather like being in a room when the telephone has rung and somebody else has answered the phone, and you only hear what they say. In this situation it is easy to get the wrong idea about what the person at the other end of the line has been saying, because you will have listened with preconceived notions. When you read an epistle, somehow you have to reconstruct the situation about which it was written and read between the lines. You must ask yourself, "What was happening that motivated Paul to write this letter?" You will find that this is a helpful way of studying the letters.

This is the method we are going to use to look at Galatians. We will be asking key questions such as:

Why was it written?

What questions was it answering?

What problems was it solving?

There may be only one issue being discussed, as with Philemon, or many issues, as with 1 Corinthians, but you need to ask these questions if the meaning of the letter is to become clear.

Paul the enthusiastic Jew

There is no doubt that the author of Galatians was Paul. It may have been the first letter that he ever wrote to a church.

By any standard, Paul was one of the greatest men who ever lived. He was born in Tarsus in what is today southern Turkey. Tarsus had the Roman world's third most important university, after Athens and Alexandria. He was Jewish, but was also a Roman citizen and spoke the Greek language – an ideal background for the task that God had in mind for him. God prepares us for ministry even before we are born, but he also prepares us through our experiences long before we know him. He is putting things into us that he can use later.

Paul was taught a trade, as every good Jewish boy was. His trade was tent-making. However, in Greek society, if you worked with your hands you were lower down the social scale than those who worked with their heads and were "pen-pushers" – an attitude that, sadly, we have inherited. But in the Bible jobs such as tent-making and fishing were well respected. Paul says, in one of his letters to Thessalonica, that the believers should all work with their hands, for he had given them an example to do that. So the Bible attaches dignity to manual labour. After all, the Lord Jesus himself had worked as a carpenter.

So Paul worked as a tent-maker, probably for the Roman army, and then studied at the university in Jerusalem under Professor Gamaliel. He became an ultra-orthodox, fanatical Jew – a "Hebrew of the Hebrews," a "Pharisee of the Pharisees," as he called himself. His attitude was: if you are going to keep the law, you must keep all of it. Just obeying the Ten Commandments was not enough. He does admit that he struggled with the tenth commandment, "Do not covet." (It is interesting that this is the one commandment that deals with inner motivation; the others deal with outward behaviour.) However, Paul believed that he had succeeded in keeping the whole of the law. He was blameless. There were not many Jews who could say that.

He had achieved a great deal of self-righteousness and attacked everybody who attacked Judaism, especially the Christians, who claimed that Jesus was God. Paul thought this claim was the ultimate blasphemy. He set out to destroy this new faith and watched Stephen being stoned to death. But from then on he began to be pricked in his conscience. As Stephen died, he said, "I can see Jesus on the right hand of God. Into your hands I commit my spirit." This stirred Paul to attack the new faith even more fiercely, because now he was also fighting his own conscience. He finally lost the fight when, on the Damascus road, he met Jesus.

Paul the fervent missionary

The man who wrote Galatians had become one of the most enthusiastic followers of Jesus ever, an ardent propagator of the faith he had once tried to destroy. He knew both Judaism and Christianity inside out, having switched from one to the other. During his missionary journeys he planted churches throughout the known world, constantly pioneering fresh territory. He called it "colonizing for Christ."

The readers

There were two geographical places called Galatia, and scholars expend a lot of ink in discussing which of these was the Galatia of Paul's letters. In what we now call Turkey there was a group of cities in the north called North Galatia, and there was a group of cities in the south called South Galatia. North Galatia is especially interesting to us in Britain because it was originally colonized by people from

Gaul (France), who were related to the Celtic peoples of the British Isles. However, I believe that Paul's letter was in fact written to Christians in South Galatia rather than North Galatia. South Galatia comprised a group of cities – Lystra, Derbe, Antioch and Iconium – which Paul had already visited. So it is understandable that he would write a letter like this, having himself planted the churches and entrusted them to new elders and to the Head of the church in heaven.

Alternative teaching

Unfortunately, what happened to them has happened to many new fellowships today. Other men came in and took over the work. We should beware of men who come and seek to take over, for they are often dangerous, building their empires by taking possession of fellowships that other people have planted. Often such leaders lead new churches down the wrong path, and Paul faced this with the Galatians. The people who did it were Jewish believers, who followed Paul around everywhere. They were his biggest problem. They said to the Gentiles, "Don't listen to Paul – he has only given you half the story. He has brought you to faith, yes, but he didn't bring you fully into the faith, because you need the law of Moses as well as Christ."

This focus upon the law is still with us today. I am amazed how often I go into churches in this country and see the Ten Commandments displayed on the wall. The first church in England that I became pastor of in 1954 had the Commandments up on the wall behind my head in the pulpit in chocolate-brown Gothic lettering! I decided that the first thing I was going to do was to paint it out, and so I got a pot of paint and painted all over it. There was a great outcry. Somebody complained that there was nothing to read during the sermon! They said they had to have something there, so I put a cross up on the wall instead.

Everywhere Paul went and brought the full gospel of Christ, these Jewish believers followed up and said, "Of course, he hasn't told you everything, and we have now come to give you the whole story." That is exactly how some leaders talk today when they try to take over other people's fellowships. They claim that the pastor's teaching is good, but that they have more wisdom.

Bad news
Paul has heard some very bad news about his young churches – the ones that he laboured to bring into being. His work was being undone, and two things were happening.

Additions to Paul's message
As in many modern cults, the new leaders were adding to the gospel – what we might call "the gospel plus." So many sects and cults around today add to the gospel, and they usually add another book to the Bible, such as Mary Baker Eddy's *Science and Health*, or Joseph Smith's *Book of Mormon*. Beware of anyone who insists that you need another book as well as your Bible, for it is the "gospel plus" argument again. Something is being added on, and you can only put so much luggage in a canoe before it overturns. Or to use another analogy, rot starts in the pulpit – dry rot. It is essential to be on our guard against bad teaching.

An attack on the messenger

It was not just that these teachers were adding to Paul's gospel – they were attacking the messenger too. They claimed that Paul was not preaching the full gospel, that he was not a true apostle, that his version of the gospel was second-hand and that he was not approved by the church. In undermining Paul's authority they sought to establish their own.

What was the issue?

On a first reading of the letter, you would think it is about circumcision, for this seems to be the thing that Paul is focusing on. The question arises: Was he making a mountain out of a molehill? Why get so concerned about this little thing? If people want to be circumcised, surely that is acceptable. Was he justified in making such a song and dance about this Jewish custom of circumcision?

Circumcision is a minor operation – the removal of part of the reproductive organ of the male. It is not practised on females in Judaism, though it is in certain tribes in Africa. It is still a widespread habit in the Semitic world, largely for hygienic reasons in that climate. But to the Jews it had a religious significance. It was the mark of a Jew. Of course, only males were circumcised, because in the Jewish world it is the male who inherits, and the promises pass down through the male line. Circumcision was a sign of eligibility to inherit the blessing promised to Abraham. It was even said by God to Abraham that if any Jewish male was not circumcised, he had to be thrown out of the people of God because he had broken the covenant. Part of the covenant with Abraham was that every male descendant would bear this mark.

So to a Jew circumcision is of crucial importance. There are things that mean everything to the Jew: the Passover, kosher diet, the Sabbath and circumcision. Whatever else they may do or not do – they may be liberal or non-practising Jews – those four things still apply.

It is important that we grasp Paul's argument concerning God's promise to Abraham. He argues in Galatians 3 that the promise made to Abraham was only intended for one male descendant of Abraham. The word that God used for "seed" was singular, so when God said "to Abraham and his seed" he did not mean to all his male descendants, but to one of them. Paul argues that when that one male seed came, which was Jesus, circumcision became obsolete, because now the promise had been inherited. The one to whom it was promised had received the inheritance, so there was no point in circumcising anybody now. So circumcision was a sign of inheritance, and Jesus had that sign. He was circumcised and he was the one who inherited.

Now, of course, Paul had been circumcised as a Jewish male, and it seemed strange, in the light of his argument, that he did actually circumcise Timothy, who came from Galatia. This may seem contradictory, but it was because he was going to accompany Paul in his missionary work, and Paul always went into the synagogue first and preached to Jews. Timothy would never have managed to get into the synagogue with him if he had not been circumcised, so Paul did it purely as an act of accommodation for evangelism. In the same way, C T Studd and other missionaries to China grew pigtails, in order to get alongside the people. But Paul, who had circumcised Timothy for that same reason, was now saying to the Galatians, "How dare you consider it!"

Circumcision was clearly very important, but behind it was something else.

Paul's very strong language in Galatians reminds me once again that the Bible is not a book for children – it is a book for adults. (The tragedy is that most people stop reading it when they become adults.) He says, "I just wish that those who would cut off your foreskins would go the whole hog and castrate themselves." Then they wouldn't be able to reproduce themselves. Strong language indeed!

Why is he so against circumcision?

The answer is that behind circumcision lay Judaism. Judaism can easily become a religion of works. It is a religion of saving oneself by keeping the Commandments. It is an impossible task, but so many people try it. This is the danger of putting the Ten Commandments up on a wall. It is communicating to people that you have got to live by these laws in order to get right with God. An outsider coming in is faced straightaway with a list of "You shall nots," which gives the impression that we are against everything, that we are negative, and that if you come anywhere near God he will stop you having fun.

Judaism

Christianity is rooted in Judaism, which is in turn rooted in the Old Testament. But how much of the Old Testament should come through to the New? How many of those 613 laws actually apply to us? That is one of the biggest questions you have got to face when you study the Old and New Testaments.

Let me give you an example. I do not ever tell Christians

to tithe, because it belongs to the law of Moses and is never mentioned in the New Testament with respect to Gentile believers. Jews did it, but no Gentile believer was ever told to tithe. We are, however, told to *give*.

I once listened to a young man preaching on tithing. Clearly, he had used his computer to search for the word *Tithing* and had got all the biblical references on the subject. He said there were blessings attached to tithing, and he gave them all. God says in Malachi, "Test me now in this and see if I will not open the windows of heaven and pour out a blessing on you" (Malachi 3:10). The preacher then added that there are also curses attached to tithing. He proceeded to tell us about a curse in the Old Testament, that our grandchildren and great-grandchildren would suffer if we did not bring our tithes. I looked at the faces of the congregation and could see their fear of causing their great-grandchildren to suffer. It is no wonder that the offering was pretty big the following Sunday! But I was horrified. In the New Testament giving is on an altogether different principle. The Lord loves a cheerful giver, which doesn't mean grin and bear it. You should give because you *want* to give, not because you are forced to, in case your great-grandchildren suffer. That belongs to the old covenant.

Another example is the Sabbath law. We must think about what we are doing before we apply old covenant laws to Christians, because if you apply some of them you must apply all of them, and if you apply the blessing, you must apply the curse. Now, are we prepared to do that? I am not. So Paul is saying, "If you get circumcised, that is just the camel's nose in the tent, and you will soon have the hump and all. If you go the way of circumcision for the reason these teachers are giving, then all the other 613 laws will follow."

That is why Paul is so anxious. The problem is not circumcision itself, but the way in which it opened the door to Judaism. He had tried Judaism, and when he considered the commandments he had kept (not just the ones he felt like keeping), he said he thanked God that he was delivered from it all. In the same way, if we tell people to keep the law of Moses, we are consigning them to hell, because they cannot do it.

It is important to put people under grace, rather than under law. There is a law we are under, but it is the law of Christ, not the law of Moses. That law is obsolete; it has been done away with. But one of the biggest problems in the church today is that we are giving people a mixture of the law of Christ and the law of Moses. Why do you think churches have vestments, altars, incense and priests? We don't need any of those things – they belong to the law of Moses, but they have crept back in.

Throughout the book of Acts we see a loosening of the ties between Judaism and Christianity. Stephen, the first martyr of the church, was stoned for this particular issue. When Philip baptized the Ethiopian eunuch, he took it a little further, and then Peter was sent by God to Cornelius, a Gentile, at Caesarea. Soon the Jewish believers in Jerusalem were very, very suspicious about this new faith being taken to Gentiles. It didn't seem Jewish enough for them, and so finally Paul went up to Jerusalem to challenge the very heart of the church that was sending out these anti-missionaries who were saying it was not enough just to believe – you had to be circumcised as well. The real issue was not circumcision, but whether Gentiles had to become Jews when they became Christians.

Salvation

The real issue was salvation itself – the whole question of how salvation is obtained. People offer several different answers to this question, and all are assumed to be Christian.

Works alone

Most religions of the world are about salvation by works. You must pray, you must fast, you must give alms and so on, and then, at the end of it all, you will get right with God. You save yourself by your own efforts. Do-it-yourself religion appeals to people because it leaves them with their pride, for they feel that they have achieved salvation. It is self-righteousness, and that is something that God hates. He would rather deal with sin than self-righteousness. Jesus just couldn't get on with self-righteous people. He was a friend of sinners, but with the self-righteous, such as the Pharisees, he couldn't get on at all.

Works plus faith

The belief about the need for works is very common. I used to be an OD (Other Denominations) chaplain in the Royal Air Force. When a new bunch of men arrived, the Anglican chaplain would walk off with 70 per cent of them, then the Roman Catholic chaplain would take everybody with an Irish accent, and I would be left with the Baptists, Methodists, Salvationists, Buddhists, Hindus, Muslims, agnostics and atheists. It was fascinating to be a chaplain to atheists.

When the men were seated before me, I would ask how many were Methodists, how many were Baptists and so on, and each group would put their hands up. In the same tone of voice I would ask how many were Christians. Dead silence! Occasionally a lad would put his hand up and smile, but usually they would all look around to see if anybody else had put their hand up.

"Come on," I would say. "You told me how many of you are Methodists and Baptists and so on. Well, how many of you are Christians?"

"But what do you mean by 'Christian,' Padre?" they would reply.

"What do you think I mean?" I would ask.

"Someone who keeps the Ten Commandments," would be the usual response.

"OK, I will accept that a Christian is someone who keeps the Ten Commandments. How many Christians are there here?"

There would be real uncertainty, and then somebody would say, "But Padre, you can't keep them all!"

"Well, how many do you have to keep to be a Christian?"

"Six out of ten."

"OK, I accept that a Christian is somebody who keeps six of the Ten Commandments. So how many Christians are there here?"

It led to a tremendous discussion of what a Christian is. You see, works plus faith implies that we keep as many commandments as we can, and then we ask God to forgive us for the commandments that we are not able to keep. That is the most common understanding of Christianity in our country. We might call it "do-gooding Christianity."

Faith plus works

Some believe that you start with faith and then you go on to works. After you have believed in Jesus, you have got to keep the law. This is what the Judaizers of Paul's time were saying.

Faith alone

Paul was saying to the Galatians, "Having started in the Spirit, are you going to continue in the flesh? The law belongs to the flesh – it is your effort, it is not the Spirit doing it in you." Paul was fighting for faith alone, faith from first to last, as he often puts it – faith from beginning to end. He said, "I am not ashamed of the gospel. It is the power of God that saves everyone who goes on believing," faith from first to last.

In other words, we cannot compromise on this – you must go on believing. That is the heart of it. You do not believe at the beginning and then work for it. There is a big difference between telling people they need to go on believing and telling them they need to keep the law now. What Paul is fighting for is Christian freedom. To introduce the law at any stage is to put people under a curse, because the only pass-mark that Jesus will accept for the law is 100 per cent. You either keep all the law or you have broken the law.

The same thing is true even with human laws. If I drove through a red light, was stopped by a policeman and I said to him, "But, Officer, I stopped at every red light on the way here," he would reply, "I don't care if you stopped at every red light – you have broken the law!" That is what God says. The law is not just a string of individual pearls – it is a necklace, it is a complete thing. If you break it at any point, the pearls all fall on the ground. You have broken the law, so it doesn't matter whether you have broken one commandment or all of them.

Imagine that three men are stranded on a rock when the tide is coming in, and there is a three-metre channel of water between the rock and the beach. If the first man manages to jump a third of the way, he will drown. If the second man is a better jumper and manages to jump two-thirds of the way, he will still drown. The third man only misses by six inches, but he is lost too.

God's word says, "Cursed be he who does not continue in all these laws, to go on doing them." This is the curse you are under if you try to keep the commandments to get to heaven under your own steam. But the gospel has a different way of righteousness altogether.

The obvious question that arises is, Why did God give the Ten Commandments? Why did he give the law of Moses at all? The answer is in Galatians.

First, God gave the law *to restrain sin*. It helps to make life livable. At least some will be kept and others attempted.

Secondly, God gave the law *to reveal sin*. It is by the straight edge of the law that we realize how crooked we are. In other words, it is only the law that tells you that you are a sinner. You don't find out how wrong you have been until you have studied the law of God. The law was introduced to prepare us for Christ by showing us that we couldn't keep that law. That is why preaching the Ten Commandments can bring a person to conviction of sin, because they know there is no way they can keep them – especially in the way that Jesus reinterpreted them.

A key theme

Liberty is a key theme in Galatians. The longing for freedom is universal, but the question is, freedom from what? The message of the Bible is that Christ came to set us free, to turn slaves into sons and heirs. So just as the Jews were liberated from Egypt, we are freed through Christ from bondage to sin. But freedom is so easily lost. As J P Curran put it, "The condition upon which God hath given liberty is eternal vigilance." The problem is not just getting freedom but *keeping* it. Liberty can be lost.

The picture below depicts the whole of Galatians. It is a very simple picture, but I need to explain it. It shows three key concepts in Galatians: legalism, liberty and licence. Legalism is clearly an enemy of liberty, but what people don't always realize is that licence is too. Galatians 1–2 talks about our liberty in Christ under the favour of the Father and in the sunshine of his love. We are in the freedom of the Spirit, and the foundation is faith in the Son. So Father, Son and Spirit are giving us the freedom of standing on top of the mountain.

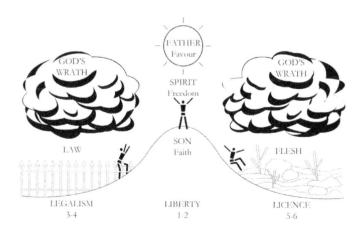

The picture shows that there are two ways of losing that freedom. One is to slip back into the law, depicted as a cage. We are trapped in it – we try to climb out, but we can't. If you get back under the law, you are under the wrath of God again, because you can't keep the law. But there is another way to lose your liberty, and that is to slip down into the swamp of the flesh. That also is bondage, but it is bondage to your own desires, and you are under the wrath of God again. You have lost your freedom.

Striding Edge on Helvellyn in the Lake District is a perfect illustration, because it is a very narrow path right along a ridge. On either side of it are two huge hollows called corries. In the last ice age they were hollowed out by two great balls of ice revolving, thus leaving this very sharp edge. The Matterhorn in Switzerland was the result of three balls of ice revolving, leaving a three-pointed peak.

It is a delicate edge that we walk in the liberty of the Spirit. It is so easy to slip one way or the other. I would say that the biggest danger to Christians in their liberty is legalism. This may surprise you. Licence is pretty obvious, but when churches start making extra rules and regulations, you get too easily into legalism, and that kills liberty. A legalistic fellowship can be easily identified – everybody has pursed lips, and there is a kind of set expression on people's faces. Trying to keep the law makes people tough and hard. Legalism makes the Christian faith a matter of rules rather than relationships. People think they are Christians because they are keeping the rules – don't smoke, don't gamble, don't drink, don't do this, don't do that – but the relationship with God has gone.

The liberty of the Spirit is not doing what you *want*, and

it is not doing what others *tell* you, *it is letting the Spirit guide you.* As Paul says in Galatians, it is not the freedom to sin, it is the freedom *not* to sin. That is real freedom. No unbeliever has that freedom – that is the freedom that God wants for us. But it is so easy to try to stop people sinning by putting them under law, and that is how some churches operate. They try to protect their members from doing this and that, without realizing that legalism is just as much an enemy of liberty as licence is.

That is the whole argument of Galatians. Chapters 1 and 2 talk about this liberty, chapters 3 and 4 talk about the legalism that can spoil it, and chapters 5 and 6 talk about the opposite danger, licence. So Paul is actually fighting on two fronts, and that is the real problem. To keep liberty and avoid both legalism and licence is quite a delicate operation.

Let us look at legalism, licence and liberty in more detail.

Legalism

Circumcision is the first link in the chain for those Galatians. It would be the beginning of legalism. It is not part of the gospel, and they would also have to keep all the rest of the law.

Some say, "But won't people take advantage when you tell them they are not under law? Won't they become lawless? If you don't give rules, won't people go and indulge themselves?"

When I was a Methodist minister there was a book half an inch thick called *The Constitutional Practice and Discipline of the Methodist Church*. It is now three and a quarter inches thick! Many loose-leaf pages are added every year. So, if rules and regulations could bring revival, the Methodists would leave us standing! But it doesn't happen that way. How easy it is to try to regulate and give rules for this, that and the other, and think that somehow our organization will bring life. It doesn't. Liberty brings life, and God set us free to be free. We must watch legalism like a hawk. If you slip into it, you invariably become hard and hypocritical, because you dare not tell other people if you are breaking the law.

Licence

There is a real danger in what Paul calls "the works of the flesh." Beware of them. They are another form of slavery. They are like a swamp which it is easy to slide into and very hard to get out of. The works of the flesh are listed by Paul in Galatians. Some are obvious, such as promiscuity and occultism. But there are also some more subtle ones, such as quarrelling, rivalry, jealousy, envy and prejudice.

"Now what happens," asks Paul, "when somebody slips into this?" There are a lot of banana skins on the Christian road. He says that if someone has slipped into sin, pick them up quickly, get them back into the fellowship and get them healed. But if someone deliberately and wilfully goes on wallowing in sin, he solemnly says that they will not inherit the kingdom. They may say, "I'm all right – I've got my ticket to heaven," but Paul says, "You're not all right – you won't inherit the kingdom." Now that is a very serious warning.

You can slip into legalism, you can slip into licence, and you need to be pulled quickly out of both. But if you deliberately and wilfully choose to live either in the cage or in the swamp, then you won't inherit the kingdom.

Liberty

Liberty is the freedom not to sin. Isn't it a lovely freedom? You are free now, in Christ, not to sin. You don't need to say yes to it. As Paul puts it in his letter to Titus, "We have been given the grace to say no." Isn't that beautiful? Let us look at what happens by referring to the picture again. Imagine a path at the top of the mountain, stretching away beyond the person on the path. We need to walk in the Spirit, along the striding edge – avoiding the pitfalls of licence and legalism. As you walk in the Spirit, something beautiful happens. Fruit grows in your life – the fruit of the Spirit. There is only one fruit of the Spirit, with nine flavours, whereas there are many works of the flesh.

There is a fruit in the Mediterranean called the *Mysterio Deliciosus*. If you take one bite, it tastes like an orange, and if you take another bite, it tastes like a lemon! It has got many different flavours in it. In the Christian you will find all the flavours of the fruit of the Spirit. You can see some of the flavours in unbelievers, don't you? Some unbelievers have joy, others have peace, but you will never see all nine together except in Christ and in those who are filled with the Spirit and walking in the Spirit. The nine flavours relate you to God, other people and yourself. Three of those flavours – love, joy and peace – bring you into perfect harmony with God. The next three – patience, kindness and goodness – bring you into harmony with other people. Then faithfulness, meekness and self-control bring you into a good relationship with yourself. What a lovely fruit it is!

The fruit of the Spirit is limited, of course, without the gifts of the Spirit, just as the gifts are inadequate without the fruit. If I went to hospital to visit a sick person, I could show them all the fruit of the Spirit – I could show them love by visiting them, joy by cheering them up, peace by calming them down, patience by listening to all the details of their operation, kindness by giving them a bunch of grapes, goodness by offering to look after their children, faithfulness by visiting them every day, meekness by leaving when the nurse tells me to, and self-control by not eating the grapes! I have demonstrated all the fruit of the Spirit in that visit, but I haven't healed them, because that is the gift of the Spirit. We need both the gifts and the fruit. We must never set these against each other.

Paul says that as you walk in the Spirit, the fruit grows. He uses the word *walk* here in two different ways, using two different Greek words. Your English translation probably has "walk" both times. In chapter 5, verses 16 and 25 he says, "walk in the Spirit". In the Greek, verse 16, "walk" is peripatetic walking – what the Australians call "walkabout". It means to go for a walk by yourself. But in verse 25 the word "walk" really means "march in the Spirit, in step with others." So there are two kinds of walking in the Spirit. There is walking in the Spirit when we are by ourselves, and there is walking in step with the rest of our Christian brothers and sisters, and we need both. True liberty is walking along that height in step with your brothers and sisters, walking in the Spirit together.

So this is the message of Paul's letter to the Galatians. It is one of the most relevant letters, although not one of the most comfortable, and I would share the opinion of Dr Merrill Tenney who called this letter the Magna Carta of Christian liberty. I really believe that is a wonderful title for it. Many people are standing for other kinds of freedom, good or bad, but the freedom we stand for is the freedom not to sin, the freedom to keep out of that cage called legalism and out of that swamp called licence, and the freedom to keep up there on the heights, enjoying the blessing of God's favour.

Legalism is still with us

Legalism is all over the place. People are trying to get to heaven by their own works. Or, having started in faith, they are going back to works, which is tragic.

The late Dr W E Sangster went to visit a dying woman in hospital. He said to her, "Are you ready to meet God? What will you say when you meet him?"

She held up her worn hands and said, "I am a widow. I have brought up five children, so I have no time for church or the Bible or anything religious. But I have done my best for my children, and when I see God I will just hold up these hands, and he will look at them and he will understand."

Now, what would you have said to a woman like that? Well, Dr Sangster just said to her, "You are too late, my dear, you are too late."

She said, "What do you mean?"

He replied, "Well, there is somebody who has got in front of you, and he is holding up his hands in front of God, and God has eyes for no other."

She asked, "What do you mean?"

He told her, "Don't put your trust in your hands – put your trust in his hands."

Legalism is still with us and it is rife. The average Briton thinks that being a Christian is being kind to their grandmother and their cat. They think, "I am as good a Christian as anybody who goes to church." When they say that, they are trapped in legalism. We need to tell them that only 100 per cent is good enough for heaven, and if they go there as they are, they will ruin it for everybody else!

We find legalism in churches too. They are so prone to add their own rules to their membership. There are four steps up to the front door of a church: repent, believe, be baptized and receive the Holy Spirit. There should be no additional steps to the front door. The staircase is inside. There are a lot of steps to climb up inside, as we find in 1 Peter and 2 Peter, but there are only four steps outside. But unfortunately churches tend to say, "You have got to be confirmed by a bishop," or, "You have got to be this or that," or, "You have got to be committed," or, "You have got to accept the leadership," and so on. Those steps all belong inside the church, not outside.

Licence is still with us

There are still those who think that adultery by an unbeliever will take them to hell, but adultery by a believer is acceptable. There are still those who believe that certain kinds of sin in believers are excused, that you may lose a bit of blessing or reward, but you cannot lose your ticket to heaven. Galatians deals with that very firmly and says that you will not inherit the kingdom of God if you deliberately go back to sin.

Liberty is still with us

We must stay and walk with others along the narrow path, the wind of the Spirit blowing in our faces and the blessing of God's grace upon us. We are free not to sin and free to be bold, if we will only walk in the Spirit. Galatians is one of the most powerful letters you will ever read.

Above all, read the letter and heed its message.

1

Galatians 1:1-10

AN EXPLOSIVE BEGINNING

A personal letter

The bondage of legalism

Two versions of Christianity

Paul's address (1:1-5)
Paul's message: the gospel
Grace and peace

Paul's admonition (1:6-9)
The storm bursts: "I am shattered"
From grace to grind
To hell with those with the wrong "gospel"

Paul's appeal (1:10)

Two conclusions

From: Paul, the Lord's emissary (not appointed by any group of human officials or even by divine guidance through a human agent, but personally sent by Jesus the Messiah and God his Father, who brought him back to life after his burial). All the Christian brothers here have read and approved my letter.

To: The gathering of God's people in the province of Galatia.

May you all enjoy the undeserved generosity and total harmony of God our Father and his Son Jesus, our Lord and Messiah. Our bad deeds cost him his life, but he gave it willingly to rescue us from the immorality of our contemporary scene. The plan of escape was decided by our Father-God, who should never cease to get the credit. So be it.

I am shattered to discover that already all of you are deserting this God who picked you out for his special offer of Christ's free gift and swinging to a different gospel, which is not even "good news." You are being muddled by certain people who aim to turn the gospel upside down. But listen – if we ourselves, or even a supernatural messenger from the other world, should bring a message to you that contradicts what I have delivered, may he be damned! We told you this before, but I must repeat it – if anyone at all preaches a gospel that varies from the one you first accepted, then to hell with him!

Now does that sound like someone who is trying to get on the right side of men, or of God? Am I being accused of seeking popularity? If I still wanted to please people, the last thing I would be is one of Christ's workers.

(Author's translation)

A personal letter

We need to remember that here we are studying a letter: a letter, not a written book. It is not a sermon that has been written down and reproduced in print but it is a letter. There are two things about letters that we need to remember.

First, the letter is one of the most revealing forms of human literature because it is so personal. The person writing a letter will reveal their mind and heart much more readily than if you asked them to write a sermon or to write a book or essay. They will give less thought and more feeling to a letter. That is why some of the great biographies of the men and women who've lived in the past are entitled *The Life and Letters of So and So* and the letters give you a real feel of the person.

Secondly, a letter is one half of a conversation. It is either a reply to a situation or a reply to another letter. Here, we've only got one half of the dialogue and so with a letter you not only have to read the lines of the actual letter, you must read between the lines of the letter to ask why it is being written: what is the situation that has demanded or prompted this Epistle?

In the case of Paul's letter to the Galatians, both these features of a letter appear very clearly. The feeling is very strong. Sometimes it's open-hearted, sometimes it's harsh; sometimes there are passages which you can't understand unless you read closely between the lines and ask what had upset Paul so deeply? What was moving him to have these passionate feelings about the people to whom he was writing?

"If Paul had not fought the battle in the Galatian controversy and won it, you and I would not be Christians today."

The bondage of legalism

As noted in the introduction, in the four churches of south Galatia, which Paul himself had started and were his spiritual children or family, there were some false teachers coming from Jerusalem. They were Jewish Christians like Paul but they did something that Paul never did. When Paul met a Gentile, he made the Gentile into a Gentile Christian, even though he was himself a Jewish Christian. But these preachers who had come into his churches, his family, his spiritual children, were trying to turn every Christian into a Jew. They believed that they were doing right. They believed that since Jesus was a Jew, every Christian ought to be also and so they were saying to these Gentile Christians, "It is not enough to believe in Jesus, you also need to become a Jew like Jesus." So they taught first of all that the Gentile Christians needed to be circumcised in their body. This was comparatively minor in itself but highly significant at a deeper level. In accepting circumcision they were accepting Judaism. In accepting Judaism they were plunging into the horror we call legalism, which is trying to get to heaven by keeping the commandments, which is a miserable, frustrating business. In accepting legalism they were coming back into bondage and losing their freedom because there is no slavery like being a slave to the laws of God. It is sheer bondage and Christ came to set us free from that kind of slavish fear of failing to keep the commandments of God.

Two versions of Christianity

This is relevant for us today. If Paul had not fought the battle in the Galatian controversy and won it, you and I would not be Christians today, for Christianity would have been limited to Jews and those willing to become Jews. It would never have spread to have become a worldwide religion to the Gentiles and you and I would not be here today if Paul had not written this letter and fought for the freedom of the Christian believer in Christ. And so that's the significance of Paul's letter to the Galatians. That's the other side of the dialogue. That's the other half of the conversation and now we can understand the letter and why Paul treats this matter so seriously. This is also why in chapters 1 to 2 Paul talks about himself so much: because these other preachers realized full well that what they taught was contrary to what he was teaching. They realized that the two versions of Christianity were incompatible. It was in fact, if you like, the first denominational difference in the Christian church and could have led to two different denominations called the "Jewish Christian" denomination and the "Gentile Christian" denomination and Paul did not say both are right. He said one is right and one is wrong. This was a rather unpopular line to take in those days but it was still right. Truth is what matters and it does not matter what our denomination thinks. Every denomination must be tested by the truth to see whether the truth lies there or not. That's what matters and so Paul tackled the issue head on, fighting with determination to win this battle for the sake of Christian freedom. Now his opponents, his rival preachers, had stooped to the lowest form of attack. Because they did not like his message, they attacked his person. Attacking the person who brought the truth is one way to try and steer people away from truth. If you cannot contradict the message, then discredit the messenger: people will then forget what he said. They were saying that Paul was not a proper apostle, he wasn't even appointed. He wasn't one of the original 12. He had got everything second hand. He managed to gain approval from some human beings; some Christians somewhere said he could go and be a missionary. He doesn't have a divine appointment: he's not a true apostle. What about his motives? Why does he not teach circumcision? Because he wants to be popular – that's why he makes Christianity easier. They were talking like this and discrediting his appointment, his motives and everything about him. They attacked Paul in the hope that people who thought less about Paul the messenger would begin to think less about his message and open the way for their own version of Christianity. Now this is exactly what happens today as well. Any preacher who preaches the freedom of Christ will be accused by other professing Christians of being worldly and making things too easy for people. Anybody who comes with the truth will be discredited in their person because that's what the devil is trying to do – thinking that if the person can be discredited, what he has said will also fall to the ground. So from the very first phrase in the letter, Paul is defending himself as God's messenger in order that his message may continue to be accepted by his spiritual children in south Galatia.

Paul's address (1:1-5)

I have divided the first ten verses of the letter into three
sections: his address (every letter has an address on the
envelope), his admonition and his appeal. And all the way
through these three sections he is defending himself as God's
messenger and the message, the gospel he preached. Now
it is normal today to use an envelope for a letter and so we
write a letter, fold it up, pop it in the envelope and then write
the address and the name of the recipient on the outside. If
it's an airmail letter we turn it over and write our own name
and address on the reverse. Now in those days when you'd
finished writing a letter on a long piece of parchment like
this, you rolled it up and you gave it to the postman to carry.
The address was written on the first few inches of the scroll
so that he could just unroll the top bit, or if he wanted to know
a bit more he could go further down. He was supposed only
to unroll that first part and read off the address. So every
letter of those days began with the address: from …, to …,
and then the postman could take it, or the series of postmen
needed would take it, from place to place. So Paul writes
the address but you know he can't even write the address
without adding something that will begin to tell them what
he's after. He could have just said "Paul, from Paul, to the
churches of Galatia," but that is not Paul. Paul is going to
start right away. He's going to write on the outside of the
envelope so they get the message even before they open the
letter. So he says "from Paul, the Lord's emissary". I thought
a lot about that word *emissary*. The word the apostle used
isn't used today in any context: *representative* or *delegate*
weren't quite strong enough. An *emissary* is a word we
still use. It means basically "sent": it's basically the same

39

word as *missile, mission, missionary* and *emissary*. It comes
from the Latin *mittere*, "to send." It is someone who has
been sent; an emissary today is someone who has been sent
to negotiate terms of peace. That seems to me to convey
something very important here. The Lord's emissary: "I've
been sent by the Lord to bring the terms of peace." That's
what an apostle was. It was the apostle who brought the
terms of peace with God, the Lord's emissary had been sent.
Now straightaway Paul, knowing what they're saying about
him, says, "I want to tell you about my appointment." What
is my authority for coming as the Lord's emissary with his
terms of peace? I was not appointed by godly men as some
Christian officials are. A group of godly men will meet
together and discuss the most suitable person and then say to
that person you are to fulfil this office. That's how it is done
in this church. Godly men, that's one level of appointment.
Another level of appointment is where God himself appoints
a person but still uses a human agent. A word of prophecy
is given and Paul was appointed by Antioch at a later stage
and set apart for his ministry in that way. "While they were
worshipping the Lord... the Holy Spirit said, 'Set apart for
me Barnabas and Saul'" (Acts 13:2, NIV). Paul claims that
his basic appointment was not like that; he went back to the
beginning when he met Jesus on the Damascus road and
Jesus said, "I am going to send you as a light to the Gentiles."
His basic authority was not from a group of godly men or
even from God through men, even though that was sent as
confirmation of his call. No, his basic authority was that he
was sent personally, directly by Jesus and God. You can't
have a better appointment than that! That's the highest level
of appointment and even if the other levels confirm it, as

they did in Paul's case, he lays it down fundamentally that from the very beginning, his appointment was from Jesus and from God his Father.

It's interesting that throughout this letter for Paul, Jesus and the Father are one. They are always described in the same terms and on the same level. So there's no question about whether his appointment is of divine origin or not. Are people saying that I was appointed by some Christians I managed to persuade to back me? No; I obtained it from Jesus and his Father. I got it from Jesus the Messiah. That's one in the eye for those Jewish Christians, for the word *Christ* to us has become a name. It was originally a title. It's the Greek for the Hebrew *Messiah*. From Jesus the Messiah I got my appointment. No Jew could argue with an appointment like that. That is the messenger. He then presents his credentials straightaway and he adds a rather subtle side comment. The other Christians here, where I'm writing, accept my authority. They have read this letter and they approve it. They're behind me. This letter is not simply from me; it's not just my own personal opinion. All the Christians here agree with what I'm going to say to you. They accept my authority: "All the Christian brothers here have read and approved my letter". I'm not just self-appointed, self-authorized. There are many Christians here who accept my authority, so this letter comes from all of us. It's as if they wrote it with me.

Paul's message: the gospel
He not only manages to say a lot about the messenger and his credentials but he also writes a lot about his message. On the outside of the envelope he's slipped in the entire

gospel. Have you noticed that? He says four things: (1) he talks about the evil of the world; (2) he talks about the will of God, to save us; (3) he talks about the redemption of Christ, his death and resurrection; and (4) he talks about the joy of the believer, the grace and peace that come to him. That's the whole gospel and it's all there in the address. Next time you write a letter, see if you can put the whole gospel on the front of the envelope! Paul did and so he says, "First of all we are all trapped... in an evil world." We're trapped. I used the word *scene* rather than *world* because the Greek word means something that's passing away, not something solid that will stay, but something that's on the move and is going to pass away; our modern word *scene* gets this across well. It is an evil scene in which we live; you just need to look around to see that, but it's a scene that's passing. The danger is that if you don't escape from it, you will pass away with it. "The world and its desires pass away" (1 John 2:17, NIV) and you're going to pass away with it unless you manage to get out of it. Our greatest need is to get out. We are in bondage; we're slaves; we're chained to our contemporary scene and God wants to rescue us from the immorality of this scene and let us escape into freedom. That's the gospel and it is the will of God that this should happen. He decided this and he desired this. Let us never fall into the trap of thinking that it was Jesus who wanted to rescue us and managed to sort of rescue us against God's wrath. God's wrath is against sin but not against sinners. It is only against sinners if they cling to their sin so long that he's got to get rid of both together, but it is God who planned it all through Jesus Christ. It is God who desired it, God who decided it, God who planned it. Have you seen any of the *Colditz* series? Its appeal lies in planning the escape, getting away into freedom. Its theme touches the human heart very deeply and this is the theme of the gospel: how to get out of the immorality of our contemporary scene, how to be free from it, how to escape from something that's passing and not ourselves pass away with it …and it was God who planned it all. How did he achieve it? Through the death and resurrection of Christ. Christ gave himself for our sins and God, who brought him back to life from the dead. It's all there in the address. It was through the death and the resurrection of Jesus that the escape was accomplished. That's what set us free.

Grace and peace

What is the result of this in your life? Grace and peace. These words need a little expansion, which I've taken the liberty of doing. What is grace? It is the undeserved generosity of God: that you could have gifts from God that you couldn't earn, that you couldn't buy, that you couldn't deserve, that you couldn't merit, that you could never be worthy of grace. It is because God planned your escape and sent Jesus to die and rise that you can have the free gift of life: grace, God's undeserved generosity, and the result of receiving grace – do you know what that is? Peace, but what kind of peace? I've paraphrased it as "total harmony." It includes at least four things: physical health, mental poise, social ease and spiritual calm. It is all-encompassing, and it is God's will that you should have such total harmony. One day you will have just that. Grace is the cause, and peace is the effect: God's undeserved generosity is the source and total harmony is the result. If there is one thing that people need today more than anything else it is total harmony and if there's one way to find it, it is the undeserved generosity of God. So there's the gospel in a nutshell. That's the message he preaches. In the address on the outside of the envelope he's presented his credentials as messenger and his message. Now we can begin to read the letter.

Paul's admonition (1:6-9)

We come now to his admonition. There was a pattern for letters in the ancient world and it's followed by most of the letters in the New Testament but not this one. The pattern in every normal letter is this: You write the name and address of the person who's sending it, the name of the person to whom it's going, then you give the greeting, which he's done, and then you always say something nice. You always say something complimentary or you say something by way of thanksgiving. Especially if you're going to say something critical or not so nice, then you must say something nice first and you'll find that in almost every other Epistle, Paul says, "I thank God for this…, I commend you for that… I'm so glad to hear about the other," but not here. This is the only letter that Paul doesn't do it. Even in his first letter to the Corinthians, when he's going to criticize them for getting drunk at the Lord's table, for being divided into cliques and groups throughout the fellowship, for being doctrinally in error about the resurrection, for condoning incest in the membership, in spite of all of that, he starts his letter: I thank God that "you do not lack any spiritual gift" (1 Corinthians 1:7, NIV). He even found something at Corinth to commend but in Galatians he does not find even a word. Why not? Because Paul is in such a state that he can't even think of anything good in their fellowship for the moment, and so he goes straight in.

The storm bursts: "I am shattered"

The storm has been rumbling on the envelope but now there's a thunderbolt and the storm bursts on these churches. Can you imagine what they felt like when it was read? He says, "I am shattered"... that's the word I used to try and get across the strength of the word he uses. To say "I am amazed" or "I am astonished" isn't strong enough. It's "I am flabbergasted; I am dumbfounded, I am stupefied. I am shattered to discover that already you're leaving this gospel and leaving this God." Now Paul had the great pain of knowing Christians who had backslidden. The New Testament church knew everything we know and here are four whole churches that probably within months, certainly just a year or two, but probably within months of being started and coming to Christ and they are already leaving the gospel. Paul is shattered. So soon are they leaving the gospel; unfortunately I have known the same thing, and so have you. People who have come to Christ and who accepted the gospel and who were set free but so soon afterwards they turn away. Fortunately it doesn't happen in the majority of cases, but it does happen in some and it happened here. Paul said you are turning away from what I gave you to something else that is far worse – indeed it's turning from the good to the bad. It's not just worse; you're turning to the opposite. It's not even a gospel you're turning to, for the word *gospel* means "good news." They are turning from good news to bad news. What fool would do that?

From grace to grind

Not far from where I am speaking is a top-security prison. I want you to imagine what we would feel if we went there one night and saw a man trying to break in. You see him crouching in the shadows, cutting the barbed wire on the outside of the prison and you say, "What are you doing?" "I'm trying to get back in." "What on earth for?" When I went to Berlin before the wall came down and looked at Checkpoint Charlie, I saw wreaths, little crosses, photographs and flowers all along the wall but only on its western side. There were none on the eastern side. One or two people have actually defected the other way and climbed over that way and we find it very difficult to understand why, because that wall was not put up as a barrier from this side, it was put up as a barrier from the other side. Why climb back into prison? Paul says, "I'm shattered at what you're doing. You're going from good news to bad news. You're going from," if I could paraphrase it, "from grace to grind. You're turning from God back to yourself. Why?" And yet people do this and I'll tell you why right at the end of this study. But Paul is shattered. I mean why do it so soon?

"To turn the gospel upside down, all you have to do is make your faith rest on your good works and it's a completely different gospel."

It's as if a man fell in love, got married and went off with his wife on their honeymoon and then after only two weeks of honeymoon that man went off with another woman. Why?

Why does somebody do this? Well, clearly somebody else must have been pushing them pretty hard and Paul says, "I'm not blaming you entirely. I know that you're being muddled, agitated, upset, confused by people who are actually turning the gospel upside down." Can you do that? Yes. I will tell you how, and you'll understand the message of Galatians very quickly. Good works are part of Christian living, but good works must rest on our faith.

To turn the gospel upside down, all you have to do is make your faith rest on your good works and it's a completely different gospel. It's not even a gospel at all; it's bad news. It's good news that your good works can rest on your faith and that God will accept you on the basis of faith, your trust in Jesus Christ, and then you can build your good works on your faith. You can express your faith as it labours through love but you've been accepted on the basis of faith and your faith is sure but if you turn it upside down, what happens? If your faith rests on your good works, how will you ever know whether you've got enough good works and what will you do with your bad deeds? You've got no assurance, no faith and you've made your good works the basis and you're saying God accepts you on the basis of your goodness – you'll never be accepted on that basis. Why? Because the right way up is the real basis: Christ himself. You build your faith on Christ and your good works on your faith. But if you follow the other way, you are building on yourself because your good works are what you do. Your faith then rests ultimately on what you do and you accept your own righteousness as the basis. The true gospel is a free gift but your own way is hard work; in fact you'll never work hard enough to achieve it. Now that's the issue. Whether you depend on Christ and believe in him and let your faith work out in goodness, or whether you build your goodness on your own efforts and hope to believe that you've got enough one day. That is the heart of the issue and Paul says there are certain people who've turned the gospel upside down and they're muddling you.

To hell with those with the wrong "gospel"

You're confused. I know someone else is attacking you and I am going to attack them. And he does attack them. He uses language which almost every version has been scared to translate literally for fear of offending the nice susceptibilities of modern congregations, but Paul says "damn him." I've translated it as Paul wrote it so that you can get the feeling. If I just read out in a nice posh accent, "Let him be anathema," you have no feeling about that. Paul literally says "to hell with him." Why? Paul, aren't you just using language that's a bit strong for a Christian? "No," says Paul, "because if that man goes on preaching that message, then he's going to drag thousands down to hell and he had better go there first before he takes others with him." Paul does not have any feeling of personal venom towards these other preachers. He says, "If I come and preach this message, if I turn the gospel upside down or even supposing an angel were to visit your church and you realized it was an angel from heaven, then status is of absolutely no importance. It's the message that matters."

Now here is a principle which cannot be underlined too much but I want to emphasize it. It is not the messenger who validates the message but the message which validates the messenger. In simple terms I do not care whether a man is a professor of theology, a denominational leader, an archbishop or even the Pope himself; that is unimportant. What matters is what he preaches. It is that which gives the person authority in the church of Christ. It does not matter what status, qualifications or anything else a man may have, it is the message that is all important and so Paul says, "If an angel steps into your assembly and he doesn't preach this gospel of free grace, then curse him. Send him to hell. He's most poisonous." You can have a drink that is good and it just needs a small amount of poison to be added and the whole thing becomes dangerous. Do you see that? Paul here is saying something very serious. He's saying something that Jesus said: "It's better for a man who does this to have a millstone, better to have a millstone round his neck and be thrown into the sea, better to be murdered physically than to kill people spiritually and send them to hell by preaching" (see Matthew 18:6). Now that's serious, and I wish the danger were over in the first century. Paul fought and won this battle then but I have to tell you seriously today that this battle is continuing. It still has to be fought and won and we still need to keep Paul's words in mind that you serve the church of Christ best by damning those who turn the gospel upside down.

Paul's appeal (1:10)

Now having said these very serious words, Paul makes a personal appeal in verse 10. Do you honestly think from what I've just said that I'm the kind of person who's seeking to be popular? I'll tell you one thing, the person who goes around pronouncing curses on other people is not likely to top the popularity polls... and neither then nor now will anybody be popular who differs from other professing Christians on the grounds of the gospel. This is not the way to be popular. It's not the way to please people but Paul makes it quite clear. Look at what I've just said, does that sound like someone who's trying to please people or someone who wants to please God? He says you can't do both. You cannot do both. There'd been a time when Paul as a Jew and as a Pharisee had wanted a good reputation. That's why the Pharisees did most of the things he did. When he gave a subscription, he blew his own trumpet and got his name on the subscription list. When he said his prayers, he didn't do it privately but he went to the street corner where people could see. He was doing it to gain a reputation with people. Paul says, "If I was still doing that," – notice the little word *still*, "if I was still someone who liked that kind of thing, then I certainly wouldn't be a worker for Christ." It's not the way to popularity. Jesus himself said so to you, that's a curse. "Woe to you when all men speak well of you" (Luke 6:26, NIV). That is something wrong, something desperately wrong. So Paul says, "I made my choice years ago. I used to try and please people, I used to consider what they thought of me, I used to be worried about my reputation and popularity but not now. I've realized that it was either Christ or my reputation and I've made my choice. I'm one of Christ's workers now and I have no motive in me to try and please others." Do you know if you read through this letter you'll realize that Paul never went out of his way to tailor his gospel to other people? He never went out of his way to please people. He never went out of his way to bring down the demands of God just for the sake of popularity. Rather he sought to lift people to the freedom of Christ. So he appeals to his language and says does that sound like the language of someone trying to please people? He also appeals to his life as a worker for Christ. Does my life look like someone who's concerned about reputation?

Two conclusions

This letter opened with an explosion; what can we conclude from these opening verses? Two things. First, the majority of people in this so-called Christian country believe the false gospel that Paul condemns in these verses. Yes, it's the majority. You ask the average man or woman in the street on what they base their faith for the future, on what grounds they hope to have a better life after this one, that is if there is a life after this one. If you ask them, then nine times out of ten, they will say something like this. "Well I've never done anybody any harm and I've tried to help my neighbours and I've tried to live a good life." Is that not true? That is the false gospel. It is a damnable gospel and I ask the sad question, where did they get it from in a so-called Christian country? Where on earth did they get that idea from? And the answer's very clear, they got it from church. They got it from Sunday School and they got it from religious knowledge lessons in day school. That is the tragedy. That's where they got it from, from this false gospel that a Christian is someone who's trying to be good. The sad thing is that they got it from those who profess to be Christians. Paul had to fight for the true gospel in the first century and we've got to fight for it even more so in our own century. There is only one gospel. I don't care what label there is outside a church and I'm not a denominational person, but I do care with all my heart what gospel is preached inside. I rejoice that under most labels you can hear the gospel but under most labels you can also hear the false gospel and the people of this country got it from us. They picked up the idea from us that they had to try and keep the commandments and try and be good. We didn't make it clear. Let's repent of that and let's pray for the church.

Secondly, we must ask why were the people so glad to accept it when it was bad news? Why were the Galatians falling for it when it's not even good news? Why were they prepared to accept bad news, a gospel which was no gospel? Because the false gospel allows you to keep your pride; it's as simple as that. If I can save myself by doing good, then I can be proud of it. That is why Paul as a Pharisee had tried to keep the law to get to heaven by his own efforts and he was proud of it. But the gospel of free grace says you're a sinner and you've got to come on your knees and say, "God be merciful to me, a sinner" and human pride doesn't like that.

In Luke 18:9-14, Jesus told a story of two men who went to the temple, one of whom was obviously of some standing in the community. He stood at the front and he said, "Lord, I'm glad I'm not like other people and I give a lot of money", and all the rest of it. Sounds familiar, doesn't it? He said, "Look at that poor chap at the back of the church, I'm glad I'm not like him." But that poor man at the back of the church said, "God, be merciful to me, a sinner." Jesus said it was the man at the back that got right with God that morning and went home justified. That's the gospel and we don't like it. Our pride says, "No, I can do good myself; I'll make it under my own efforts." George Bernard Shaw said, "Forgiveness is a beggar's refuge, I'll pay my own debts, thank you" and he did. The gospel of free grace humbles

a man. It says you'll never save yourself. God needs to
save you and he planned it. He sent Jesus Christ who gave
himself for your sins and he brought him back to life from
the dead so that you could be rescued from the immorality
of our contemporary scene and given the grace of God that
would bring total harmony into your life. That's freedom
and may anybody who preaches any gospel other than that
go to hell where he belongs.

2

Galatians 1:11 – 2:14

THE SOURCE OF
THE GOSPEL

The "gospel of Jesus" and the
"gospel of Paul" (1:11-12)
False teachers
Two simple facts

Contradiction (1:13-14)
He was violently against Christianity
He was forcefully in favour of Judaism

Contemplation (1:15-17)

Conversation (1:18-24)

Consultation (2:1-10)

Confrontation (2:11-14)

My dear brothers, I must make it quite clear to all of you that the Good News I tell is no human tale. I neither heard others relating it, nor did anyone pass it on to me. I got it direct from Jesus the Messiah, as the events of my life prove.

You must have heard about my earlier career in the Jewish religion. In my extreme fanaticism I was hunting down God's company of Christian believers and playing havoc with them. As an ardent supporter of Judaism, I forged ahead of many fellow-nationals of my own age, because I was so enthusiastic about the established customs of my ancestors.

Then God took a hand. He had marked me out before I left my mother's womb and generously chose me of all people to show others what his Son was really like, especially those I used to call foreigners. At once I decided not to seek anybody's advice. So I did not go to Jerusalem to consult those who were already working as emissaries of the Lord. Instead I went off alone into the Arabian desert to think it all over; and from there I returned straight to Damascus.

It was not until three years later that I finally got to know Peter in Jerusalem. Even then I only stayed two weeks and saw none of the other apostles, though I did meet James, our divine leader's own brother (as God watches what I write, I'm not making any of this up). After that I went to various places in Syria and Cilicia, so the Christian gatherings in Judea would still not have recognized my face. All they knew of me was hearsay – that their bitter enemy was now spreading the very beliefs he had tried so hard to wreck – and they thanked God for the transformation.

Another fourteen years passed before I paid another visit to Jerusalem. This time Barnabas and Titus went with me. It was God who prompted me to go and have a private discussion with the reputed leaders of the Jewish Christians. I intended to check with them the gospel I had been spreading among other nations, lest all my efforts were being wasted. I took Titus as a kind of test case, for he was a Greek Christian. But they never once insisted that he go through the initiation rite of being circumcised. In fact, the question would never have arisen but for some interlopers who had no right to be in the meeting at all. They sneaked in to spy on the freedom we enjoy in our relationship with Christ; they were looking for some way of getting us back under the control of their system. But not for one minute did we give way to their demands, or you would have lost what is truly good news.

As far as the apparent leaders were concerned (their exact position doesn't bother me, for God pays no attention to status; I mean those who were obviously looked up to by the others), they added nothing whatever to the teaching I had outlined. On the contrary, they could see that I was as qualified to take the good news to uncircumcised people as Peter had been to the circumcised. For the same God who was working so effectively through Peter's outreach to the Jews was obviously doing the same through mine to the Gentiles. James, John and Cephas (Peter was using his Hebrew name) seemed to be the three mainstays and when they realized how much God was blessing my work, they shook hands with Barnabas and myself as a token of full partnership, on the understanding that they would concentrate on the Jews and we on the non-Jews. The only plea they made was that we should not forget to send financial aid to poor Jewish Christians and I was more than ready to go on with this.

But a serious crisis arose when Peter returned our visit and came to Antioch. I had to oppose him to his face, for he was clearly in the wrong. When he first came, he was quite happy to eat with the Gentile converts. Then some colleagues of James arrived and Peter was afraid of what they might think, so he began to have his meals separately. The other Jewish believers pretended to agree with him and even my friend Barnabas was swept into the hypocrisy. When I saw that such behaviour could not be squared with the reality of the gospel, I said to Peter in front of everybody, 'You are a Jewish national, but you dropped your scruples and adopted the lifestyle of Gentile foreigners. Why all of a sudden are you now trying to make them accept Jewish customs?'

(Author's translation)

The "gospel of Jesus" and the "gospel of Paul" (1:11-12)
For 2,000 years people have been criticizing Paul for spoiling Christianity. And they have tried to drive a wedge in public opinion between Jesus on the one hand and the "lovely simple gospel" telling us how to live, and Paul on the other with his complicated theological system, his letters, many of them hard to understand. Lord Beaverbrook was one of those who tried to drive this wedge. He was the owner, as you may remember, of the *Daily Express*, and he wrote a book on the life of Christ. He called it *The Divine Propagandist*. That said more about Lord Beaverbrook I think than about the Lord Jesus. Nevertheless that is what he said in that book. He said that Paul was responsible for changing the simple gospel. And that by following St Paul, the church had misunderstood and misrepresented Jesus Christ for 2,000

years. He said about Paul that he was incapable by nature of understanding the spirit of the master, and that he damaged Christianity and left his imprint by wiping out many of the traces of the footprints of his master. I always find it interesting that those who want to divide Paul from Jesus in this way invariably call Jesus Master rather than Lord. They talk about the Master. Maybe because Paul loved to talk about the Lord Jesus and you can tell someone who loves the teachings of Paul because they talk about the Lord as he did. But those who tend to use the phrase "The Master" tend to go back as it were to the four Gospels, Matthew, Mark, Luke and John, and say that's where they get their Christianity. Such people say they have no time for Paul. Even scholars have been known to talk about the "Pauline gospel," as if this was somehow different from the one Jesus taught.

It may well be that the first time you read Paul's letters you found them much tougher going than the Gospels Matthew, Mark and Luke wrote for you. And maybe you even were tempted to think that there was a difference. Maybe you have thought that as a Christian you are to believe everything Jesus taught, but that you're perfectly free to pick and choose among Paul's teachings. You may think you can say, "Oh well, that was only Paul, or that's what Paul said, but I follow Jesus Christ." I've heard all this many times before. Indeed, someone who didn't know that we preach the whole New Testament said to me, "Don't you get sick of St Paul and wouldn't you love to have some 'gospel' preaching?" Well, there it is – I don't think that person realized that we preach through the four Gospels as much as we preach through Paul's letters. But don't you find there's a popular division in people's minds between Jesus and Paul as if

Paul somehow took a beautiful flower and by analysing and dissecting it, pulling the petals to pieces has destroyed something fragrant? Do you know they were saying that 2,000 years ago? Poor Paul has suffered from this from the very beginning. And the people who followed him around, these false teachers that we are considering while we study his letter to the Galatians, were saying, "You know Paul has given you a garbled account of Christianity: he has twisted and distorted it. Some of what he says is right, but some of what he says is way off beam. But we have come to teach you the whole truth and to put it all right." Poor Paul suffered from this. The only difference was this: today people say that Paul distorted the gospel by making it up himself. In those days they were saying that Paul had distorted it because he'd got it second hand. He didn't get it first hand; he wasn't one of the original 12 apostles, he didn't walk with Jesus, he wasn't there at the cross, he wasn't there at the resurrection, he got it all second hand and when you pick a thing second hand it's liable to have changed. They thought he'd garbled the "true" gospel.

The modern version of saying this is what I heard recently when I was speaking to a group. One of the questions that somebody asked was an old chestnut. As soon as I quoted part of the New Testament they didn't like, or that didn't fit in with their ideas, they immediately said, "Ah, but how do we know we've got an accurate copy? How do we know it's come down to us accurately?" I notice they only say it with a text they don't like. Where they like a text and it fits in with what they believe, then they are perfectly happy to quote it against me. But if it's something they don't like then they ask, "How do we know it's accurate? How do we know it's come down to us? How do we know it's been passed down in all its fullness? How do we know that's what Jesus really said?" This is how the human mind evades the challenge of the gospel.

They were saying this about Paul: "How do you know, Paul? You got it second hand, so you don't really know you've got it accurately. But we have come to give you the true version of Christianity." Now what was Paul's answer to that? It's very simple. He said, "I didn't get it second hand. What I told you was no human tale. I didn't hear somebody else preaching it. Nor did somebody else preach it to me. I got it direct from Jesus the Messiah, and you can't get it more direct than that." If that claim of Paul is true, then nobody dare ever say that I can't accept what Paul says, I only accept what Jesus says. You can never divide these two people if what Paul claims here is right. But if his claim is false, then not one of his epistles ought to be in the New Testament. If he did not get the gospel directly from the Lord, then he is not an apostle; he ought not to be writing the New Testament, and we can safely dismiss everything he said. Now that's the choice. And here we face Paul's claim to have got the gospel not from any human source but a divine source. That is not true of any one of us. Each of us got the gospel second hand. Everyone of us. You either got it from the church, or you got it from the Bible, or from a Christian from the Church, or a Christian quoting the Bible. But you got it second hand. Paul got it directly from Jesus Christ and that's what made him an apostle. He had the gospel passed onto him. Some of you had it passed on to you or you overheard someone else telling it. But none of us can say we got it through no human channel whatever and directly from the Lord. We didn't.

You got it second hand. But Paul says he got it first hand. And that's his answer to this criticism that he garbled it. If he got it straight from the Lord, you can't say he changed it in the process of being passed on. You can't say that people forgot bits of it or added bits of it. If you get it from first-hand sources, then it's accurate. Now Paul has to prove this claim because his message is at stake.

False teachers
Let me remind you what the false teachers were trying to say. There were following Paul round to the very churches he'd built and saying he missed one thing out. "He told you," they said, "to believe in Jesus but he missed out something important. That is not enough. Faith only takes you part of the way. You need to believe and also do something else." The thing they said Paul had missed out was an initiation rite, a branding of the flesh called circumcision. They were saying Jesus was a Jew. Jesus was circumcised. All the 12 apostles were circumcised. "If you have not been circumcised," they said, "you do not belong fully to the people of God."

Now that sounds a simple little thing in itself. Why make all this fuss about a little operation that's over in a few minutes? And if they said that's the right way, well why not submit to it? But Paul says this: If you submit to this one little operation, you are actually changing the whole of the Christian religion. You're changing it from a religion of believing to a religion of achieving. You're changing it from a religion that puts its trust in what the Lord does for you to a religion that puts its trust in what you do for the Lord. And that's a totally different religion, because circumcision will lead you on to the law and the law will lead you into bondage, and you'll go right back to the religion of trying hard to be good enough to get to heaven. And that's a miserable religion, because the harder you try, the further heaven seems, and the further off you are. You don't know how bad you are till you've tried to be good. This is an important point: you will never know how bad you are until you really try to be good.

It's only those who try to be good who discover they're bad. It's those who don't try who think they're good. But you try; try as hard as John Wesley tried as a student in Oxford, rising at four o'clock in the morning to begin his religious exercises, visiting the poor and the sick, doing everything he could to be good enough for God. You try as hard as Martin Luther tried, whipping himself, whipping his own body in his cell in the monastery to try and be good enough for God and whip out the badness in him. You try as hard as some of the saints have tried and then you'll discover how bad you are. It is those who want to serve him best that are most conscious of wrong within.

"Now which religion are you going to have?" asks Paul. "The religion of circumcision and the law, in which you try and try and try but you never get there – and it's sheer bondage and it's 'You shall not' all the time or the religion of Jesus that says 'Put your trust wholly in me. It's what I'm going to do in you that matters, not what you do for me.'"

It's a totally different religion. And so in saying that there was just one little thing that Paul missed out – circumcision – they were actually turning the gospel upside down. And Paul said that is a damnable heresy, but I'm sad to say it's the religion of 90% of the people living in this country: "Do your best." But Paul came with a gospel of freedom, of liberty and of truth that sets people free and says now it's the Lord who will get you to heaven, not you. It's the Lord you can trust, not yourself. And when you trust in him, you discover how good he is. Not how bad you are, but how good he is. That's the difference. And his goodness replaces your attempt at goodness. And when you stand before God, you don't present your own good deeds and say, "Lord, I did this, that and the other," you stand before God and present the good deeds of Jesus that he accomplished in your place, and you offer his goodness, and that gets you in.

Two simple facts

Paul says, "I'm going to prove to you by the events of my life that on the one hand I didn't get my gospel from anybody else, from the apostles, that I didn't get it from them. But on the other hand I'm going to prove to you that they agreed with my gospel. I got it independently but it was not different. I got it direct but it was the same as the one they preached." And so he selects five periods of his life to show these two simple facts. I didn't get it from man, but men agreed with what I preached.

"When your sins have been forgiven, you are free to talk to others about them without fear or bitterness."

Contradiction (1:13-14)

The first period Paul chooses is from the sad period of his pre-Christian life. We now have a lot of personal autobiography. Do you know one of the best arguments you can ever use is personal testimony? If you really want to convince people of something, then tell them what has happened to you. This first period of Paul's life was a period of contradiction, in which he was totally opposed to Christianity. Now he couldn't possibly have picked it up from Christians when he was totally opposed to them could he? You don't go learning from people and then throwing them into jail. And in this period of contradiction, there were two things in his life:

He was violently against Christianity

He was violently against Christians and he violently supported his own religion, Judaism. He looks back with sadness now but it's a mark of forgiveness that you can talk about your past sins. If you can't talk about your sins, they're not yet forgiven. Think that one through. When your sins have been forgiven, you are free to talk to others about them without fear or bitterness. And Paul could say this is what he was like. You can only do that after you've received forgiveness, because until you've been forgiven you don't want to let people know what you're like. But when you're forgiven, you can tell them quite frankly this is what you used to be like. And Paul says, "Let me tell you what I used to be like. I'm sure you've heard how fanatical I was about my religion. I used to hunt down Christians. I used to go as a missionary against Christians." He even left his own country to go and fight Christians. It's one thing to go and be a missionary for Christ, but imagine going to be a missionary against Christ! But first of all, he was a missionary against Christ. He left his own country and he hunted them down, men, women and children who met in fear. Everywhere Christians fled; they met in secret. They asked, "Is Paul on his way here?" They feared they'd be thrown into prison. Paul got a name as the Christians' worst enemy. He was a missionary against Christ. And Christians were separated from their loved ones, thrown into prison and lost their lives, because of this man. He said that's how he used to be. "Do you think I picked up the gospel second hand? Far from it. I couldn't stand them."

He was forcefully in favour of Judaism
Paul added, "As far as my own religion is concerned, you must have heard I got ahead of most of my contemporaries; I really was a Jewish Jew, a Pharisee of the Pharisees, a Hebrew of the Hebrews. [See Philippians 3.] I got further on in my religion than most of the people of my own age because I loved the traditions of my ancestors – I loved to keep their customs. I was full on in my religion. In other words, I had no intention whatsoever of becoming a Christian, or of preaching the gospel – absolutely none. That was my life and it was a life of stark contradiction."

This brings me to something important to all of us. All along Paul knew one thing was true – that Christianity and Judaism as religions will never mix. He realized that Judaism was the cradle of Christianity but could easily become its grave. Now let me express that differently to make it clear. Our religion, the Christian religion was born within the cradle of Judaism. We use the Jewish scriptures. All the apostles were Jews. Jesus was a Jew. Our future is bound up with the people of Israel. But Judaism as a religion will never mix with Christianity, and Paul realized he'd got to be one or the other. If he was a Jew, he would be against Christianity, and if he is a Christian, then he would be against Judaism. You can never mix the two. And that is why it is so hard for God's chosen people to accept Christ. They have to leave their Judaism to do so. And it really is very tough to do so. You're leaving Judaism to follow a Jewish Messiah. That's the problem. And Paul knew that they were utterly incompatible, a contradiction. That's why he tried to stamp out Christianity, because if Christians were right, then he was wrong. And he didn't want that. And it's been so ever since; there has always been this tension between Judaism and Christianity. You simply cannot avoid it because it's there. They are two different religions trying to get to heaven by totally different ways. That's the first event in his life and Paul says, "How do you imagine I picked up the gospel from people I was throwing into prison and when I was such a fanatical Jew?"

Contemplation (1:15-17)

The second period of his life was one of contemplation. Paul believes in predestination. The reason he believed it was the reason that I believed it, namely that it was God who made me a Christian. That's what makes Christians believe in predestination. It's not a theory; it's not a philosophy; it's a fact in their lives. Then God stepped in. I didn't take the first step towards God; he was hunting me down. That's true of me in my own simple way, and it's also true of you if you're a Christian. Looking back now over your life, would you say that you chose God or that God chose you? The glory of it is that even though at the time you think you decided for Christ, you look back and you say, "Oh Christ, thank you that you wanted me, that you marked me out and set me apart." It is a fact that Paul had no intention whatever of becoming a Christian, and much less a missionary for Christ. Then God took over. And do you know that God had been watching Paul before any human being had seen him? God had had his eye on Paul even before his own mother had seen him; God watches us while we're in our mother's womb. He notices us when he's knitting us together in our mother's womb. And he'd watched Paul develop in his mother's womb and said, "That's the man I want. That's the man I'm going to have." And he waited many years until this man had spent all his hatred on Christians and then God met Paul on the road to Damascus, on his way to kill some more Christians and he said, "Paul, you're going to become my missionary. You're going to be a missionary for Christ, not against him. And you're to go to the foreigners, not to the Jews. You're to take me to the world." Paul replied, "Me of all people? Me?" He chose Paul, the greatest enemy of all.

But that's how God works. I went and spoke at a youth club recently to about 30 young people. When I came back home, my wife asked me how I had got on and I replied, "Most of them couldn't care that much. It was like speaking to a brick wall, but there were two who were terribly cross with me. They were really angry – a boy and a girl. The girl was so cross there were tears in her eyes; she was arguing so heartily. I think there's hope for those two." The Lord had his hand on those two and I baptized both of them within the following year. None of the others that I spoke to that night were interested.

It seems as if God said to Paul, "You're fighting me, are you? Well, at least you're interested! At least you've got energy and you've got purpose. Right, you're my man!" Sunday School teachers sometimes find this. The worst child in the Sunday School may later turn out to be the greatest Christian. There's a little comfort for those of you who have struggled with a really naughty child. But isn't it true? And God says, "That's the man I want – Paul." And God took over and he stepped into his life. Paul says, "Do you think that was anything to do with me or anybody else? I didn't even have a missionary trying to talk to me. I never had an apostle come and preach the gospel to me. God just stepped into my life. And because it was clear that God wanted to deal with me in a special way, I didn't even go and consult anyone else. I didn't go and talk it over with the apostles. I didn't even stay in Damascus. I went off into the desert, alone, to think it all over." He'd done a mental somersault, experienced a revolution. He had been totally opposed to Christ and now he was faced with the fact that Christ was right and he was wrong. What a moment! That's enough to turn a man insane. Except that it turned him sane! And he went out into the desert to try and think it all through. And he went there for just under three years, by himself. Those of you who want to get off into full-time Christian service by the end of next week at the latest, just you remember, Paul went off for three years to think it over. That's why he could keep it up for forty years and more later. He went off to prepare, to think it through.

As somebody has pointed out, all the other apostles had had three years with Jesus, so Paul went and did the same. He got alone. And the Lord told him many things in the desert.

Do you know the Lord even told him about Communion, the Lord's Supper then? He wasn't even told about that by anyone else, because in 1 Corinthians 11, he said, "I received from the Lord what I passed on to you, on the night he was betrayed he took bread and broke it" (see 11:23-24). How did he know that had happened on the last night of Jesus' life? Jesus told him; nobody else did: "I received from the Lord." The Lord told him all the gospel, all the Christian gospel, all that he was to believe and everything he was to preach. Paul says that's how he got it. And then he came preaching the gospel in Damascus. "I went to no theological seminary. I sat as a pupil under no apostle. I got it from the Lord in the desert. That's my gospel. And you tell me I've garbled it, got it second hand, that I've muddled it because it was passed onto me badly! Then you're blaming Jesus for passing it on badly. I got it from him." So he came back to Damascus.

Conversation (1:18-24)

The third period, after three years of contemplation by himself, he had a conversation with Peter; "I finally went up to meet him. But I only stayed a fortnight, so I didn't do a theological course even then. I didn't get my degree in Jerusalem. I just went up to say hello to Peter. And I didn't even meet any of the other apostles, I met only James, the Lord's brother. I was there only briefly, for two weeks. So I still didn't go to learn anything from them. You know, this may sound a bit incredible, but as God is my witness, I'm not making it up, this is how I got my gospel. It does sound incredible, doesn't it, that a man could go off by himself into the desert without a Bible, a missionary or a teacher, and come back with the whole of Christianity. I admit it sounds incredible. But I'm not making it up. I swear before God – he is watching what I write. He's my witness. I got it this way: I had a chat with Peter when I went up to see him."

Now that settles one question, doesn't it? The question where Paul got his gospel from. If he's right in what he claims, and as God is his witness, he's not making it up, then you do not dare question what Paul has said and say that's not Christianity. He got it from the Lord.

Consultation (2:1-10)

The next question is: does the gospel Paul preached agree with what the other apostles were preaching? Was it the same gospel or was it different? And so Paul picks out two more events in his life. He says, "I went on preaching this gospel for another 14 years. I preached all over the place. Everywhere I went, people came after me from Jerusalem and said I hadn't preached the true gospel. What was I to do about this? I know, I'll go up to Jerusalem and we'll sort it out." He'd been a missionary for 14 years before he did this, but God told him – prompted him – to go. God said, "Paul, go to Jerusalem and have it out with them. Go and see whether what you preach is the same as they preach." And Paul said, "Yes, Lord, I'll go – and now I'll take Barnabas with me. He's a Jew, but he's a man with a big heart and a big mind and he was big enough to see that Gentiles were now believers. And I'll also take Titus, a Greek Christian, who's never been circumcised, and see if they let him in." It was all somewhat contrived, but it was nevertheless a very wise deputation. They selected three marvellous people to go, and those three were going to confront Peter, James and John and the other leaders, and have a consultation about it. And off they set.

I want you to note that these three – Paul, Barnabas and Titus – went from Antioch to Jerusalem, to meet Peter, James and John. What was significant about Antioch? Just this: it was in Antioch that for the first time people realized that Christianity was a new religion. It was there that for the first time it got its label. Up till then, Christians had been regarded as eccentric Jews, a minority that felt the Messiah had come over against the majority who felt he hadn't. But in Antioch, so many Gentiles believed that they realized Christianity was not a Jewish sect and they were called "Christians" for the very first time (Acts 11:26). It is this that marked out Christianity as a new religion. Even though we use a Jewish Bible, even though I speak about a Jewish Messiah, we are not eccentric Jews. We are a different religion: we are Christians. Paul took Barnabas, a Jewish Christian, and Titus, a Gentile Christian, and said, "Come on, God has told me we are going to have a showdown at Jerusalem. We're going to have this out." And they went up to Jerusalem. They had a private meeting with the reputed leaders of the fellowship. Unfortunately some interlopers got into the meeting, false brothers who shouldn't have been there at all. They were clearly those people who'd followed Paul around and spoiled his ministry. They got into the meeting and said, "Titus has not been circumcised." Paul responded by saying that he and the others wouldn't yield an inch to those people. Paul, Barnabas and Titus had come to meet the leaders of the church, and the leaders of the church welcomed Titus without any qualification. Praise God for that moment, when the Jewish Christians were big enough to see that God was bigger than their little ideas.

There was complete harmony between the three and the three and Peter, James and John were so thrilled with what God was doing that they said, "Paul, let's shake hands on it. God is blessing you. Do you know in the last analysis that is what matters, God is blessing that ministry. That's the important thing. God is honouring it. You look after the Gentiles, and we'll look after the Jews, but we're partners in the gospel. We're not going to divide. You're preaching the same gospel as we are." They added nothing to what Paul had outlined. And you and I must never add anything to the gospel. Take the tricky subject of Sunday observance. It's one of those issues where we've been tempted to add something to the gospel and bring people back into bondage as people remember the traditions of their fathers; "This is the way we've always done it in this church and this is the way we're always going to do it." That can lead to a fanaticism that divides Christians from one another. Praise God when we see that customs don't matter. The gospel is what we're agreed on, nothing more, nothing less. And if we're agreed on the gospel, we can shake hands with a person and say, "Even if God has called you to work in a different way, in a different sphere, may God bless you, we belong to each other. We're partners. Let's shake on it." And so this consultation made it quite clear that even though Paul got his gospel independently, it was the same one that the Lord Jesus gave Peter, James and John. That's proof that God was in it. And I will tell you this, that you can go up and down this land to churches of different denominations, with different labels, and hear ministers who have never met each other, and never been trained by the same people, and you can hear the same gospel. Isn't that marvellous? There are others where you will hear a different gospel. To me the greatest proof of the unity of God to our land is not for churches with the same label outside with a uniformity from Land's End to John o'Groats, but the fact that you could go into any church anywhere in this country and hear the same gospel. And if they worship the same Lord and listen to the same apostles they preach the same gospel. What a unity that would be! So Paul says he got it separately, but it was still the same as theirs.

Confrontation (2:11-14)

Now comes the final event in his life. It is a rather sad and difficult one. In the last few verses of this section, Paul relates an event which clinches his argument that his gospel is the right one. It must have been a painful event for him to recall and relate. It was the time when the two greatest apostles of Jesus – Peter and Paul – had an argument. Their names have gone down as two great people in the Christian gospel. Their names have been linked even in folklore and in proverbs: we talk about robbing Peter to pay Paul. It goes back to this very thing. Peter and Paul, the two great pillars, the two great founders of Christianity, under Christ. And one day they had an argument, and Paul relates that argument to show that he even had to correct Peter's gospel. What a claim to make! This is how it happened. It's very simple. Dear old Peter reverted to type as we all do from time to time and as even Paul did on occasion. Peter at heart was a coward. It was only the Holy Spirit who gave him boldness. At heart, Peter was afraid of people and that's why he'd once denied his Lord – a servant girl had made Peter scared by asking him if he belonged to Jesus and he denied that he did. Peter had the weakness that he was scared of what people thought. When Peter came down to Antioch, he was perfectly happy. God had dealt with Peter in the matter of Cornelius, and God had shown Peter that Gentiles were just as much part of his people as Jews, and Peter came down to Antioch and he was perfectly happy to sit down and eat food that was not kosher, that hadn't come from a proper butcher; he was perfectly happy to eat without washing his hands and eat Gentile food in Gentile ways, because he was a brother with them.

Then some other visitors came from Jerusalem and he got scared of what they would think, and the tragedy is he denied his Lord again. And when they came, he said, "I'm afraid I think I ought to have my meals separately." And so within the one fellowship, with one Lord, you had two Lord's tables. Because the Communion service was taken at an ordinary meal, they literally had separated at the Communion table: they broke bread separately. They acknowledged one Lord Jesus Christ, but they couldn't sit down and eat together.

"Peter was a coward. He was afraid of what people would think: he lost the courage of his convictions. Before we blame Peter, let's admit we have done the same thing. We have been in situations when we have known what was right, but we have just been scared of what people would say or think and we have not done what we've known to be right."

It was Peter's cowardliness that did it. He was afraid of what people would think: he lost the courage of his convictions. Before we blame Peter, let's freely admit that you and I have done exactly the same thing. There have been situations when we have known what was right, but we have just been scared of what people would say or think and we have not done what we have known to be right. This is what happened to Peter here. But Paul saw that having achieved a unity of the gospel, if Peter went on doing this, then there would for the first time be two denominations in Christianity. This was the first point at which two denominations could have started. They would have been called "the Peterites" and "the Paulites." And so Paul, with great courage, said that he had rebuked Simon Peter, the first pastor of the church, to his face. He said, "Peter, what you are doing is not true to the gospel. It doesn't line up with it. You were perfectly prepared to eat with Gentiles when you came, so this is not your true conviction. You're doing it out of pretence; you're doing it out of fear; I rebuke you, Peter. You're saying to these Gentile brothers, you'll have to get circumcised before you can come and eat with us. Eating together is a token of friendship and fellowship." We know from other Christian bodies, what devilish things follow when people refuse to eat with others. And Peter was doing this. "Peter, how dare you! Don't you remember that we Jews had to believe in Jesus to get right with God?"

And so Paul, having started this passage by speaking of the source of his gospel, not human but divine, finishes by speaking of the substance of his gospel, not achieving, but believing. We know we could never make it through life if God told us to do what we could. We thank God that Jesus has done what he did. We need not come in cringing fear to God lest we have failed to meet his standard, but we can come to him in simple faith, trusting him to lead us in the paths of righteousness, for his name's sake.

3

Galatians 2:15-21

TRUTH MATTERS MORE THAN UNITY

Truth matters more than unity
Peter's hypocrisy

Christianity became a different religion
Paul's words to Peter

Paul and Peter:
our Jewish failure with the law (2:15-17)
The evidence of experience
A statement of Scripture
The limitation of logic

Paul: "my" Christian experience (2:18-21)
I, through the law, died to the law
I died with Christ
Christ lives in me
Trusting Jesus Christ to live in me

Concluding thoughts

We were born within God's chosen people and not among the lawless outsiders of other nations. Yet we know perfectly well that a man cannot be innocent in God's sight by trying to obey the commandments but only by trusting Jesus Christ to take away his sins. So even we Jews had to get right with God by relying on the work of Jesus the Messiah rather than on our own attempts to live up to God's standards. Our sacred writings freely admit that "judged by God's laws, no man living could ever be acquitted" (Psalm 143:2). But suppose our quest to be right with God through Christ does find us living outside the Jewish law. Does that make Christ an anarchist, deliberately encouraging lawlessness? Never!

What would really make me a lawbreaker would be to erect again the whole legal system I demolished. I discovered long ago that trying to keep God's laws was a deadly business. The failure killed my ego – but that gave me the very break I needed to live as God wanted me to. For when I realized that Jesus died on the cross for me, the person I used to be died as well. I know I'm still around, but it's not really me; it's Christ living his life in me. So the real life I'm now living in this mortal body springs from continual trust in God's Son, who loved me so much he sacrificed his life for me. Whatever anyone else does, I'm not going to be the one to make God's generosity redundant. For if I could get to heaven by keeping the commandments then Christ's death is utterly meaningless.

(Author's translation)

During the first 30 years of Christianity the two great outstanding leaders were Peter and Paul. Peter and Paul were the greatest in those early years and the book of the Acts of the Apostles is divided between them. The first twelve chapters tell us about Peter's ministry which was primarily among Jewish believers, and then the next half of the book tells us about Paul's ministry which was primarily to the Gentiles. These two men were the two greatest missionaries and preachers of the gospel. But one day they had an argument and it was a public disagreement. It was a very embarrassing experience.

It's an incident that we might never had known about unless Paul, many years after it happened, had written it all down in God's word. This means God wanted us to know about the disagreement that came between Peter and Paul and the open confrontation. From this little incident we learn one profound truth and it's this: that truth matters more than unity.

Truth matters more than unity

That is a lesson that we need to have written in golden letters in the sky in these days. If truth is at stake, then even Peter and Paul must be seen to be publicly at variance with each other. What was the issue in this disagreement between Peter and Paul in front of everybody, facing each other in opposition? At first sight it looked a trivial matter, as many disagreements do. It was not trivial, however. It was "simply" which table Peter had his breakfast at and you'd have thought that was a matter of his personal choice. If he wanted to have his meals with certain people then why was Paul to argue about that? But behind this simple matter lay a whole issue.

Why was Peter choosing a certain table to have his

meals? Because he'd been born and bred a Jew and Jews were rightly very particular about their eating habits. They wanted kosher food. They even went so far as to be careful that they did not use a table, dishes or cups that might have been used by those who did not regard their kosher laws as important. So no Jew would sit down and eat a meal that was not kosher. I remember the evening that we had as a church when we invited as many Jews as we knew to come and spend an evening with us. We had a lovely, happy evening; our ladies laid on one of their usual magnificent spreads on the table in the lounge. I remember our Jewish friends coming in and looking at the table and I saw them cast their eyes along it. I saw the relief that came when they realized we'd put on a kosher meal for them. It was there: you could see it straightaway, as soon as they saw the food.

Peter had been brought up with this kind of hesitation. He had scruples about what he ate and whom he ate with. It took Jesus Christ to break that tradition of centuries. It took many years after Peter became a Christian before he really learned. It took a direct vision from God before Peter would go into the house of a Gentile and sit down and eat. You remember it was in the house of Cornelius that Peter first broke all his lifetime's scruples and went into that house – you can read it in Acts chapters 10 and 11. Years later, Peter was at Antioch where most of the believers were not of Jewish background but Gentile and he was quite happy to sit down and eat with them until some of his old friends arrived, and then he stopped doing it. In fact, he let them think that he hadn't broken any kosher food laws since he'd been there and he ate very carefully in a corner of the room away from the others. Then Paul said, "Peter, how dare you do that?"

And with one word Paul stripped away all the veneer and he gave the show away to Peter's friends that he'd actually been eating with the Gentiles when they hadn't been there. He said, "There you are, you were born a Jew, you dropped your scruples, you ate with the Gentiles; you adopted their lifestyle. Why, all of a sudden, have you changed?"

"Christianity was becoming a different religion from Judaism. This is the tension through the early chapters of Acts. Paul realized this: Christianity and Judaism will never mix. They are two different religions and you can't put them together."

Peter's hypocrisy

Paul knew perfectly well why Peter had suddenly changed: because his friends had arrived. But Paul highlighted it and stripped away Peter's hypocrisy – that's what Paul calls it – stripped away his pretence and said, "Peter, why did you change?" Now, why do that publicly and why embarrass Peter like that? Why didn't he take him quietly to one side and say, "Look, Peter, what you are doing is creating a bad impression. You just put it right." Why did he say publicly in front of everybody, "Peter!"? I'll tell you why: because there was a huge issue at stake. The gospel hung on this incident. It was at Antioch that for the first time you had a church that was largely made up of non-Jews and it was at Antioch that they first thought of the name that now distinguishes our religion from others. It was at Antioch that they were first called Christians: *Christ-ians* (Acts 11:26), *Messianites*, if you like. Until that time, everybody thought that Christianity was simply a Jewish sect, a group of Jews who believed the Messiah had come in contrast to all the Jews who believed that he hadn't come, but were still Jews.

Christianity became a different religion

But now Christianity was being set free from Judaism. It was becoming a different religion and this is the tension right through the early chapters of the book of Acts, a tension which Stephen broke with his very blood. And Paul, who had been present at Stephen's death, realized this: that Christianity and Judaism will never mix. They are two different religions and you can't put them together. Even though Christianity was born in the Jewish cradle, if it had stayed there, it would have become a Jewish grave for this new religion. And here we are with a Jewish Bible, as I have frequently said, worshipping a Jewish Messiah and praising the God of the Jews but we are Gentiles. Christianity is our faith and our religion and Christ is our Christ, our Messiah. That might never have been so if Peter had not been publicly rebuked by Paul on that day. But it wasn't just the issue of the relationship between Judaism and Christianity, it was literally a matter of life and death. The difference between the two religions is the difference between heaven and hell. Judaism as a religion, like every other religion in the world, will take a person straight to hell. Christianity will get a person to heaven. It is that issue that caused Paul, with amazing courage, to dare to disagree with the very first pastor of the Christian church, Simon Peter, who had been appointed by Jesus himself to feed the lambs of Jesus. But it does not matter who a man is; it does not matter what his ecclesiastical position is, if he is not true to the gospel, then someone must have the courage to stand up and differ from him and rebuke him, to save the truth that sets us free. Thank God this argument occurred! Thank God we know about it! Thank God for Paul, daring to stand up even to Simon Peter and say, "Peter, you are wrong. Peter, what you're doing doesn't square with the gospel. Peter, it just doesn't line up with what you know to be true." Now, here we have the heart of the issue: a man who tries to keep the Ten Commandments in order to be good enough to get to heaven will find himself in hell. That's the issue. But a man, no matter how bad he has been, who comes to Jesus Christ and trusts him will find that he's got a right straightaway to look forward to heaven. That's the difference.

Paul's words to Peter

Now let's go into the passage and see what Paul said to Peter. Scholars have variously disagreed as to how much of chapter 2 was actually said to Peter. In other words, where do you start and where do you finish the quotation marks of what Paul says to Peter? And if you take many different Bibles, you'll find that the quotation marks finish in different places. They all start at the same place: "I said to Peter in front of everybody, "You are a Jewish national" (2:14) That's where they start. Some Bibles finish the quotation at the end of verse 14, some finish at the end of verse 15, some in verse 16, some in verse 17. I have finished the quotes at verse 21, at the end of chapter 2. And as soon as you do that, the whole passage makes much more sense.

Throughout this passage Paul is talking to Peter and when you realize that you understand why he spoke as he did.

And you can divide what he said into three paragraphs by the personal pronouns that Paul used. First paragraph (verse 14): "you" – "you, Peter." Second paragraph (verses 15-17): "we," "we," "we": "You, Peter and myself, Paul." Third paragraph (verses 18-21): "I," "I," "I": Paul. So in the first paragraph, Paul is saying, "First of all, I've got something to say about you." Then in the second paragraph, "I've got something to say about the two of us, we Jews." Then in the third paragraph, "I've got something to say about myself and my own personal experience and testimony."

Now, I'm going to deal primarily with the second and third paragraphs because we have looked at the first one in the previous chapter of this book. Paul is blazing away with both barrels of his gun. I wouldn't like to have been in Peter's shoes, on the receiving end of these second and third paragraphs. Paul reduces Peter to jelly, I think, from what he said. His argument is carefully worked out. By the time Paul has finished, poor Peter hasn't got a leg left to stand on. No reply is recorded – I think because there wasn't one. To argue with Paul was a dangerous thing to do. For one thing, he had such a brilliant mind but for another thing, he had the truth with him and it does not matter what your IQ is, how brilliant your logic may be, if you've got the truth with you, you are in the stronger position.

Paul and Peter: our Jewish failure with the law (2:15-17)
Let's see what he said to Peter about this dangerous thing that Peter was doing, slipping back into Jewish habits. Paul is saying, "You are betraying the truth." We are looking at verses 15 to 17 in which Paul uses the plural *we* and *our*. He's including Peter and himself. He's appealing to Peter

as his brother and he talks about the two of them. The key word in verses 15-17 is a word that we don't use much today, *justification*. The verb is used four times, *justified*, and the noun once, *justification*. I've deliberately not left in that word in my translation. I've tried to paraphrase it each time. What does this word *justified* mean? It's a word that is cold to us because it means nothing. We do use it occasionally in the sense of proving someone blameless. You know, a husband arrives home from the office at 10.30 pm. His wife says to him, "Come on, justify yourself. Where have you been since you left the office?" In other words, "prove yourself blameless." "Prove yourself to be in the right, coming home at this time of night." Or the boss calls you in and says, "I've been going through the accounts and all this money – can you justify these expenses on your account? Can you justify them?" What does he mean? He means: "Can you prove yourself blameless, can you prove yourself to be in the right, to be innocent?" So our English usage of the term, even though it's rare, is right.

In the Greek world it was a word used in the law court. The judge sat there and looked at the prisoner in the dock and, after hearing the case, the judge said either, "Guilty" or "Justified" – innocent. Innocent or guilty or, in those terms of those days, condemned or justified. Those two words were the words that a prisoner waited with bated breath to hear and wondered which it would be as he stood there in the dock, accused of certain crimes. If he heard the judge say, "Condemned", off he went to prison or almost certainly to death in many cases. But if he heard the word "Justified", he walked out of court free, never again to be charged with that crime. Recently we had a rather unusual example of that. A man was charged with doing away with his wife. They hadn't enough evidence and the case was dismissed. He walked out of the court a free man. Only God knows the full truth about the case. But I mention that case because instinctively I can see from the look on your faces that you wonder whether he was guilty. And here is the problem for God. Why do I need to be justified? Why should I be bothered about Paul's teaching on justification? For precisely this reason: that God has already ringed the date on the calendar when you and I stand in the dock before him. He has appointed the day on which he will judge the world, one by one. It's all fixed. You are only out on bail at the moment. That is my position, and that is your position. We're on bail and God has already fixed the date when we are to stand before him and justify before him the way we've lived, the words we've spoken, the thoughts we've had, the deeds we've done, the feelings that have entered our heart. We have to justify them before God. He gave us our life and he expected us to live blamelessly. One day you and I will have to stand before God and justify the way we've lived and prove that we were right.

"The pidgin English version of the New Testament used in New Guinea translates 'justified' as 'God, 'e say I'm all right.' That is a perfect translation: 'God, 'e say I'm all right.'"

I recently saw the pidgin English version of the New Testament. It's a fascinating document; it's used in New

Guinea among those whose language is very simple and picked up second hand from Australian traders. When they came to the word "justified" do you know what they translated it with? This little phrase: "God, 'e say I'm all right." That is a perfect translation: "God, 'e say I'm all right." Now one day I've got to stand before God and he will look at every part of my life, even every idle word that slipped out of my tongue, and every thought that went through my mind. And one day he will say either, "Condemned" or "Justified". But you and I know perfectly well that God cannot say about one person here now, "He's all right" or "She's all right." How can I ever get right with God? How can I ever be justified in his sight? How can he ever say, "I'm all right?" That is the biggest question of life and the greatest need you have as you read this. Your greatest need is not food, clothes, education or money. Your greatest need is to be justified, to get right with God, to be innocent in his sight so that, in the day when the whole world is gathered before him, he points to you and says, "He's all right. He's in my good books. He is innocent. You can justify everything he's done." How will that ever be? The one thing that Paul makes quite clear to Peter here is this: you will never get that way by trying to keep the Ten Commandments. Never. And so he brings to Peter three arguments.

The evidence of experience

"Peter, the two of us were born within the Jewish nation. The two of us were born within God's people. Peter, we were given every chance we could have had to keep the Ten Commandments. We took them in with our mothers' milk. When we were little kids we learned to recite them on the ten fingers of our two hands. Peter, we were brought up in this. From our earliest days we knew the Ten Commandments and we lived among people all around us who tried to keep them. Then when we were 12 years old, we were taken to the Bar Mitzvah ceremony and we were made sons of the Lord and we promised to keep the Ten Commandments ourselves. Peter, we've had every possible opportunity to keep the law. And what did we find? We found we couldn't keep it. And if we couldn't, when we were brought up in that way, how do you expect these Gentiles to do it?" That's his first argument. He says, "Peter, when you were trying to keep the Ten Commandments, when I was too, we had no peace. We had no clear conscience. We had no sense of God's love. We were afraid of God all the time because we knew we'd done things wrong and we knew we'd broken the law." Just one law alone was enough to kill Paul, and that was: "Don't be greedy." That's all: "Don't be greedy." And Paul says, "I found all kinds of coveting in my heart." And so Paul says, "Peter, we were brought up in this. We've tried it. We've done everything we could to get there under our own steam and what happened? We were afraid of God, we were the wrong side of God, we were in God's bad books and we knew that if we stood before him, he'd have to say, "Condemned." Then we put our trust in Jesus, Peter. And do you know what happened? Suddenly we knew the love of God. Suddenly peace flooded into our soul. Suddenly we were right with God and we knew it. And that if we died the next minute God would look at us and say, "Justified," "innocent," "righteous." It was a matter of experience to Peter and Paul that that's what happened. So Paul says, "Peter, just think – look at what you were and look at the way we were brought up and look what happened to us. As soon as you dropped the Commandments and turned to Christ, what happened? You got right with God." That's the argument from experience.

A statement of Scripture

Peter has a second argument from Paul, a statement of Scripture: "If you can speak to people from your experience and from the Bible and the two match up, you've got an invincible case. Peter, do you remember what you read in your Bible, in the book of Psalms?" The greatest king of Israel, a man after God's own heart, David, wrote his innermost thoughts in poems – we call them psalms. And David wrote in one psalm, "Judged by God's law no man living could ever be acquitted" (Psalm 143:2). Paul says, "Peter, it's in your own Bible, your Old Testament, your Jewish Scriptures; they admit that a man after God's own heart, King David himself, acknowledges he couldn't make it that way. It's also written all over the Old Testament. The laws are there, the standards are there, but what is also in the Old Testament is that nobody ever reached them. Nobody ever kept them; no one managed it. Nobody was acquitted in God's sight because of keeping the law. Not one single Jew, ever." And the tragedy is that even now, 2,000 years later, there are still sincere, honest Jews trying to get to heaven by keeping the Commandments. If they're honest, they're still failing. Not only in the religion of Judaism but also when you look at every other religion in the world and every other religion says, "Do this and you'll get there." There are hundreds of millions of people struggling to do it and not getting there.

The limitation of logic

The third argument that Paul uses to Peter is the argument about the limitation of logic. There comes a point where experience and Scripture say one thing but logic says something different and Paul makes it totally clear that when your experience of Christ and Scripture are on one side and logic is on the other, it is logic that is wrong. Now, I want to develop this because with logic you can prove black is white and white is black. With logic you can prove that God is an evil god. Look what logic has done with the lovely truth of predestination. Logic proves that God is evil from the doctrine of predestination, but logic is wrong. You can prove that God is unfair by logic. For example, here are two people. One has spent a lifetime trying to be kind to their neighbour and trying to do good. They've had a few failures but they've tried hard. The other man has been a criminal all life. He's been selfish, he's done bad things to people all his life and he's hurt many people. But in the last moment of his life he puts his trust in Jesus. Then: the man who has tried to do good all his life goes to hell, but the man who's not done good but has trusted Jesus goes to heaven. Logic says that's not fair. Logic says God is unjust. Logic says God is an evil god to do that. And logic is wrong, terribly wrong. Because those who know God well know that God never does anything unfair; they know that God is never unjust. You know God so well that you know he'd never do this. This is what Peter is saying, what he is being told here. Paul says, "Peter, you've allowed your logic to run away with you. Your logic has taken you away from your experience and has taken you away from Scripture." How? Because Paul knew why Peter had really separated at meal tables.

Peter was here not afraid of what others might think about himself; he'd gone beyond that. He was afraid of what others would think about Jesus Christ. And logically he was right. Logically he was thinking like this: "If these people see me ignoring the Jewish laws, they may come to the conclusion that Jesus encourages lawlessness, that he's an anarchist, and I don't want to give that impression of Jesus." So Peter was not considering what people thought of himself. He was considering at the highest level what people would think of Jesus Christ and he'd got all the consequences worked out logically. "They will think wrongly of Jesus if I behave in this loose manner." Paul then says, "Peter, logically you're right. But in real life you're wrong. You know Jesus better than that. Just because my quest to get right with God through Christ leads me to live outside the Jewish law, does that make Jesus an anarchist? Does that make him a lawbreaker? Does that mean that Jesus encourages you to lower your standards? Never! Never."

That is Paul's reply. He doesn't argue it because he's showing how logic is weak. So he doesn't answer logic with logic. He just says, "Never!" That word he uses, in Greek it's *me genoito* – a funny word. It means the exact opposite of *Amen*. Amen "let it be." *Me genoito*, "never let it be." It's better translated by just one English word: *never*. It's translated in the King James Version usually as "God forbid." That's an expression Paul wouldn't use; the word "God" isn't there. The NIV has "Absolutely not!" It's the opposite of the word *Amen*, which says "that is certainly going to be." But this word means "never." Make Christ an anarchist? Never! Peter and Paul knew Jesus better than that. Jesus didn't lower his standards. In taking us away from the Commandments, he wasn't dragging us down; he was lifting us higher. It was the Commandments that dragged us down and Jesus set us free from that, that he might lift us up. Just because Peter is living away from the Commandments now, that doesn't make Christ a lawbreaker or someone who is going around stirring up rebellion and lowering standards. On the contrary, he set us free: he set us free from the Commandments that he might lift us up. Does that make Christ an anarchist? "Peter, your logic has run away with you!"

The lesson I want you to learn from this argument is this: Follow the Scripture and your experience of Christ. Let those who want to argue logically that it's unjust or unfair or wrong argue all they like. There's a limit to what logic can see. Paul says, "Peter, forget the logic. You know from your own experience and from the Bible what the truth is. Then throw logic away if it's going to start making deductions that don't fit in with what you know of Jesus Christ." And I say the same thing. There are mysteries of life. Suffering is one. We were discussing it with students recently. It's so easy to argue logically from the facts that God is unfair. If that's where you're driving, then throw logic away. We know from Scripture that God has no pleasure in hurting anybody. We know that it's wrong to say that he is the cause of suffering in our world; however logically it may seem to us that he is responsible; Scripture and our experience tell us that God is not like that. He does not willingly hurt or grieve people. Logic is helpful up to a point, but where it goes against Scripture and Christian experience, it is an enemy of the gospel and it will cause us to do silly things. So let us rather go by the revealed word of God, confirmed by our experience of the Lord Jesus.

Paul: "my" Christian experience (2:18-21)

Now I come to the third paragraph in verses 18 to 21. Paul has just proved in three ways that Peter is wrong because he has proved that the Jewish way of law is a failure and that you will never get to heaven by keeping the Ten Commandments and you'll never live right. And Paul now goes on to his personal experience and he speaks about his own discovery – "I," "I," "I." Although he writes "I," it is not a self-centred paragraph but a deep, personal testimony. He says, "Peter, I've told you what I believe is wrong with your behaviour. Now I'm going to tell you why I could not do the same thing as you. I just couldn't go back from being Christian to being a Jew again. I couldn't return. I'll tell you why, Peter. Do you feel guilty about having left the Commandments? I would feel guilty if I went back to them. You feel guilty because you've left the law and turned to Christ. I would feel guilty if I left Christ and turned back to the law. If I rebuilt the things that I've demolished, the only thing I'd achieve would be this."

In my translation, it is there at the beginning of the sentence: "What would really make me a lawbreaker would be to erect again the whole legal system I demolished." In other words, you don't become a lawbreaker by leaving the Commandments behind. You would become a lawbreaker by going back to them. Does that sound a bit funny? Let me explain. If there were no laws, there would be no criminals. If nobody had ever made the laws, then nobody could ever break them. In fact, there weren't any such things as crimes until laws were passed. The only thing you achieve by making a law is to prove that people are breaking it. Do you understand that? Every new traffic law that comes in creates a new set of criminals and I guess quite a lot of us are criminals in this respect. You parked your car in the place you used to park in but there's now a yellow line underneath it. You're a criminal. You used to park there and until the law was made – until the yellow line was painted – you weren't a criminal, but now you are. Every law that has been introduced produces a new crop of criminals. All it does is prove that people break the law. Paul says, "If you go back to the old system of laws, all you will achieve is to prove that you've broken them." Going back to the laws won't help you keep them. That doesn't help anybody keep them. It just proves you break them. If that's all you achieve, then what have you really achieved?

I, through the law, died to the law

"Now, let me tell you about my experiences," says Paul. "I'll tell you in three stages what I discovered." "I, through the law, died." He's expressing himself in simple language: it's a deadly business to try and live a good life. Have you ever tried it? You'll know that it kills you. You try and do it for just one day. Just try to live a really good life for even one day. Do it seriously; really try. At the end of the day you'll feel dead. It will kill your ego terribly. The reason why most people don't feel unhappy about their life is that they don't try to live a good one. If they really tried, they'd feel dead. Trying to be good kills you. Trying to be bad is child's play! You can see it even on the stage. Most actors and actresses find it far easier to act a bad person – a bad character, a villain – than a good person, without seeming false and artificial. It is much easier to act a bad part than a good part. You try and live the good life – it'll kill you. Paul says, "It killed me, it really did. It killed me. I tried keeping the law." And nobody ever tried it harder than Paul. He got ahead of everybody else in keeping it. In other people's eyes he was blameless, but in God's eyes he was not. He said, "It killed me dead. My ego just went down and down and down." I remember a man telling me that he was a good man, a group Scoutmaster for an area, and was constantly engaged in good service. The world would have said there's never been a better man. But I remember him saying to me, "Over about a year God took down my self-respect like a brick wall, one brick at a time until there was nothing left." He was a good man, engaged in many acts of good service, kind to his fellow men and yet his self-respect was taken down brick by brick by God's law, till he was nothing. Paul said, "That's what happened to me. The law just killed me dead and the Ten Commandments would kill every one of you if you tried to keep them." Do you think that's bad news? No. Paul says, "That gave me the very break I needed. So I finished with it." Only when the law has killed your ego dead do you finish with it. At the beginning, you're trying so hard that you build up your ego because you manage a little bit and then a little bit more and you build up what the Bible calls "self-righteousness" and even though you get very far along that road, the trouble is that all your righteousness is still self, self, and more self. That is the real problem: self.

"Paul says something amazing: 'When you come to the cross and see that Jesus died for you, something will happen. You will also die with him. You look at a cross not on which your Saviour died alone but on which you also died.' The cross finishes off your self. The cross says, 'You are dead. You are finished.' The cross spells death to self."

I died with Christ

How do you get rid of self? There's only one answer: You'll never improve self. The best thing is to kill self. Kill it dead. You will never improve your life. Kill it. Get rid of it. "I, through the law, died to the law. I got to the point where I realized it was a dead end. It was full of good intentions but it was the road to hell and so I finished with it, I died to it, I finished with it altogether. How? How did my self die? I'll tell you. It wasn't just the Commandments that killed it, it was the cross too." Here Paul says something amazing. He says, "When you come to the cross and see that Jesus died for you, something will happen. You will also die with him. You look at a cross not on which your Saviour died alone but on which you also died." The cross finishes off your self. The cross says, "You are dead. You are finished." The cross spells death to self. I wonder if you understand what I'm saying? It's a deep truth, this. It's one thing to believe that Jesus died for me. But it's another thing to understand that I died with him. But when you come to the cross, that's what happens and your self dies. You are crucified with

Christ. There's something radical that changes and you have died. That's why we have funeral services here, in water, for people who have died with Christ. That's what baptism is all about. And next time we have a baptism I want you to remember this. We're burying those who've died. Their self died with Christ. They were crucified with Christ so we're holding the funeral. We're burying what has died.

Paul said, "That's what the law did for me. Thank God it did. It did something good for me. It got me to a dead end where I finished with the law. It brought me to the point where I died to the law. I washed my hands of it. It was clearly not going to help me, so I finished with it and that set me free to live for God." That's an extraordinary statement. "As soon as I finished with the Ten Commandments I was able to live for God." Think that through.

Christ lives in me

Paul is giving his personal testimony. We're now looking at the cross and Paul is getting nearer and nearer to one of the best texts in the Bible. If we set this verse in its lovely context, then the beauty of this jewel shines out even more. Many people just lift it out of context and take verse 20 by itself and treasure it but we are to put it in its setting, in the brooch that God gave it. Put it in this whole interview between Peter and Paul and Peter now is told this lovely truth: "Peter, when you've been to the cross you're on the way to the resurrection." Look at the word that comes in now – 'life,' 'live,' 'alive,' 'life'. "The law brought me to death but I came to the cross. That completed the death of self. But it brought me life." The cross of Jesus led to the resurrection for Jesus and his life after his resurrection was different from his life before his death. No longer was he troubled with Satan. He was alive to God. He was finished with Satan.

Paul is saying, "You and I, Peter, can have resurrection life now. You see after I had died at the cross, people said, "But you're still around. I still saw Paul's body." No, you didn't, it wasn't really me! You saw somebody else: Christ living in me. Never try to improve your life. Kill it and let Christ live in you." That's the message. That's the way to keep the law. That's the way to live a truly good life. That's the way to get right in God's sight. Cancel your old life altogether so that you're dead. Do you know, a dead man can't be tried. In the Nuremberg war trials, when the Nazi war criminals were put on trial, two or three of them managed to commit suicide during the trial in their prison cell. And then their trial stopped immediately. They were just finished with. The court had finished with them. When you've died, the law can't touch you any more. Isn't that exciting? When you've died to the law, God's law can't touch you any more. Not any more. You are dead and the life that you now live, you live by faith, by trust.

You don't just start being a Christian by faith; that's also the way it goes on. "The life I now live," says Paul, "after 30 years, I'm not going to go back to keeping the Commandments. I'm not going to go back to observance. I'm not going back to that outward ritual and regulation. I'm not going to go back to that. That killed me and I'm finished with it. I'm dead as far as the law is concerned. But now, now, now the real life that I live is by constantly trusting Jesus every day, every moment. To live his life in me."

Trusting Jesus Christ to live in me

Two parents came to a Christian minister one day and said, "You know, we're terribly worried because we get so impatient with our children and we lose our temper with them and we know it's wrong. It's upsetting the home, but will you tell us how we can have more patience with our children and will you pray for us that we may be more patient?" And the minister said, "No, I won't. That's not the answer. You don't need more patience." And they said, "Well, what is the answer?" He said, "You are not patient people. You never will have patience. It's no use trying to be patient with your children. What you must do is let the patience of Jesus live in you. And instead of saying, "Lord, give me patience," you should say, "Lord, you be patient with my children through me." There is a world of difference. You're not trying to be patient any more. The life you're now living is by trusting Jesus Christ to live in you. That's different, and that's successful and effective.

Whenever you live that way, you'll find that you don't need to bother with the laws because you keep them. You'll find you don't need to bother about being good because Christ is living his good life in you. You are living by continually trusting in Jesus. What kind of a Jesus? You will never get further than the cross. It will always be by continually trusting the Son of God who loved you and gave himself for you. You must live in the shadow of the cross. You must stay at the cross. You don't just go there for salvation, you stay there all your life. As the hymn put it, "Beneath the cross of Jesus I fain would take my stand." That's where you have to stay. And at the cross of Jesus you trust the Jesus who loved you enough to give his life for you. And you say, "Jesus,

I'm going to trust you the whole way. Every day, in every situation, in every crisis." And Paul says, "Peter, do you think I could go back from that kind of a life? Never! Do you think I would give up this life of faith in Jesus? Trusting him to do it for me and in me instead of trying to do it for him? Do you think I'd go back? No. If I did, do you know what I'd be doing? I would be nullifying the grace of God." To express that more simply, I would be throwing God's gift back in his face. I would be saying, "God, I don't want what you give me. God, I don't want to receive anything. I'm going to get there myself. I'm not going to be a beggar. I'm going to stand on my own two feet." I've quoted to you before George Bernard Shaw's words when he was told about the grace of God: "Forgiveness is a beggar's refuge. I will pay my own debts." Poor soul. I'm not going to make the grace of God redundant. Here is God, holding out an offer of life and I am going back to the demands of the law. Here is God saying, "I'll give you goodness. I'll give you life." And I'm saying, "No, I'm going to try and get it for myself and I'll kill myself in the process." That's what you're doing. And above all, Paul says, "If I try to get to heaven by keeping the law, I make the death of Christ utterly meaningless."

When we take bread and wine in Communion, we remember Jesus Christ on a cross. If I'm trying to be good, I'm saying to Jesus on his cross, "You're wasting your time as far as I'm concerned." Dare you say that? That's what you're doing. So Paul says, "As for me, I'm not going to throw God's generosity back in his face. As for me, I'm not going to say that Jesus wasted his time dying to make me good. I'm going to come and I'm going to trust Jesus. I'm going to live that way for evermore." Poor Peter, he probably said nothing at all after all that. Would you? Do you?

Concluding thoughts

I want to close with two thoughts. One, I want to say that if you're not yet a Christian, then this is how you begin, not by trying to be a Christian, not by trying to do good, not by trying to live up to your standards or God's or anybody else's but by coming to the cross and saying, "Jesus, take away my sin." Jesus told that lovely story of the Pharisee at the front of the temple saying, "Oh God, I thank you that I'm not as other men are, especially that chap at the back. I fast twice a week and I put a lot in the collection and I do good when I can." And this poor man at the back beat his chest and said, "Oh God, have mercy on me. I am a sinner." And Jesus says, "I tell you, that man at the back went home justified." "Justified" – he used the word – rather than the other (see Luke 18:9-14). That's Christianity.

Finally, a word to those who are Christians. Do you know one of the most dangerous temptations to a Christian? It is this: having started by faith, to go back to works. Having started by trusting Christ to make you a Christian, then to go back to trying to be one. Having started by letting him do it, to go back to trying to do it all yourself. And then religion becomes fearful and miserable. Keeping observances and outward ritual; it becomes a bondage. The life I now live, right now, the life I now live I live by faith in the Son of God who loved me. The message here to us, from the Lord, is this: stop trying and start trusting. Lord Jesus, keep us near the cross. Never let us leave the place where self died and life was born.

4

Galatians 3:1-18

TRYING OR TRUSTING?

Only two sorts of religion in the world
Summary of the letter so far
Rowing or sailing?

Paul's argument from his experience (3:1-5)
The beginning of your experience
The cross portrayed
The Spirit received
They have abandoned their mind
They have trusted their flesh
The middle of your experience

Paul's argument from Scripture (3:6-18)
Abraham
Moses
Jesus

Conclusions

You stupid Galatians! Who has hoodwinked you, so that you no longer act on what is true? Your eyes were fastened on Jesus Christ by our vivid description of his death by crucifixion. Just answer me one simple question – when you first experienced God's Spirit, was that because you had done what the law demands or because you believed what you heard?

Right! Then have you gone out of your minds? Having got started by the supernatural power of God's Spirit, do you think you can reach the finish by the natural energy of your own constitution?

Have you learned nothing from all you've been through? Surely you won't throw it all away now. Tell me, when God went on giving you a liberal supply of his Spirit, so that real miracles were happening among you, was this while you were trying to obey his laws or while you listened to what he said with complete trust?

Your experience is identical with Abraham's, for he "believed that God could do what he promised, and because of this trust he was listed in God's records as a good man" (Genesis 15:6). You realize, then, that the true descendants of Abraham are those who have this same trust in God. And the Bible, looking forward to the days when God would accept other races on exactly the same basis of faith, includes the announcement of this good news to Abraham himself – "Through you all the peoples of the world will enjoy God's blessing with this man Abraham, who was so full of faith."

But those who rely on keeping the commandments are actually under God's curse, not his blessing. For the law of Moses states quite clearly that "anyone who fails to keep all the rules of this book all the time will be cursed"

(Deuteronomy 27:26). It is patently obvious that nobody could possibly reach such a standard, if this is how God looks at us. So even the Old Testament points to another way to get right with God – "The good man will live by trusting" (Habakkuk 2:4). The law never mentions this matter of believing, its emphasis is all on achieving – "The man who obeys these rules will live well" (Leviticus 18:5).

Christ has ransomed us from this binding curse of the law and the price was to be cursed in our place. Quite literally, he paid the supreme penalty of the law – "The body of a man under God's curse is to be hanged on the bough of a tree" (Deuteronomy 21:23). By removing the curse in this way, Jesus our Messiah released the blessing of Abraham to non-Jews. So we could now receive the promised power of the Spirit, simply by believing.

Brothers, all this is nothing out of the ordinary: I can illustrate what has happened from everyday human affairs. Once a man's will has been sealed, it cannot be cancelled nor can any other provisions be added. Now God made his testament in favour of Abraham "and his issue" (Genesis 22:18). Just note that the word is singular rather than plural, indicating one surviving descendant rather than many; actually, it referred to Christ. But my main point is this – an agreement already ratified by God cannot be cancelled by a legal code introduced four hundred and thirty years later, or else the promise was worthless. The two are incompatible. If the blessing is now inherited by keeping the commandments, it is no longer available on the original terms. But God generously gave that first promise to Abraham and he will always stand by it.

(Author's translation)

Only two sorts of religion in the world

There are only two sorts of religion in the whole world. There are the religions that are based on trying and the religions that are based on trusting. All the other religions in the world, including the religion we call Judaism, belong to the category of trying. They tell you what you must do in order to be good, and then they leave you to try and do it. There is only one religion in the world in the second category and that is the religion of Abraham and of Jesus: it is not a religion of trying to be good, but one of trusting a good God. There is no comparability whatever between these two different kinds of religion. The writer of this letter, Paul himself, had learned the difference the hard way. He'd been brought up in an atmosphere of trying to be good. He had tried harder than anyone else in the whole of that religion. He had gone further than anyone else, but he was frustrated by constant failure to achieve his ideal, as everyone does who tries to be good, if they are sincere and honest in their attempt. And then one day this good doer, this do-gooder, this man who tried hard, met Jesus Christ face to face. And a revolution took place, and what he'd been trying to achieve was given to him on a plate: a relationship of joy and peace, of being right with God and finding that he was living a good life – it happened. His whole ideas of religion were turned upside down – or rather, the right way up. He saw the truth and he set off after some years of thinking it through to spread this good news throughout the world. The gospel is not good advice, it's *good news*. It's not telling you what you must try and do in order to be a good person and get to heaven; it's telling you that a good person came down from heaven because he loved you. It's saying trust him to do what you will never achieve.

Paul went everywhere preaching this good news. Having been liberated from the frustration and the bondage of trying to keep the commandments, he now preached Christ and Christ's free love. But the trouble was, wherever he went, there were those of his former Jewish compatriots who came along afterwards and spoiled his work by telling Christians, "No, you must not only trust Christ, you must also try to do good." Just to focus this, to show you that the danger is still present, 2,000 years later, that the battle is not over, let me quote you a hymn that you sing and that you love. I love it too; I love its first verses but I don't like the last verse. This is because it spoils the whole hymn. It's a beautiful hymn about Christ's death on the cross:

There is a green hill far away,
outside a city wall
where the dear Lord was crucified
who died to save us all.

There was no other good enough
to pay the price of sin;
he only could unlock the gate
of heaven and let us in.

He died that we might be forgiven,
he died to make us good;
that we might go at last to heaven
saved by his precious blood.

That is the gospel, that's good news, that's great – and

then suddenly and unfortunately, the last verse is:

> *Oh dearly, dearly has he loved*
> *and we must love him too*
> *and trust in his redeeming blood*
> *and try his works to do.*

The whole thing is spoiled. This is the danger today, not that people drop their faith altogether and stop trusting, but they think that Christianity is a mixture of trusting and trying, that you've got to do both. But I tell you: the two will not mix. They are two totally different ways of getting right with God. Paul's argument in Galatians 3 is never try and mix them up. So I want to rewrite that last verse as: "Oh dearly, dearly has he loved / and we can love him too,/ and trust in his redeeming blood, not try his works to do." You even have my permission to change it in your hymnbook. I may get into trouble, but that's the gospel, that's the good news of Jesus Christ.

Summary of the letter so far
Paul in Galatians is arguing very closely, he's making you stretch your mind, he makes you think it through, and he wants you to follow the argument every step of the way and his first statement was that if somebody comes to you and tells you to try to be good, then damn him (1:9); it's not the gospel. He's putting you under a curse; he'll drag you to hell because the road to hell is paved with people trying to be good – it's paved with good intentions. He then goes on as we have seen in Galatians chapter 1 and chapter 2 to describe from his own experience how he got free of trying

and found that the way was trusting. Nobody taught it him; he found it by himself. Christ gave it him direct. Out in the Arabian desert he rethought his entire approach to the religious life and he realized it was good news. We have seen how he argued even with Simon Peter himself over this matter and accused Peter of compromise and bringing back the "trying" approach. And then in the previous chapter of this book we considered that wonderful statement, where Paul is saying, "Not only did I get right with God in the beginning by trusting the Son of God, that's how I've also continued my life. In fact, the life I now live 30 years later I'm living by continually trusting in the Son of God who loved me and gave himself for me – I'm still under the cross. I'm not going away from the cross into what I do for the Lord; it is what he does for me the whole way. I'm still living by faith."

"Are you rowing or sailing as a Christian? If I can put it this way, instead of your religion being a sailing boat, it's become a rowing boat. Now there's still work to be done on a sailing boat. But it isn't your work that's carrying you along. And that's the difference. If you're rowing and if you're having to pull hard, is it because you've stopped trusting and you're going back to trying?"

Rowing or sailing?

So Paul has spoken from his own experience, and now in Galatians chapter 3 he begins a much tighter and closer argument, with almost a legal mind ... arguing against legalism. Paul is now going to turn from his own life to the life of the Galatians, the people he's writing to, who have actually stopped trusting and have gone back to trying to be Christian. You can do that, as some of you have done. You've lost your peace, you've lost your joy and you've lost the sense of victory in life for this one reason, that years ago when you were converted and came to Christ you came by trusting... and you lived by trusting. Somehow over the years, however, the delight has become a duty and now it's what you do for him that matters and you very loyally keep up the good deeds and support things at the church, but it's all become a drudgery. It's become something that you do because you feel you ought to. If I can put it this way, instead of your religion being a sailing boat, it's become a rowing boat. Now there's still work to be done on a sailing boat. But it isn't your work that's carrying you along. And that's the difference. So are you rowing or sailing as a Christian? If you're rowing and if you're having to pull hard, is it because you've stopped trusting and you're going back to trying? So Paul says, "O you stupid Galatians." He does not say "sinful Galatians." It's not a sin to go back to trying; it's just silly, foolish. He says, "You're stupid." He must have known that Jesus said, "Be careful if you call anybody stupid – that's verbal murder. You can be in danger of hellfire by calling somebody a fool" (see Matthew 5:21-22). Jesus was very careful about whom he called a fool. He said that a man who lived for money and built up his business so that he could have a wonderful retirement was a fool, because he could die the day he retired (Luke 12:20). Paul says to the Galatians, "You're just stupid. Stupid! Just fancy, when the wind was blowing you along – and you were having a great sail – you pulled your sail down, took the oars out and you started pulling as hard as you could. The tide was too much – fancy doing it! It's stupid when there's a wind blowing, and when the Holy Spirit has been given to you; why do this?" And yet we do it. All of us here have got to confess that we are silly Christians and from time to time we go back to trying and make it all a duty, and a matter of "oughts." That's not the good news. It's only good advice.

He argues with the Galatians under two main headings in this passage: two arguments that will appeal to the Christian: first, the argument from his experience, and secondly, the argument from his Bible. These are the two things that will convince a Christian of what is right: what a Christian knows in their heart from their own experience of the Lord, and what they see in their Bible from their own study. These are two very powerful arguments, and they are both needed, because our experience can be deluded.

You can have false experiences. People who've been on a trip with LSD or heroin have told me that they've met God, that they've had experiences of heaven and the infinite, but that experience has not been real – it's been a fantasy. They've had to come back from that trip to reality. It is not a way to God that is borne out by Scripture, We've got to test our experience all the time by Scripture, but when experience and Scripture say the same thing for the Christian, that settles it. When it's there in the book and there in my heart, nothing more needs be said.

Paul's argument from his experience (3:1-5)

The beginning of your experience

Paul says, "Now, you stupid Galatians, stop and think about your Christian experience. First, let's go back to its beginnings when you were first converted. Then let's look at how you're going to complete what's begun, and then let's look at the middle in between and everything that has happened between when you began and now you're contemplating its completion. Let's go back to the beginning."

The cross portrayed

He asks, "Has somebody put a spell on you? Has somebody cast an evil eye on you? Has somebody bewitched you? Hoodwinked you? I fixed your eyes on Jesus, on Jesus crucified. If you take your eyes off him, you'll soon come under some hypnotic influence. You've taken your eyes off the cross."

This is the fundamental secret of it all: how did you begin the Christian life, how did you come to Christ? The answer is by somebody telling you about Jesus' death on the cross. The more vivid the description, the more your eyes are fixed on the cross. Paul literally says in the Greek, "I placarded Christ before your very eyes, I posted him up. I painted a picture of him dying for you to fix your eyes on the cross." Now who's been taking your eyes away from him and hypnotizing you to some other view?

I've told you before about the evangelist who went to Cambridge to conduct a mission amongst students. One day he was holding a discussion group in a study and in the study above in the same college was a group of students having a bit of a drunken party. When they'd got merry and got a little bold and were doing silly things, some of the students said to the boldest one, "I dare you to go downstairs and ask that chap to convert you." So down came this drunken student who lurched into the room below and said to this evangelist, "I want to be converted." The evangelist summed the situation up in a glance, put him in a room by himself and took out of his pocket a picture postcard of Jesus hanging on the cross. He gave it to him and said, "Sit there and look at that, and I'll come back in ten minutes." He came back, with the student still looking at the postcard. The student said, "What's this supposed to do then?" "Go on looking at it," the missioner replied, and he left again, came back in another 10 minutes, the student still looking at it, with nothing happening. So the evangelist went away again, and came back a third time. Then the student was on his knees, praying... and do you know he became a bishop in the Church of England in Australia? You see this is how you get people right with God. You paint a picture of the cross; you say to them, "Jesus Christ died for you." That's how it begins. It's the cross that spells the death knell of all your good deeds. It's the cross that brings you to the end of yourself. It kills your ego dead; you're finished with yourself and you're face to face with God.

Paul says, "Then who has hypnotized you? – I painted a vivid description for you of Christ on the cross and your eyes were fixed there and you got the message. But now who's taken your eyes away?" If you are trying today to be a Christian, I'll tell you this, somebody's got your eyes off the cross. Somebody's turned your attention away, and you've been hoodwinked.

The Spirit received

The second thing is this. As Paul looked back to the beginning of the Galatians' experience of Christ, he says, "When you came to the cross and you saw the truth – when you received Christ as Saviour – the next thing that happened was that God confirmed that by giving you his Holy Spirit, and you received the Spirit. Let me read some words from Dr William Barclay's commentary on this verse. He says "... for the early church, converts nearly always received the Holy Spirit in a perfectly visible and manifest way. There came to them a new surge of life and power that anyone could see." I'm sure he's making a good comment there.

So when Paul asked them, "Did you receive the Spirit by observing the law, or by believing what you heard?" although it was a rhetorical question, Paul expected his readers to think of the answer. He was absolutely confident what that answer would be – a confirmation that God's gifts are received through faith, not by attempting to keep his commandments. Paul expected them to answer directly from their experience at the time, not by deduction from anything that happened later. The aorist tense of the verb *receive* points to that initial event, although he later (3:5) goes on to ask a similar question about the continued supply of the Spirit, of which they have also been fully aware because the power to "work miracles" was the evidence, again the result of believing, not keeping the law. Both the initial reception and continual supply of the Spirit were self-evident experiences.

Paul is saying to the Galatians, "Look what happened – you

received the Saviour by faith. You believe that he died for you – what was the next thing that happened to you? The Spirit of God was poured into your life and God confirmed your faith by giving you his Spirit. Now tell me this," he continues, "I'm not so concerned at the moment with what happened when the Spirit came on you, I'm more concerned with why it happened and how it happened, and the simple truth is this: Tell me did you receive the Holy Spirit by trying to keep the Ten Commandments or when you believed what you'd been told?" And there is only one answer. I would like to guarantee that you could go to any Christian in the whole wide world, who has had the Holy Spirit poured out on them and say, "Now tell me how did you receive that experience? Was it by trying to be good? Or believing what you heard?" And you will get the same answer from every one of them, "It was by believing what we'd been told." It wasn't by attempting to keep the Ten Commandments.

Now that's the argument from the beginning of your Christian life. If you are struggling and trying to be a Christian today, then I say go back to the beginning of your Christian life, how did you get going? By trying to be good? By trying to be a Christian? Or was it through surrendering to the Lord and saying, "Lord I can't make it – you do it?" And suddenly the kingdom of heaven burst open on you. You'd been banging on the gates of glory with the fists of your good deeds for so long, and then suddenly you knocked and humbly said, "Please," ... and the gates swung open. Isn't it amazing? That's how you began.

> "Paul says, 'Look at the completion of your Christian life. If that's how you began, how are you going to finish?' They're not even changing horses midstream, they've actually *abandoned* the horse in midstream! They've left behind the gospel that was carrying them through and they've switched from trusting to trying. He says, 'Look, do you realize what you've done? Have you gone out of your mind? You've abandoned something that was succeeding for something that is failing.'"

They have abandoned their mind

Now says Paul, "Let's look at the completion of your Christian life. If that's how you began, how are you going to finish?" They're not even changing horses midstream, they've actually *abandoned* the horse in midstream! They've left behind the gospel that was carrying them through and they've switched from trusting to trying and he says, "Look, do you realize what you've done? Have you gone out of your mind? You've abandoned something that was succeeding for something that is failing." A man who does that has gone out of his mind; he's gone crazy. Have you gone out of your mind? There's a place for the mind in the Christian life and the place is to be sensible, to be rational about your experience and to look back, and let your mind work it out from your experience. He says, "You've gone out of your mind – having begun one way are you thinking of finishing another? Having begun by letting God do it, are you now thinking you can finish by you doing it? Having begun with supernatural power are you going to finish with natural power? Having started with the Spirit are you going to finish in the flesh? Do you think that having begun with God's grace, your own constitution can carry you through?"

They have trusted their flesh

Here we're touching on a second reason why people go back to trying in the Christian life. They get to the point where they think they can manage their own Christian life themselves. God has enabled you to be fairly successful so far in your Christian life. You've trusted him and God has enabled you to succeed and then there comes the point where you think you can succeed in the Christian life and back you go. Samson is a marvellous example of this. The Spirit of the Lord came on Samson and he killed the Philistines with the jawbone of an ass. The Spirit of the Lord came on Samson and he carried the gates of a city away on his own shoulders. The Spirit of the Lord came on Samson and he did this, that and the other. And then one day Samson said, when somebody shouted, "The Philistines are upon you," he said "I will arise, I will go out as I've always done, I'll deal with these Philistines." But you see he was now saying, "I will do it." And he went out, but wasn't strong; he was the weakest man in the Bible. And he was like a kitten; they bound him up and they took him away and they gouged his eyes out. Samson learned his lesson of the discipline of the Lord. There he was, brought out as a public spectacle. Chained, blind, helpless for the crowds of the Philistines to laugh at, but Samson learned his lesson. He felt in his arms the pillars that held the roof up and he said, "Oh God, sorry.

It was you all along. Now you do it again." He pulled and he heaved and his strength was there again and his greatest victory followed. You can read it for yourself in Judges chapters 13 to 16 and you'll find the same message right the way through the Bible. Just because God gave you success, don't reach the point where having begun by the Spirit, you think you can now complete the job in the flesh.

The middle of your experience

Now Paul goes on to consider their experience between the beginning of the Christian life and looking forward to its end. He says, "Just look back over your experience" ... you didn't just receive one filling of the Spirit, you didn't just have a once-and-for-all experience of the Spirit, but God went on supplying you with his Holy Spirit. He generously went on moving with his Spirit and there was a constant stream of miracles happening in your church. But reading between the lines, Paul is also saying, "Those miracles have stopped, haven't they? When God was going on working miracles for you, constantly supplying his Spirit to you, was that when you were trying to be good or when you believed what you listened to?" The lesson is obvious. The moment a church is filled with do-gooders, the moment a church is filled with Christians who are trying to do the Christian thing, then that is the moment that miracles stop. But when a church is filled with people who believe that God can do what he promised, miracles happen and go on happening. That's the secret. And Paul says to them, "You Galatians, just look back, have the miracles stopped? It's all you now, isn't it?" So let's examine ourselves as a church and say this, "Let's not make a list of what we've done for God." It's not very impressive in the sight of heaven, whatever people may think. The important list to make is what God has done in this place and what God continues to do. He doesn't do it among people who are trying to be good, trying to get the church going, trying to support meetings; he does it among people who believe that God means what he says.

Can I put it this way: you become a Christian, not with your hands but with your ears. The emphasis here is on listening. Using your ears and believing what you hear – that's what's going to see God work. And in the last analysis what matters in the church is what God does there, not what we do. That is Paul's appeal to their experience and what an argument it is! It is a profound lesson. Don't be so busy concentrating on what you're doing for the Lord, that God can't get in with his miracles. Instead, use your ears and believe what you hear, and then see what happens.

Paul's argument from Scripture (3:6-18)

I now move on to his argument in verses 6 to 18 from Scripture. Here, instead of a series of questions, which we had in the first part of this study, he now gives a series of quotations. In appealing to people's experience you ask them questions. Now what have you found – isn't this true in your life? – but when you come to the Bible you don't bring questions, you bring quotations. There are now seven quotations from the Bible, and in a brilliant way six of them are from the law of Moses. He's going to use Moses to confound Moses. He's going to show that even the five books of Moses point to this same truth. Now you can prove anything by text, I know that. I know that a person who doesn't really know their Bible can just pick one verse here and another verse there and you can make the Bible say almost anything. Even the devil did that to Jesus (Matthew 4:1-10): in the temptations the devil chose one text to try and get Jesus off balance. But what Paul is doing here is not just quoting seven texts; he's looking at the whole sweep of Scripture. He's only quoting those texts in the context of the whole unfolding story of God's pattern of how to be good.

The theme he's going to draw out is "The two greats of the Old Testament were Abraham and Moses." Moses talks about Abraham in his books. The greatest person in the New Testament is Jesus. Now here is the simple question: does the religion of Jesus follow Abraham or Moses? Because the things that Abraham learned and the things that Moses taught are incompatible with each other. Now that's the problem. This is where we get a little deeper. Let's look at the argument, which has three sections: Abraham, Moses and Jesus.

Abraham

We look first at Abraham. We go back to the very beginning, back to the first Jew, back to the father of all the Jews, Abraham. This dear old man who lived in a town and in a house where there was central heating and running water in the bedrooms. He was a man who at the age of 80 set off into the unknown and lived in tents for the rest of his life. The man who went out wandering, looking for a little patch of land that God said could be his. What a man, what a spiritual giant! Everybody acknowledges that Abraham was a good man. In the current Middle East crisis one of the anomalies of the situation is that all the Arabs look back to Abraham as their good father and all the Israelis look back

to Abraham as their good father because they were both
descended from Abraham: it's a family feud in the Middle
East. Through Ishmael to the Arabs and Isaac to the Jews,
"Abraham" they all say in the Middle East. The Egyptians
will say it; the Libyans, the Syrians and the Israelis also say
that Abraham was a good man.

But how did he get that way? How did he become a good
man? Let's go back to one night when Abraham stood at
his tent door. The sky was that deep midnight black and
twinkling all over the sky were the stars. Abraham looked
up at the starlit night sky. He was lonely; he had no son, no
children, and he heard a voice that said, "Abraham, look at
those stars. You will have a bigger family than those stars.
You'll have more children than all those stars in heaven."
Abraham could probably have seen about six thousand stars
from where he stood, if he'd been able to count them. "But
more than all that, you'll have a family." Abraham was a
hundred years old and his wife not far behind, but Abraham
said, "God, I believe you. I know it. I trust you." And the
Bible records that night Abraham became a good man. God
reckoned him as righteous. From then on he was a good
man; it's written there (Genesis 15:6). Paul says, "Can't
you see that those who are the true sons of Abraham are not
the Jews and not the Arabs or anybody else descended from
either? The true sons of Abraham are those who say to God,
'I believe you.'"

This means that you and I are descendants of Abraham.
What God promised him he promised us. Don't you find
that exciting? I'm a Gentile and here I am a son of Abraham!
If you believe God and trust his word, you're a descendant
of Abraham. Because not only does the Bible say that

Abraham became a good man that day, it also records that God said, "Abraham, through you, I'm going to bless all the nations of the world. What I'm giving to you, Abraham, you're going to share with all sorts of people, not even your physical descendants, but all the nations of the world." Do you know we're nearly at the point where that's literally true? Everywhere you go in the world you'll find true sons of Abraham who trust his God. So that's Abraham: read your Old Testament – you are a son or daughter of Abraham and he's your father – read that story of Abraham and see how he became a good man and that's how it was shared. In a nutshell, God's purpose was to call Abraham out of the nations, to bless him and send that blessing through him back into the nations. So he called Abraham out to be a special nation and to start the Jews, and then through them to send the blessing back to everybody. That's the story of the Bible. The sad part of the Bible is the story of the descendants, the physical descendants of Abraham, failing to realize the blessing. But it still came to us through the Jews. It came to us through a Jewish Messiah. It came to us through Jewish apostles.

Moses

What about Moses? 430 years later Moses comes, staggering down Mount Sinai with two great lumps of granite in his arms, and saying, "From now on, you keep the law." Do you notice the difference between promise and law? Promise says, "I will, I will, I will." That's why in a marriage service the key words are, "I will." The bridegroom doesn't say to the bride, "You shall." and the bride doesn't reply, "Well all right, if you shall also." The bride says, as the bridegroom says to his bride, "I will do this for you, no matter how bad it turns out, no matter how bad you are, for better, for worse, I will." The promise stands by the person. "I will." And God didn't say to Abraham, "You shall or you shall not." Did you notice? God said to Abraham, "I will make you a blessing. I will give you this land." And along comes Moses with "You shall, you shall not." The law is totally different from the promise; the law in fact puts you not into blessing but under a curse, because the law of Moses clearly states that if you don't keep all the commandments all the time, God will curse you (Deuteronomy 27:26), which is literally true. He will.

If you choose to try and be good by keeping the commandments, then that's the standard you've got to reach. What is the standard? The law demands perfection. The pass mark is 100%. I used to have fun in the RAF with boys joining the RAF discussing what it was to be a Christian and invariably they said, "You know it's about keeping the commandments." I said, "Keeping how many commandments? How many do you think you should have to keep before you're good enough?" They usually came down to six out of ten, slightly above half way. They recognized plainly that not everybody can. But they came down just above halfway out of ten. That's not what God says. He doesn't say students may need only attempt five questions out of ten – he says ten out of ten. The law can't cope with failure. The law can't offer forgiveness; the law can only tell you what to do and then punish you when you don't do it. That's the limit of law; it can't do anything else. The law can't make a single person good; it can only tell them that they're bad. And so the Ten Commandments came not with "I will" but "You shall, you shall not." Not only is perfection demanded in the law but also faith is ignored in the law – the law of Moses does not say a word about believing. It's all about achieving, it's all do, do, do, do, do ... and Paul says: You know, though the law of Moses demands perfection and ignores faith, even your own Old Testament recognizes that's not going to get anybody anywhere. Take the prophet Habakkuk. Habakkuk was a prophet who could see that the punishment of God was coming on the Israelites through the Babylonians. And he saw this ... and he realized that every one of the Israelites deserved punishment at the hands of God and so he thought well, the whole nation will be destroyed by these Babylonians, there'll be no one left, we all deserve it, how can we possibly survive? And then he saw, and God put these words on his lips, "The good man will live by trusting" (Habakkuk 2:4). And those who trusted survived.

Today we face the punishment of God because he's already appointed the day on the calendar when he will judge all of us. We already face it and not one of us can say we've kept the Ten Commandments – how are we going to survive that judgment? The answer is simple. "The just shall live by faith." "The good man will survive by trusting." It's all there in Habakkuk in the Old Testament.

Jesus

So we come finally to Jesus. Here we have the promise of Abraham, "I will" and the blessing to be shared with all the nations, and then 430 years later, Moses comes along with a law that curses us with a punishment for failing to live up to God's standards. Now which of these two are we going to pay attention to? Which did Jesus take into account? The answer is both, because both came from God – that's the dilemma. The promise to Abraham was from God and the "You shall not" to Moses came from God, so we can't set them over against each other and say Abraham's was God and this was Moses. They both came from God, so when Jesus came which was he going to take up? The answer is both.

But what if we ask which did Jesus pass on? The answer then is only Abraham. Let me explain. Which did Jesus take up? Both. He took up the law of Moses; he was born under the law; he was made a son of the law; he was circumcised on the eighth day and taken to the temple at 12 years old. He kept the law, every single law of Moses. He took up the law of Moses in life. And then what happened? At the age of 33 they strung him to a block of wood, to a tree trunk stuck in a socket in the rock and he died. He was under the curse of God crying out, "My God, my God why have you left me?" He kept the law and here he was being strung up according to the letter of the law of Moses, being under God's curse. When he was put to death, his body must be strung up on the bough of a tree: it's there in the law of Moses. What was he doing? He was ending the law for us. Jesus was saying the curse of the law is not on him because he had failed to keep the law – no, he had kept it. But the curse of the law is on everybody else and so he takes that curse. He said, "I take that curse on myself to set them all free." This is the glorious good news of the cross, that the curse that is on everybody who's broken any of the commandments of God – and there are not just ten there are 630 – anybody who's broken any of them, that curse, Jesus said, is on him (Jesus). He said,

"I'll pay the ransom and set them free." And the price he paid was to be cursed on the tree. That's why we preach the cross. That's why we placard it, that's why we paint a picture of it, that's why we want you to see it and fix your eyes on it. Because it's the end of the law of Moses for you. The law of Moses has now extracted its final penalty. It's been paid. Jesus took up the law of Moses on your behalf. He both kept it, and was punished as if he'd broken every part of it. He did it for us. Did you notice that little phrase in verse 13? He became "a curse for us." So now what can happen? Now that the curse of the law of Moses has come to its final consummation in the death of Christ, then the blessing promised to Abraham is released. That's what passes on – do you see? The law of Moses kept every Jew away from the blessing of Abraham. But not us. Now it is released, to everybody, non-Jews included.

The blessing that Abraham promised has been fulfilled, and the Holy Spirit of promise has been poured out, and now we've got a totally new way of living and a totally new experience of God's love and grace – and it's all based on Christ's merit.

Conclusions

Let me conclude. The real link between Christianity and the religion of the Old Testament is to be found in Abraham, rather than in Moses. It's to be found in this man who was full of faith, who went out into the unknown, and who looked up at the God of those stars and said, "I believe you." If you have believed in the same God, then you're a son of Abraham.

A final small legal argument: Paul says, "Look there's

nothing extraordinary about this whole relationship between Jesus, Moses and Abraham ... I'll give you an everyday human illustration of it." I have checked this with a local solicitor and I said I thought you could alter a will once you'd made it and add a codicil and do all kinds of things with it. The lawyer told me quite simply, "Yes you can alter a will and testament until it has been sealed. But if you seal it and put a seal on the bottom, then it's a legal contract in perpetuity and you can never alter it. So if you're making your will and you think you might fall out with those relatives later, don't put a seal on it and you can change it. But if you put a seal on your last will and testament, you'll never be able to alter it. It's fixed for ever." And Paul says, "Look, when a last will and testament is sealed, it can't be altered. It can't be added to. It can't be amplified; it's settled. You have willed something to someone else for ever." And so he says, "Don't you see that's what God did. God made his will and testament to Abraham, and even though the law came in later that can't alter the promise which was ratified to Abraham, sworn to by God on his own name, as an oath."

There's one little thing about the last will and testament to Abraham: it was God's last will and testament. It's never been altered and it needs never to be changed. There was one little word and, and you know if you've had anything to do with solicitors how even one word alters the whole situation, there was one little word, to Abraham and it is issue (NIV "seed"). Not everybody has noticed that in the Bible the word issue was in the singular, not the plural. Only one male descendant of Abraham would share it with him – and that was to be Christ, and if you and I have believed in Christ we are now in Christ and we are now one man in

Christ Jesus as the end of Galatians 3 says, "We're not a bunch of different individuals. We're not male and female, Greek and Barbarian, slave and free. We are one person in Christ Jesus. We are the one issue that inherits the blessing."

Do you understand? It's all come down to us through inheritance. "You cannot have it both ways," says Paul, as he concludes this argument. They are utterly incompatible. If you inherit blessing through keeping the commandments, then the promise to Abraham was worthless, but the simple fact is that God stands by his will and testament. You in Christ are the male descendant, the issue to whom that inheritance comes from Abraham. The blessing is yours.

Paul draws attention to one word in God's covenant (his will and testament) with Abraham, namely *seed*. Paul is quoting three passages in Genesis, which all use seed in the singular, never the plural. He argues that therefore only one physical descendant can qualify to inherit the promises, namely Christ. But this one person includes all who have come to be "in" him through faith. So all Christians, Jewish or Gentile, are the seed of Abraham.

There are four problems with this line of reasoning. First, *seed* is a collective noun, even in the singular, meaning one of many. *Sheep* is the same: a shepherd looking for his *lost sheep* can mean one or more. *Offspring* is another. Second, *seed* in Genesis clearly means many. God defines it as like the dust of the earth and the stars in heaven, too many to count. Third, God made the promise to Abraham's physical descendants (the Hebrew is the equivalent of "sperm," male seed). Fourth, the content of the promise was also physical, even territorial (the "land").

On all four counts Paul appears to be stretching things a

bit, in a somewhat rabbinic fashion. I doubt if he intended to imply that Christ was the *only* legitimate heir of the Abrahamic covenant. His eagerness to include Gentile believers in Galatia may explain his overstatement in this context. He was right to "single" out Christ as the only link between them as Abraham, thus sharing in the promised blessing; it would be wrong to cut out all Abraham's physical descendants.

One further question remains, "Why did God add the law of Moses?" We will consider the answer in our next study, because Paul does so. But meanwhile, may I ask you to examine your own heart very carefully. Are you trying or trusting? Are you in blessing or under curse? Are you struggling to be a Christian or are you just letting go and letting Christ take over?

5

Galatians 3:19-29

THE PURPOSE OF THE LAW

What is the purpose of the law?
Paul has argued against religion based on struggle
The purpose of the law

The law shuts us in (3:19-22)
An interim measure
Why was the law necessary?
The law's limited application
An indirect measure
A mediated covenant
A mutual contract
An inadequate measure

The promise lets us out (3:23-29)
Baptized in Christ
New dress
No distinctions
Blessed in Abraham

Conclusions

Then what was the point of the law? It was a temporary addition to deal with human lawlessness! Until Abraham's "issue" arrived to inherit the promised blessing, wrongdoing had to be exposed for what it was and kept under some control. Unlike the promise, the law was not given direct to men. God communicated it through heavenly messengers and an earthly intermediary handed it on. Normally a middleman is used to negotiate between two parties; and in a sense the law was a mutual contract, in that the conditions had to be accepted by the people. But our belief is that God stands alone. He is not an equal to be bargained with, but can act entirely on his own terms, as he did in giving the promise direct.

Do these differences mean that God introduced two rival religious systems, the law as an alternative to the promise? Never! If passing a law could make people live good lives, then legislation would be the answer. But the laws of the Bible simply shut down this possibility by proving that everybody does wrong, leaving the only way out that of believing God's promise by trusting in Jesus the Messiah.

Until the opportunity of faith came, we had to be remanded in custody and kept under the strong guard of the law, waiting for the day when we would be shown how to believe. Putting it another way, we were like children and the law was a strict guardian, keeping us under firm discipline until Christ could take over and put us right through our trust in him. Believing in Jesus Christ brought the full status and freedom which belongs to grown-up sons of God.

All of you who were initiated into the Christian life by immersion in water are now wrapped up in Christ. So you are no longer separate individuals – one a Jew and another a Greek, one a slave and another free, one male and another female. All of you make up just one person inside Jesus. As parts of Christ you belong to him, which makes you that single descendant of Abraham who is entitled to claim the blessing promised to his "issue."

(Author's translation)

What is the purpose of the law?

One of the questions that troubles many Christians is what to do with the Old Testament. It's the major part of our Bible, and we believe it to be the word of God, yet not a single Christian keeps all the commandments of the Old Testament. Neither do I know of a single Christian who feels under the obligation to do so, which is rather extraordinary.

Considering that Jesus was a Jew, considering that the Old Testament was his Bible, considering that he endorsed every part of it and that he said not one jot or one tittle would pass away from it, even though heaven and earth pass away (Matthew 5:18), isn't it extraordinary that Christians sit so lightly to the Old Testament? Are they right or wrong? I wish the answer to that question were simple. I wish we could just say that the Old Testament is the Jewish book and the New Testament is the Christian book and that all that Christians need is to know the New Testament and base their lives on it, but it's not as simple as that, and Jesus didn't make it as simple as that.

The clue to unravelling the Old Testament is to realize that it's like an electric flex. There are two strands, twined together through the Old Testament. One of them is linked to Abraham and the other to Moses, and from these two great men of God to whom God spoke come the two strands of promise and law, which come right through to Jesus Christ. What Jesus did was to unwind the flex, to separate these two strands, and to do different things with them both.

As far as the law of Moses was concerned, Jesus took that law and he stopped it. He brought it all down to himself. He took every penalty the law has mentioned and he drew it all into his own person and at the cross he suffered the supreme penalty and curse the law pronounced on those who broke it. And at the cross, the strand of law through Moses was stopped ... and we are no longer under law. The law which came from God and down to Moses carried with it a curse on those who broke it, which went right through for many centuries, 14 centuries, to the cross and it stopped there. The curse of the law was then fulfilled. Jesus paid the supreme penalty and in so doing, if I can put it reverently, washed his hands of the law. He completed the law, fulfilled it and finished it.

The other strand which in fact came earlier to Abraham, 430 years, nearly half a millennium, earlier, the strand of promise went underground through the period of the Old Testament and the promise was not enjoyed by the Jews. They knew it was there; they knew it was continuing through the generations as the promise, but the fulfilment never came. As Paul has argued earlier in Galatians 3, which we considered in our previous study, when God made the promise, he did not make it to every descendant of Abraham but to one. The promise went on being passed down, until the one male descendant would come, who would inherit

God's will and testament made to Abraham.

Jesus was that issue; he was that male descendant. He has inherited the promise. But whereas he took the curse of Moses and stopped it, he took the blessing of Abraham and passed it on. The result is now that whereas the Jews lived under the curse of the law of Moses, Gentiles now live in the blessing of Abraham.

Paul has argued against religion based on struggle

Paul has been arguing against the kind of religion that is based on struggle, or as I put it, don't try, just trust, or as someone else has said, don't wrestle just nestle. We tend to take religion and make it an effort. We take what is an offer and turn it into a demand. We take what God meant to be a delight and make it a duty – it's a constant temptation and even Christians can do it. Unfortunately, the Galatians were doing it; they were going back from Christianity to Judaism, back from the freedom of Christ to the bondage of the commandment, back from trusting him the whole way in everything to trying to be good… and it's a very backward step. Now in Galatians 3 he argued very persuasively, from their experience and from his Bible, as we saw in our previous study, that this was a wrong step to take. Some may feel he overstated his case and left no room for the law whatever. Indeed if you're not careful, you could get the impression from Paul that God made an awful blunder when he gave the Ten Commandments, that it was God who messed it all up, that it was God who gave us the impression we had to try by saying, "You shall not… You shall not…" and setting such a high standard.

The purpose of the law

So there is one question we must ask and try and answer and it is: "Why the law? If God wanted to give us all this, if God wanted us not to try but to trust, if God wanted us just to come with open hands and receive what he had to give, why ever did he give the Ten Commandments in the first place?" Surely that is what has caused us to have the impression that you become a Christian by trying to live a good life, surely this has really thrown the whole thing out of gear – "God, why did you give us the law? Why didn't you just leave the promise?" Paul in the rest of Galatians 3 is going to say that God knew perfectly well what he was doing, and the law has indeed a very important place in human religion. What is that place?

"You can't set a man free till you've locked him in. You can't relieve his sin till you've shown him he's a sinner. Provided he thinks he's not a sinner, and provided he thinks he is free, then the message of forgiveness is wasted on him and will do him no good whatever. The gospel does not make sense until a person realizes how much they need it."

The law shuts us in (3:19-22)

An interim measure

The answer comes in two parts: the law shuts us in, and the promise lets us out. You can't be let out until you've been shut in. Now, if that sounds a bit odd, as if God simply locks you in a room so that he can have the privilege of unlocking the door and letting you out again ... we'll see that it's not quite like that. But that is what Paul is saying here, that it is necessary to shut a person in before they can be set free. I can put it another way and you'll straightaway realize what Paul is saying: you can't forgive a man until he knows he's guilty, can you? If a person is not sorry, you cannot forgive them. Try it with your children. If they are not sorry for what they've done, you can't forgive them. In some way you have to show them that they're in the wrong before you can put it right and this was God's supreme design in giving the Ten Commandments, that he might lock us into guilt ... and then set us free for forgiveness. You can't set a man free till you've locked him in. You can't relieve his sin till you've shown him he's a sinner. Provided he thinks he's not a sinner, and provided he thinks he is free, then the message of forgiveness is wasted on him and will do him no good whatever. The gospel does not make sense until a person realizes how much they need it. Now are you beginning to see why the law was added? It was a temporary addition. It was added after the promise and it was made obsolete before the promise. The promise continues right on through. The law was added as an interim, temporary measure; it was not meant to be a permanent feature in your religion. It is a temporary stage to lead you to something else, but it was necessary.

Why was the law necessary?

Because of human lawlessness. The law does two things; whatever rules you make, whatever laws are passed, two effects occur. First, you simply prove that people are breaking the law. But secondly, you actually do put a brake on wrongdoing. When MPs vote for a new measure, they know that people are going to break that law. That's why we have the police. Wouldn't it be marvellous if the House of Commons just passed a law and suddenly everybody in the UK kept it? What a wonderful thing it would be to be an MP in that case. I could imagine Christians flocking to the House of Commons, if that was the effect, but you and I know that it is not so. The effect is twofold: a law does control wrongdoing to some degree, but it doesn't stop crime and sin, but it does put a brake on it and thank God for good laws that put a brake on evildoing. There is a restraint – if there were no traffic laws, the situation would be far worse than it is. But on the other hand, it does reveal that people break the laws, frequently. For example the traffic laws do just that: they expose what is wrong. The law is needed for these two purposes: first, to show up wrongdoing for what it is, to let people know that this is considered wrong, and secondly, to put some kind of a brake because of the sanctions and penalties attached so that it is under some control. It is God's will for all society that there should be laws which will do precisely those two things. Until there are laws, I have no idea how lawless I am in my behaviour. But when there are laws, I know, and it helps to keep me from getting worse. Can I put it this way quite simply: God never gave you the Ten Commandments to make you good, but to show you that you are bad, and to stop you from getting worse. If you think that through, you will realize how wise God is and how he knows exactly what he's doing. So it was a later addition.

The law's limited application

It also has a limited application in time; it is only "until." It is a temporary stage and God wants us to grow out of it, to get beyond it and to become mature enough not to need it. That's the aim of most school rules, which is why they are relaxed in the 6th form (year 13) – you must wear uniform in year 7, but in year 13, you can wear your own choice of clothes. Why do schools do this? Because they know that rules are needed. But they hope that they are needed only temporarily, until a person has grown mature enough not to need them and can discipline themselves. It's the hope of every parent. We parents make mistakes if we say that as long as our children are in our house they will never have the key to the front door, we will see that they are in on time. A wise parent disciplines their child in such a way that they know when to realize the child has grown up and ought to be trusted with the front-door key. And that's a small illustration of God's love for us. The law is an interim, temporary stage, a later addition, and of limited application in time. It is therefore inferior to the promise.

An indirect measure

A mediated covenant

The second way in which the law is inferior to the promise is a more difficult argument. Peter said there are many things in Paul's letters that are hard to understand, and I agree wholeheartedly with him. In the next few verses Paul is making a rather difficult point, again to show that the law is in a sense inferior to the promise. The first point he makes here I think is fairly straightforward and it's that if you have a very important message to pass on to someone, and it's very personal, important and vital that you would not send it through a lot of other channels. You would take it yourself direct. For example, if a headmaster wants to say something important to a boy, he doesn't give a message to a teacher and tell the teacher to give it to a prefect and the prefect to give it to the boy ... he sends for the boy. Or if a boss has something important to say to an employee, he doesn't give the message to a secretary to give to the office boy to pass on to the employee ... he sends for the employee and gives it to him or her directly. Therefore Paul says, "You can see that in some way the law of God was not so important as the promise. The law was given, by God, to angels to give to Moses, to hand on to the people. However, when he gave the promise, he said, 'Abraham I have something to say direct to you.'" This is why some theologians have called the law God's "strange" work; it is less personal, somehow more secondary than what he says directly. So, law and promise again appear to be rather different.

A mutual contract

Now here comes Paul's second point, and I'm going to be frank with you and say that we now come to one of the most difficult verses Paul ever wrote. In the King James Version, it reads: "Now a mediator is not a mediator of one, but God is one"; in the NIV, it reads: "A mediator, however, does not represent just one party; but God is one." It is one of those verses that go in one ear and out the other and you miss it. Normally when a preacher reads Galatians 3 you just switch off for that verse and pick the threads up later.

What is Paul saying? Did you know that there are 600 different ideas as to what he was saying? 600! Study the commentaries that have been written and you can take your pick of 600 meanings. I'm going to give you one of those 600 and you can virtually make up your own, and you'll probably find it's been thought of but you're entitled to it. But what is Paul saying? I believe he's still pointing out that there is a difference between the law and the promise. I've paraphrased what I believe is the sense in about four sentences to try and explain it. If you use a middleman, it's usually because you are in a state of negotiation. You have a go-between to go and ask the other party if this is acceptable. Or to put it this way, why do you employ a solicitor when you buy a house? And why does the other person employ a solicitor? Two go-betweens? The answer is because you're working out a contract, and you make an offer and that goes through the middlemen and then a further figure comes back from the other side so you offer another figure – a contract is being negotiated and you use a middleman because it's in the nature of a two-sided contract. Now in one sense, the law given by God to Moses is a two-sided contract. God says, "If you keep the commandments, I will bless you." So there are conditions being passed through the go-between to us. Moses brought the conditions to Israel who then said, "All that the Lord says we will do," and Moses went back to God and said they would.

Now the law is in the nature of a contract between two parties, God and humanity. There are conditions on both sides – if we keep our side of it, God must keep his. If God keeps his side of it, we must keep ours – it's a contract. But the promise is not like that a bit. The promise is not a contract; it is a covenant. And a covenant is a one-sided thing with no conditions. It is a promise. When we marry two people in this church, it's not a contract. The bride doesn't say to the groom, "If you'll cook my breakfast every morning and warm my slippers every night then I will be faithful to you." And the bride does not say, "If you bring home your pay packet, all of it every week, then I'll be faithful to you" – it is a covenant. It is one-sided, and in fact each makes a promise as a single party: "I will be faithful."

When God made a promise to Abraham there was no contract in it. There were no ifs and buts; God said, "I will": "I will bless you and all nations through you." "I will." So the promise is much more like God's character than the law. It's not like God to make a contract because we believe that God is one. He's not one of two parties – he stands alone and God has the right to tell me whatever conditions he likes; he can make any promises he wishes. I cannot bargain with my creator; I can't say, "Lord, I'll do this if you'll do that." I am not in such a position; God is one: he is one party. So let's never get the idea from the law that you can actually bargain with God. He is one. God is one party and therefore he makes covenants, rather than contracts. I hope that's perhaps enabled you to understand just a little of that difficult verse.

An inadequate measure

The third contrast between law and promise which Paul makes is this. He says, "I'm quite sure by now you're thinking that the law and the promise are opposites, that God in fact gave us two rival systems ... and you can choose between them. You can either believe the promise or keep the law." In providing these two strands in the Old Testament, God was in fact giving us a choice between two ways of getting saved. "You can either get saved by believing my promise through Abraham, or you can get saved through keeping the commandments." It seems as if there are in fact two religions in the Old Testament. What is Paul's reaction to that? Never! Never! It is the same strong expression that he used in 2:18, which is the opposite of the word *Amen* ... never. Never let it be! "Absolutely not!" (NIV), for the simple reason that the law, as far as a religion goes, is a non-starter: it is completely inadequate. It was not only an interim measure; it was not only an indirect measure given through others, it is also an inadequate measure to deal with your wrongdoing and mine. It's a complete non-starter.

Now let's look at this in more detail. If passing a law could make people lead good lives, then it really would be an answer, wouldn't it? Have you heard the proverb, "You'll never make a man good by an Act of Parliament?" Have you heard that? But more than that – you can't cure sin by an Act of Parliament. I'm going to be bold and simply express an opinion, that the Industrial Relations Act thought it could and it can't. You can't make honest workers by Act of Parliament. And it never will. Why we hope we can put a situation right – when it's clearly due to human sin – and think that an Act of Parliament will bring us out of all our troubles is beyond my comprehension. All it can do is demonstrate how evil we are and also put some kind of a brake on it. But to hope that an industrial relations act would cure strikes and would lead us all to peace and prosperity was utterly naive. Paul says, "If you could pass a law to make people good, then it would be an alternative." But there's no such law. And though there are over 630 laws in the Bible not one of them can make you good. What do they do? They just shut down – that's the literal word – they shut down every possibility of making law your religion ... and trying to get saved by doing good. Every commandment that's written closes down the possibility and proves that everybody has done wrong.

That is what the law does. We've got to get it absolutely right: the law will not make you good ... it will simply show that you are bad and stop you getting worse. And so law and promise are not rivals, because the promise can make you good – the law can't but, the promise can. The law can only show that you are bad and stop you from becoming worse, but the promise can lift you into a good life. The law therefore was utterly inadequate and couldn't do the job.

Now let's move on; we've virtually said that the law puts us in prison. Again I remind you of that form that was filled in by somebody and the question was "Have you ever been in prison?" He answered, "No," which was an honest answer and the next question was, "Why?" And he just wrote, "I've never been found out." In fact as far as the law of God is concerned, we have been found out. Every one of us is at this moment remanded in custody until the day of our trial. Every one of us is at this moment under the guard of the law ... awaiting the day of our trial. That's the situation and the law can do nothing about it. All that the law can do is prove that you're guilty and shut you up in your guilt. You are in a condemned cell if you make the law the basis of your religion. If you try to keep the Ten Commandments, you'll just put yourself in the dock.

"Which would you rather be: a man on the run, knowing that one day the police will catch up with you, or a man with your case being taken now and get acquitted? Do you see the difference? One is a false freedom; the other is true freedom."

The promise lets us out (3:23-29)

Now let's turn to the glorious side of the promise. He has shown that the law is necessary to shut us in, to imprison us, to remand us in custody. But the promise is what anticipates your day of trial, brings it forward and says, "You are acquitted!" Now which would you rather be: a man on the run, knowing that one day the police will catch up with you, or a man with your case being taken now and get acquitted? Do you see the difference? One is a false freedom; the other is true freedom. So it isn't just a case of the law shutting you in so that God can let you out. It is the fact that each of us is in the situation where the law is going to catch up with us. Think of the train robbers and the miserable life they lived after the Great Train Robbery of 1963. They were on the run all the time – they knew a freedom of sorts but what kind of freedom is it when you are afraid of every knock on the door, afraid of being recognized, moving from country to country – what kind of freedom is that? But supposing you get caught, and your judge says, "We'll take the case now" and then the judge says, "Acquitted." You walk out of that court into a different kind of freedom, don't you? It's a true freedom, a real freedom. Now the world is in a measure free, people walking around our towns and cities today, going out and enjoying the sunshine in their cars without a thought of God – they are free in a measure, but only in so far as they are on the run. They show every sign of it – you talk to them about God and they run faster. Try and open a conversation on the Ten Commandments and see where it gets you. People know that they're on the run. They don't like religion and they don't like religious people. They never open their Bible because deep down they know that the law of God is after them, and they're trying to put off the evil day and trying to avoid thinking about it altogether. That's not real freedom. But true freedom comes to those who come to Christ and believe the promise. They receive salvation as a free gift. They hear God say, "I've taken your case now, not at the day of judgment. I'm taking it now, and you are acquitted. You are justified through faith." You walk out of that court into true freedom. Now you are free to read your Bible; you're free to worship God. You are no longer on the run from him, his word or his people. Now you're free, really free. It's the promise that did it for you.

Now Paul describes three stages here from prison to freedom. The first stage he recaps a bit and he says, "I'm going to paint the kind of bondage you were under in two pictures. The first one is prison. You were remanded in custody. You were kept under a strong guard of the law. It was always there to say, 'You shall not.' Everywhere you went it escorted you and your conscience; you were remanded in custody."

Then perhaps Paul is thinking that is a little too tough or strong a picture so he give us another. He says the law was like a strict guardian, to make you behave when you were a child. At one stage in my life for just a few years I had a nanny – and she was given full authority over me. And she wielded it! She applied the "board of education" to the "seat of learning" in true nanny fashion. She exercised discipline. In a sense there was a delegated authority from my parents. It was only for a few years but I remember it quite vividly and I have fond memories of that nanny who now lives on a farm in Northumberland.

In ancient times, it was the job of a slave to do this. Until a child came of age the parents did not discipline their own children; did you know that? They got an older slave, who was given a Greek title *paidagogos*, which means "childminder or babysitter." That child minder was given the task of punishment and discipline. The parents never punished their own children; the slave did that. Moreover, some of those slaves were very tough. They walked with the child all the way to the school playground ... until they went to the school, and then they waited for them at the end of school in the afternoon and brought them all the way back home. They saw they didn't get into mischief on the way home. Everywhere the child went, the slave went, and the slave had full authority to punish that child in any way, short of killing them. The slave looked after the child in this way until the child reached anywhere between the age of 14 and 17. Then the father took over, and the child was given full freedom from punishment. The child was for the first time called a son ... prior to that *child* – now *son* and for the first time the son could use the word *father.* The son was given full freedom, the key of the door. The father did not replace the slave with discipline; the father trusted the mature son.

Now that is a lovely picture that Paul takes out of domestic life and he says, "Can't you see that's what the Ten

Commandments were to you. They were your governess, your guardian, your childminder. When you were immature, you needed someone to follow you around wherever you went, to make sure you weren't naughty, that you didn't get into mischief." You see, a child doesn't know what's naughty until you tell a child. You've got to say, "That's naughty," and the childminder did just that. Now the law was your childminder, and all through those years before you met Christ, the law was given to you to look after you, to show you that you were doing wrong, to punish you when you did it. The law was there to bring you up properly. You needed that discipline. But the childminder always had to pass a child on at a certain age. The childminder always passed on to a schoolteacher when the child went to school, but the main task of the childminder was to pass the child to the father. When the child became a son, the childminder's job was finished. Now do you begin to see what that says? The law was your childminder, and when you were an immature person, you needed the law. But one day you met Jesus Christ, and you changed from being a child of God – every person in the world is in a sense a child of God – you now became for the first time *a son of God*. "But as many as received him, to them gave he power to become the sons of God, even to them that believe on his name" (John 1:12, KJV).

Is God the father of all people ... or just Christians? The answer is that all people are his children, but only Christians are his sons, according to the Bible. Do you see the distinction? And when you came to Christ, the law completed its job. It had shown you that you were a sinner: it had shown you your guilt; it had kept you from getting worse. It had kept you under strict control until you met Christ, but now you've met Christ you're a son. You can look up to heaven and say, "Dad, Abba, Father," and your heavenly Father says, "From now on here's the key of the door, son. From now on, I trust you. From now on, you're self-disciplined." What a freedom!

I remember when I left school for the last time, I went dancing away. I remember the lightness, as if I was walking on air. I had left school, I was away from that headmaster, away from those prefects, away from being kept in which tended to happen … I was away from all that … I was free! Of course I didn't then realize what the rest of life was going to be like, but do you remember how you felt when you were let out of school? Do you remember as a child when the bell sounded at the end of the school day, you felt you were free. I have not been to prison so I don't know what it's like when the gates close behind you when you leave having served your sentence but I would imagine it's quite a feeling. Free, at last! And when you came to Christ, that's how you can feel now about the law. It's been with you wherever you went; it's escorted you; it's been your guardian; you've been under its custody. You've been waiting for the day of your trial but now in Christ, your trial has been held and you've been acquitted, so you're free! You're no longer in custody, you're no longer in the hands of the law – you're free!

Baptized in Christ

New dress

That is what Paul is saying now. In fact, he says it really happened when you were baptized. It's interesting that

Paul rarely says when you were converted; he always takes baptism as the key point in your initiation. He doesn't say, "When you were converted this happened"; he says, "All of you who were immersed." I wish all Bibles would translate the Greek word *baptized*; it's not an English word, it means "immerse, dip, plunge, sink." "When you were sunk, when you were immersed, when you were dipped, when you were baptized, do you know what happened? You were wrapped up in Christ"; he says, "You put Christ on like a new suit of clothes. You put on Christ; you clothed yourself in Christ." I've chosen the word *wrap* because it implies dress. When you were baptized, not only did the water enclose you, but also Christ enclosed you. When you were identified fully with him in his death, burial and resurrection, you were wrapped up in Christ. You put on some new clothes. Now do you know that when a Roman boy became a son and came of age, his father said, "From now on you're my son. From now on the slave who's looked after you has finished. From now on you're free, and here's the key of the door," the father would hold out a new robe? A new toga. It was called the *toga virilis*. It was the first suit with long trousers, did you know? The father would say, "Now put this on." And the boy would put on his *toga virilis* and he'd walk down the street, and he'd say, "Look at my new suit. I'm a man now, with long trousers!" It's quite a moment in a boy's life when he puts on his first long trousers. So he'd walk down the street – he was a man now. When you were baptized, you put on Christ. God held out Christ to you and said, "Put him on. You're a man now. You're my son now, so put on my son."

I had a thought recently, supposing someone found an old

garment and an old pair of sandals and discovered that they'd actually found something that Christ wore while he was on earth. Supposing they brought them here to the church and said, "Would anybody like to put these on?" How would you feel? Would you want to? Or would you shrink from putting that robe and those sandals on and think, "I'm wearing what Christ wore"? It would give you a funny feeling, wouldn't it? I'll tell you something much more marvellous than that. If you're a Christian and you've been baptized, you are wrapped up in Christ; you are wearing him now.

No distinctions

What does that mean? How does this teaching work out? It means that all of you who belong to Christ are not separate individuals anymore. You are just one person. So you can't look at people and say he's this and she's that and he's the other, you cannot say that's a Jew and that's a Gentile. You can't say he's male and she's female, you can't say he's a slave and he's free ... all you can say is we are all just one person now. I wonder if I can put it this way and it might just get it across ... you have not only become sons of God, you have each become part of the Son of God. You see the difference? We're not just sons, we are all parts of him. And so since we are all just one person, it means, if I may say it, we are all Jewish ... we are all male ... and we are all free. Because Jesus is Jewish, male and free. And so we are all one person.

We can consider verse 28 from another dimension too. Verse 28 has been compared to the English Magna Carta and the American Declaration of Independence as a proclamation of human freedom – from all the distinctions of race, sex and class that divide humanity. Christ has abolished them. They are obsolete. Christians are therefore committed to advocating and advancing a totally egalitarian order in society. The church is called to model this for the world to follow.

Verse 28 is thought to have political as well as social implications. The divisions between rich and poor, black and white are also included. The recent wave of "Liberation Theology", spreading among South Americans, South Africans and Palestinians is not unrelated.

Let us consider the gender clause: "neither male nor female." This is the clearest distinction of all, dividing humanity into two. Feminist theologians revel in this verse and use it to counteract almost everything else Paul said on the subject of gender. His teaching on male headship in marriage, male eldership in the church, restrictions on female ministry – all this "Jewish paternalism" must yield to this one supreme Christian illumination, when he was free from his traditional prejudice!

Practising homosexuals also rejoice in verse 28. If gender is eradicated, what is wrong with one-sex loving relationships, provided they are also loyal? Why do Christians frown on same-sex marriage? Again this verse is used to cancel out Paul's teaching in other letters (eg Romans 1:26-27; 1 Corinthians 6:9-10).

It is pretty obvious that as long as we are in this world we have not been sexually neutered. Christians still have sexual temptations. Husbands are still husbands and wives are still wives, with different roles and responsibilities.

The important thing to realize is that Galatians 3:28 is dealing with our *vertical* relationships with the Lord rather than our *horizontal* relationships with each other or, to put it another way, our heavenly privileges rather than our earthly responsibilities. Paul deals with the latter in other letters and contexts (Ephesians 5:22-6:9 and Colossians 3:18-4:1), where human distinctions are accepted.

But there may be more to it than that. The immediate context of 3:28 is the paragraph 26-29. Verses 26 and 27 tell us that through faith in Christ Jesus we become sons of God, as he was, baptized into him (and his name), "clothed" with him (from then on), we have taken on his identity. So in God's eyes we are all Jewish, male and free. All of us, even women believers, are "sons." We are all one person (significantly in verse 29 the word for "one" is not the impersonal Greek for "united" but the personal word for one individual, as in English "every*one*" and "any*one*").

Blessed in Abraham

Now if you are that one person, here comes the exciting bit, if you are that one person, you can go to God and say, "I claim the promise. Because I am that single descendant of Abraham to whom you left it in your will and testament, I can claim the promised Holy Spirit." You can claim that promise; you can go to God and say, "Bless me with the Holy Spirit because you promised him ... to the seed of Abraham and I'm wrapped up in Christ, I'm part of your son, I am that seed. I am that issue, I'm the one person who inherits. I claim my blessing." You have the authority and freedom to do so. This may seem a deep argument to you and rather intellectual. But Paul is stating the sober truth that in Christ we are no longer a lot of separate and different individuals – we are one person.

155

There are still differences of function within the body. It does not mean we can all do the same thing, because within one body there are different limbs and organs and there are different functions. And within the one body, male and female still have different functions; they do in a Christian family. But they are doing it as members of one individual ... not as separate individuals. They are doing it as different parts of the whole, not different whole people. So the blessing has come down.

Since biblical inheritance comes down through the male, the fact that we are all sons means that we are also heirs. Belonging to Christ we are Abraham's (single) "seed" (verse 29) eligible for the promise made to him that "all peoples on earth will be blessed through you" (Genesis 12:3, NIV). We are Abraham's sons if we share his absolute trust in God's word and his complete obedience to it.

Conclusions

Has the law – the Ten Commandments – any place in religion today? Only, if they act as a guardian to lead you to Christ. That's their function, and I believe that in that capacity the law has a function still. First it has a function for those who do not yet know Christ. The Ten Commandments drive us to Christ. Dr Billy Graham has found again and again that whenever he preaches the Ten Commandments, more people come to Christ. And the reason is simple: it is the needle of the law that penetrates our soul, to pull the thread of the gospel in. It is the law that brings you down low, so that God may lift you up high. It's the law that makes you guilty, that God may forgive. It's the law that shuts you in so that God may let you out.

We're living in times when many people are coming to Christ without having first faced up to the commandments and the result is a very shallow Christianity. It's a Christianity that lacks the joy of forgiveness. It's a Christianity that has not faced the demands of God and just wants the free offer. The healthy conversion is the conversion of someone who's been to the law first and realized from the law how far they've fallen short, and then coming to Christ: their freedom is so real. The great preacher P T Forsyth used to say why are the churches so full of nice, kind people who have never known the despair of guilt, or the breathless wonder of forgiveness? And the answer is they've never been to the law. They've had the gospel without the law.

But now that we've come to Christ, has the law anything to say to us now? Now that we've been set free, yes I believe it has. To go back and look at the guardian and see what the guardian said to us drives us further to Christ, doesn't it? When as Christians we read the Ten Commandments, it just makes us realize much more how we need the promise of free grace. We don't try to keep the commandments, we go back to Christ, for more forgiveness, more grace and more of God's love. And so I believe that God uses the law all the time to bring us to Christ, to lead us to him, to drive us to grace, to show us our utter inadequacy without him. Then we come to Christ and we discover what freedom really is.

6

Galatians 4:1-11

IS GOD YOUR BOSS
OR YOUR DAD?

"We" Jewish believers (4:1-5)
Estate
Elements
The gift of God's Son
Becoming sons of God

"You" Gentile believers (4:6-10)
God has sent the Spirit of his Son
We cry out "Abba! Daddy!"
How can you go back to being slaves?
Superstitions
Special days
God wants sons not servants

Look at it like this – a child can inherit a business, but as long as he is under age he is no better off than one of the employees, even though he owns the whole lot. He is supervised by guardians and his affairs are managed by trustees, until the date set by his father. In much the same way, when we were spiritual infants, our behaviour was governed by the world's childish superstitions.

But God had appointed a time for our coming-of-age and when it was ripe, he sent his Son into our world. He came in the same way as we did, from a woman's body. She was a Jew, so he was born subject to the law. This enabled him to purchase the freedom of those who lived under its tyranny and give us the full status of grown-up sons.

Because you too have been recognized as God's sons, he sent the Spirit of his Son into our inmost beings, so that we call out instinctively, "Abba! Dad!" (which is exactly how Jesus addressed his heavenly Father). This proves that each of you is a son of God and no longer his servant; and if you are his son you are also his heir, and he will make sure you get the estate.

There was a time when you had no personal relationship with God. But your religion bound you to do so much for 'gods' who weren't even real! But now that you know God as he is (or rather, now that he has introduced himself to you) how can you possibly go back to those feeble and needy superstitions? Do you really want to be in their grip again? Already you're observing a calendar of so-called "sacred" days and months and seasons and years. I am beginning to have a horrible fear that all my efforts to help you have been wasted.

(Author's translation)

Our generation has become obsessed with relationships. We're trying to work out what the right relationship between parents and children is, the relationship between the public and the police, between people of different ethnic origins, between Jews and Arabs, between students and university staff. There are new sciences like group dynamics being studied and whereas once the popular subject at university was psychology, the study of the individuals and their behaviour, the most popular one currently is sociology and the humanities in which we study how people relate to each other and behave as groups.

The Bible is concerned from cover to cover with relationships. But it begins with the first and most important relationship in your life which is not that between you and your husband or wife, or between you and your parents or children, or you and your brothers and sisters, or you and your friends. The most important relationship in your life and the one that will determine all the rest of your life is your relationship with God. How would you describe that relationship? If I can paraphrase the question that Paul is raising in this section of his letter to the Galatians in a rather simple and perhaps rather crude way but it'll make my point. Is God your boss or your dad? That's what he's saying. Is your relationship with your creator that of a servant or a son? Is he your boss or your dad?

As we have studied Galatians, we have been looking at the same question from different angles. We've looked at it from the point of view of the relationship between the Old Testament and the New Testament and from the point of view of the relationship between Judaism and Christianity, from the point of view of that kind of religion that is based on trying to that kind of religion that is based on trusting, the one that is built on law compared with the one that is built on love.

In this study, we are looking at the same question but from the point of view of are you a son or a servant of God? Can I express it in this way? Is an act of worship for you a service or a celebration? Now that's the question we're considering.

"We" Jewish believers (4:1-5)

I've divided this portion of Galatians into two parts by the personal pronouns used. In the first half Paul uses the pronoun *we* and in the second half *you*. There are one or two exceptions which I'll note but this is a generalized distinction. When Paul says *we* he is generally speaking about the Jews who have believed in Jesus: "we Jewish believers." But when he says *you* he is referring primarily to you Gentile believers who did not originally belong to God's people. The amazing thing is that Paul applies the same term to both himself and his fellow Jews who believe in Jesus and the Gentiles and that word is *son*. And since he applies the word *sons* to them, he is also prepared to say *brother*. There was a time when Paul confronted with a Gentile would have called him "a sinner" and said, "I belong to the people of God – you're a sinner." But when Paul came to know Jesus he could look at Gentile believers and say, "You're a son and therefore you're my brother. We're in the same family." That's the kind of transforming relationship that comes into a life when Jesus Christ is Saviour and Lord. Welcome to the family!

"Paul uses an analogy from ordinary life: 'Grow up!' Far too many people have never really studied much since they were children. So their faith has never become mature. The Bible was written so that we might grow up, that our relationship with God might be mature."

Let's consider what he has to say about the Jews. Paul is going to use an analogy from ordinary life and his message is this: "Grow up!" Far too many people suffer from childish religion. They've never really learned much or studied much since they were a child in Sunday School or at day school and so their faith has never become an adult mature faith. The Bible was not written for children even though it contains some parts that we can give to children. This book was written for adults, for those with a mature faith. It was written that we might grow up, that our relationship with God might be mature. Paul says, "Grow up." We have grown up. We Jewish believers had to leave behind our childish religion and grow up. Now the illustration he uses is a very common one. I'm going to twist it slightly to bring it more within the realm of your experience. Have you ever been to a country house, and gone down into the basement kitchen in the cellar and seen rules hanging up on the wall – rules for the servants? "Rules to be observed." There are some fascinating rules about them – they mustn't wear their overcoats while they're having meals and mustn't let the dogs lick the plates and all sorts of things like this. Rules. Rules. Rules. There were servants who were bound by these rules. I want you to notice the key word in the middle at the top: Observed. But if you go round the same country house, there is another room that was the nursery for the children. They too were under rules and there would be a strict governess or nanny or someone looking after the children while they were under age. They were the children who would inherit the whole of that estate, but as long as they were infants, they were no better off than the servants down in the cellar.

Rules to be observed. One day those children would grow up and one day the boy who'd been kept under rules like any of the servants up to a certain age would be set free and the whole estate would be his. He would walk around that estate ten feet tall. He was the son and the heir. Now the point is this: he could have been the son, the whole estate could have been his, if his father had died while he was an infant but as long as he was a minor under age he was no better off than a servant.

Estate

The tragedy is that the whole estate belongs to us and we are meant to walk ten feet tall in God's sight as sons and heirs, but we stick so easily to a childish religion which puts us under observance of rules, as if we were still minors, still infants – we cling to these things. So Paul says, "Grow up." God wants sons, not servants. He doesn't want you to come to church because you're observing a lot of rules. He wants you to come and celebrate that you're the son and heir of God and that all things are yours in Christ. That's what he wants. Grow up – don't be a minor – don't put yourself under a governess. Don't put yourself on the same level as a servant of God. He wants you to be a son.

He then describes what he means by being a servant, what he means by putting yourself under rules. He uses a rather funny word, which we're going to have to explain a little; it's a word translated in normal Bibles as *elements* or *basic principles*.

Elements

Elements. You were bound by elements. Now the simple meaning of that is "ABC; elementary education." That's the simple meaning, but it's hard to say that Paul was meaning that because that would not bind us. That helps to set us free; to teach a person to read sets them free to read. Why then does Paul say you were bound by these elements if he simply means "elementary ABC education; learning the alphabet"? There is another meaning for the word *elements*. It was used for example to describe earth, air, fire and water, which are the four elements. It was used to describe the sun, moon and stars. People in those days sometimes felt that they were in the grip of the sun, moon and stars and they would read the zodiac. They would read their horoscopes and they were born under this or that sign and this was not a very good day to do this or that – you know there are people still like this today. They are in the grip of elements and they believe the stars decide what's going to happen for you; they read their horoscope in their daily paper or magazine. There are very few popular papers would dare to go to press today without including a horoscope.

But the Jews, apart from one or two sad lapses, didn't worship the stars. They did on occasion but on the whole they didn't. So what does Paul mean here? There is one word that seems to me to combine elementary ideas with the sense of being bound and it is *superstition*. Paul is saying when you're a child, you turn religion into a superstition.

I was talking recently to a very clever businessman with all his mental faculties; he's got on well in the world. He's done very well for himself and made a lot of money. I asked him, "How are you?" and he replied, "I'm very well, touch wood." A man with all his senses and yet he wouldn't answer without saying that! He's in the grip of a childish superstition. You would be astonished how many great people in this world are in the grip of such superstitions. How many have their advisors? How many read their horoscopes? How much business there is in such superstition! A superstition is a religious idea that's been twisted until it's become childish and it's based on fear. For example throwing salt over your shoulder. Why do you do that? Simply because if you'd lived a few thousand years ago, you'd have taken some salt and you'd have thrown it onto the altar of your god. Why do you get all worried if you see a black cat? Because black cats were used by the druids, as was mistletoe. Why do you get worried about sitting 13 at a table because Jesus and the 12 disciples sat 13 at a table and one went out and hanged himself and that's why Friday the 13th is considered unlucky. People are in the grip of such superstitions. The only one that isn't really silly is walking under a ladder, which has a profound and rational basis to it, but Paul is saying that the Jews had turned their religion into a superstition and were bound by it and the fact is they had. They were scared stiff of putting a foot wrong. They were scared stiff of offending God. They were scared stiff of eating without washing their hands. Or of brushing against a Gentile in the marketplace. They were full of superstition, and yet they were God's chosen people meant to show the world how to relate to God properly.

Paul says when we were spiritual infants we were in the grip of childish superstitions. The one thing about coming to Christ is you're set free from superstition. You need never again touch wood or worry about a broken mirror or look at the calendar before you go out. You're free. All those ways are childish. Actually, it's astonishing how childish some people are. When I was a chaplain in the Royal Air Force, pilots – brilliant young men trained up with all their technical knowledge and flying the latest jet aircraft – used to tuck a rabbit's foot in their pocket before they took off. They would not take off before they had done so. That is the kind of religion that grips infants who have never grown up, and it's Paul's description of the Jewish minority. They were underage; and he goes on to say, one day we grew up. That happened when Jesus came – that's when you grow up and become an adult. It's when you stand in God's presence, but not as a subservient, fearing and cringing slave but as a son.

The gift of God's Son

Then Jesus came. God had appointed a time. I've heard many sermons and I've preached one myself on the phrase "when the time had fully come" (4:4, NIV). I've usually pointed out, as other preachers have, that the Roman roads had been built and the Greek language had been started and the world was ripe. But in fact the phrase means a lot more than that. It means when the Jews had had enough of the law; when God saw that the law had taught them all it could; when God saw that they were ready for maturity, he said, "Now I'm going to give them a Son."

The next few verses say this. God's Son became a servant so that those who were his servants might become his sons. That is the gospel in a nutshell: God's Son became a servant so that God's servants might become sons. Take the first part. God sent his Son on a mission to our world and he came into our world in the same way as we came. He didn't come down from the clouds the first time, although he will when he comes the second. When he came the first time, he came in the role of a humble person to a working home. He was born in a dirty manger. He became a servant. Some people think that the phrase "born of a woman" refers to the virgin birth. If it is, it's the only time Paul ever mentions the virgin birth. But the phrase "born of a woman" in the Bible is used of everybody else. Every one of us was born of a woman. You need to remember that, you owe your very existence to the pain of some woman. Christ, too, was born of a woman. He was conceived differently from us but he was born in exactly the same way. He came to help me so he had to be like me. He came right into my circumstances. He was born as a little crying baby, as I was.

Because his mother was a Jew, he was born under the law and he had to keep it. On the eighth day, he was circumcised and presented in the temple and in the 12th year, he was made a son of the law in the same temple. He grew up under the law and he had to keep it and he did keep it. He was the first man who has ever done so. See what he was doing: he was getting under our load so that he might lift us up. He was getting inside our skin so that he might let us out. He was coming into our life so that we might have his life. Praise God that he didn't remain in heaven and say, "Here is the way – you can find your way to me." God said, "Son, you'll have to go and you'll have to get right into their lives and you'll have to lift the load from inside." So he was born of a woman, born under the law.   That was how he could purchase freedom for those who lived under the tyranny of the law. There is only one way to set a slave free and that's to buy him.   I heard of a missionary who went out to Africa and found himself in a market where slaves were being sold. The missionary was so touched by his first real glimpse of men being sold like cattle and women and children too in a market that he put together all his money and he bought a slave, and then he set that slave free. This was the first thing he did in Africa... and Jesus purchased freedom for those who were in slavery to superstition. He came right under the law which had been turned into superstition, something fearful that was binding people. He got under it and he paid the supreme price to set them free.

Becoming sons of God

What was the result of him setting them free? They were adopted by God as sons.   I've not used the word *adopted* in my translation for a very simple reason. It is a misleading word in the English language. In our language *adoption* usually means having someone else's child in your family. But in those days the word referred far more frequently to having your own child as your son. It was a ceremony that took place between the ages of 14 and 17 and the boy put off his toga which he wore as a boy and he put on this *toga virilis*, the man's garment. He took his toys and he got rid of them, he put away childish things. He walked down the main street with his dad to the forum. It was a great moment in a boy's life. He was accepted in male society as a man;

he was now adopted. His father said, "I adopt you and you can now call me 'father.' My own business is yours. You will inherit it; you're a son and heir." A man didn't do this until his boy got into his mid-teens. Sometimes he looked around his boys and saw how they were turning out and said, "I think I'll make that one my son and heir," and so he might only adopt one of his children. They were already his children but he would adopt one and give that one the status of son and heir. That is the adoption Paul is referring to here without a doubt. He says once Christ had set you free from slavery to superstition, God could adopt you as his son.

Paul believed firmly that all people are God's offspring. When he was in Athens, he quoted a Greek poet: "For we are all his offspring" (Acts 17:28). He quoted it with approval. Here comes the tension I mentioned in our previous study that we are all God's offspring but not everybody is his son. Therefore not everybody can call him "Father" and not everybody is going to inherit his estate. But when Jesus came, born of a woman, born under the law, he lifted the load. He paid the price; he purchased our freedom and God said, "Now call me Father. You're my son and heir." That is the description of what had happened to the Jews.

"You" Gentile believers (4:6-10)

Now we go on to Paul's remarks about the Gentile believers. He's now turning to the Galatians who came from a very mixed background, one that was totally different from Paul's. Paul had only believed in one God; they had believed in many gods. And yet Paul says, "You are sons". It does not matter what a person's cultural background has been… if months ago he was a cannibal on a South Sea island or if he's

IS GOD YOUR BOSS OR YOUR DAD? *4:1-11*

been the worst criminal on earth. The day he comes to know Jesus, he's a son of God. My brother! He is going to inherit God's estate – that's the glory of it all! Paul says, "Now you Gentiles, how did this happen to you? It happened when Jesus came to you but not in the same way as he came to us Jews. To us Jews, he came in the flesh but to you Gentiles he came in his Spirit."

God has sent the Spirit of his Son

There's a very clear difference here: Jesus came born of a woman in the flesh to the Jews and those who believed in him became grown-up sons. But to the Gentiles he's never come in the flesh. Jesus has never visited this country in the flesh. One sect believes he visited the United States in the flesh, but I'm sure they're wrong. He never left his own land in the flesh; from that land perhaps he slipped over the border to Syro-Phoenicia once but from that land he slipped straight back to glory. He's never been to this country in the flesh. The funny thing is sometimes we wish he would, but if he did, I think we would think again. Just imagine Jesus is here in the flesh at a service this morning. Which of you is going to speak to him afterwards? Who's going to get the chance to have a word? A few of you might if you pushed hard, but some of you would not get near him for the press. Some of you might have to climb into the balcony to see like Zacchaeus climbed a tree. He hasn't come to us in the flesh and thank God he has not in one way. He's come to us in the Spirit. Paul says as God sent his son to us Jews in the flesh, he has sent the Spirit of his Son. That's what made you his sons. Now because he's come in the Spirit, he's come right inside. Deep inside, right into our hearts. That is something he couldn't do if he was here in the flesh. So praise God that he sent his Spirit and Jesus came right into our hearts.

We cry out "Abba! Daddy!"

What is the result of his sending the Spirit of his Son right into our hearts? It is that people shout out. It says so here. The Greek word is *krazon* which means "to cry out." I had a funny thought this week that some poker-faced, stiff and starchy people are going to shout *hallelujah* in heaven. You'll surprise yourselves, so maybe it is better to get used to it here and then it doesn't make it so difficult to adjust there! When the Spirit gets right into a person, he has to get out again. That's the law of Scripture and you will find if you go through Scripture carefully, you will find that whenever the Holy Spirit comes on people, their mouth does something. You read your Bible right through and study it every time. You'll find that when the Spirit gets into the heart, he comes out of the mouth. That is the proof that something has happened. That's how it always has been. That's how it was on the Day of Pentecost and there was the sound like a mighty rushing wind; there were tongues of flame on each of them and they were all filled with the Holy Spirit... and they began to speak. The devil has had great use of your tongue and mine. Why shouldn't the Lord have it? And if you can control your tongue, you're perfect, so the way to be perfect is to let the Lord have your tongue.

"When the Holy Spirit gets right in, something comes out. Paul describes one of the loveliest things in Scripture. One commentator said it was a quiet inward witness. That's rubbish! The word is *calling out, crying out*. No 'quiet inward witness'! For too long we've liked our religion to be quiet and inward but that is not New Testament religion. New Testament religion was rather noisy and was outward. It came out."

When the Holy Spirit gets right in, something comes out. Paul now describes one of the loveliest things in Scripture, but this is often misunderstood. One commentator I looked up said it was a quiet inward witness. That is rubbish! The word is *calling out, crying out*. No "quiet inward witness"! For too long we've liked our religion to be quiet and inward but that is not New Testament religion. New Testament religion was rather noisy and was outward. It came out. "Now there were staying in Jerusalem God-fearing Jews from every nation under heaven. When they heard this sound, a crowd came together in bewilderment, because each one heard them speaking in his own language" (Acts 2:5-6, NIV). "Shout for joy to the LORD, all the earth" (Psalm 100:1, NIV). I know quietness has its place and is scriptural too. What comes out here? Paul says, "The Spirit of his Son in your heart will cry out, '*Abba*.'" That's not even your language. It's not translated into English in the Bible deliberately. I haven't translated it into English because Paul kept that in the original language for a specific reason: you don't know what language you'll use when the Holy Spirit gets your tongue.

This is the language of Aramaic – which Paul did not speak as far as we know – but which Jesus did. Abba. What Paul is saying is this: "When the Spirit gets right into your heart, you will find yourself addressing yourself to God in maybe quite a new way and a new language. But what the language is saying is this: 'Dad, dad.'" That's what *Abba* means. It is the little Jewish word that a Jewish baby is taught: "Dada, dada. *Abba*. *Abba*. Dad. Daddy." At prayer meetings we have been moved by the use of that word in our prayers; as we look up to heaven to our creator; we say "*Abba*, Daddy."

What does that mean? It means that you're no longer a servant but a son. A son. Servants never dare to address their employer by saying, "Dad." Never, but sons do. When the Spirit gets right into you, you will find yourself talking to God as a son, as a daughter. You will find yourself speaking as a member of the family. That's what the Spirit does. Romans 8:15-16 is perhaps the best commentary on this verse. It amplifies it a bit: "For you did not receive a spirit that makes you a slave again to fear, but you received the Spirit of sonship. And by him we cry 'Abba, Father.'" We have received the Spirit of adoption by whom we cry out. It's we who'll cry. The Spirit doesn't make a noise; we do that. We cry out, "*Abba*. Dad. Father." It's the instinctive cry of a child, a child in need crying out, "*Abba*. Father."

How can you go back to being slaves?

Now let's consider the mature relationship that these Galatians had received. They had received the Spirit. Paul says in Galatians 3, "How did you receive the Spirit? By works of the law or by faith?" They knew what it was to receive the Spirit. The Spirit had gone on being supplied to them so that God did miracles among them regularly. Now Paul says, "Not only does he do miracles; he also makes you cry out, doesn't he? You shout out as a son or daughter of God and you're a member of the family. Now," he continues, "how can you go back from that to being a slave again? You're holding out your hands and saying, 'Put the chains on again.' You're climbing back over the prison wall back into your cell. How can you possibly go back from being a son to being a slave?"

The tragic truth, however, is that many of us Christians do just that. You cast your minds back to that carefree initial love you had for the Lord when you were free, when you really enjoyed sonship and now, years later, you must ask yourself has your religion become a drudgery? A chore? Has it become a matter of being doggedly loyal to the fellowship, to the church, to keep it all going? To grind away at the machine? Why go back to being a slave again? Has it become a superstition again? Yes it can. Even Holy Communion can be made into a superstition. People can come out of fear.

Superstitions

Now had the Galatians been doing it? Paul goes back to their childhood, to their spiritual childhood, their infancy. He describes what they were redeemed from. He says, "You used to believe in a lot of gods." Have you ever realized how complicated it is to believe in many gods? Most of you have no idea what it's like because you've only had to deal with one. You were brought up to believe that there was only one. People generally in this country believe in only one God. But I wonder if you can imagine what it's like to come into this building and try and keep a whole lot of gods happy? And to have one god for Sunday and one for Monday and one for Tuesday and so on, one god for your food and one god for your health and another god for your crops? Another god for this and another god for that? Can you imagine what it's like? It binds you in superstition. You've got to do something about it. And you are bound by rules and this, that and the other. It's an awful bondage. The tragedy of it all is the gods aren't even real. They're not even there. There is something very sad about a Hindu going from shrine to shrine, leaving a pound of butter here and a pound of butter there, going from god to god trying to find reality.

I remember meeting a man who was once a Hindu who became a Christian and who eventually became a bishop; he was one of the loveliest Christians I've ever met. He told us how, as a Hindu boy, he had tried to find the truth and his mother had taken him to shrine after shrine in her sincerity trying to do her bit and taking their little offering for the gods here and there. As a boy he was puzzled because they never got through to God. They were bound. Then one day he met Jesus, and he was free from all the superstition. He found out the gods weren't even real and the whole thing was a gigantic bluff of Satan and superstition is a bluff. I tell you: call Satan's bluff. Challenge it in the name of Jesus. The gods aren't real. The stars do not decide what you do. You can be free now and you can sing, "Sun, moon and stars in their courses above" without worshipping the sun, moon and stars. You've got no bondage to the sun, moon and stars. You can enjoy the sun and thank God for it; so we're not victims of superstition.

Now Paul says, "Look, you got out of those superstitions." They had two characteristics. They were feeble and they were beggarly. What does he mean? He means first superstition is feeble. It can't help you one bit. Not only can it not do anything for you, it's always demanding that you do something for it. It's beggarly. And every superstition has those two characteristics. It can't do a thing for you but it makes you do things for it all the time. So there's that poor businessman touching wood every time somebody asks him "How are you?" and he's got to do it. He's bound to do it and he goes on doing things for the superstition and what does it do for him? Absolutely nothing. These are weak and beggarly superstitions.

Paul says, "Now you're going back to them." How were they going back to them? Are they going back to many deities? No. Are they going back to pagan worship? No. I'll tell you what they're going back to. He says, "You are already turning Christianity into a calendar. You're already having special sacred days and months and seasons and years just like the Jews did."

Special days

I want you to notice, and I realize I'm going to tread on some people's toes here, but I've got to say it. I want you to notice that that is just as bad as paganism. In Paul's sight to start making Christianity a matter of dates and calendars is to do exactly the same kind of thing as the poor pagan in his superstition bound by a god who doesn't exist. I'm aware I'm saying this at the beginning of Lent. I find nothing in my Bible about Lent. Do you know I received through my door this week a suggestion from a dear brother for a rule of life for Lent, suggesting rules and regulations for me to keep in Lent? Thank God I'm free! There is no calendar in the Bible. Every Sunday is resurrection day. Every day is the Lord's day. Once we start getting confined and bound to observe rules of Lent and do without sweets and things and think that somehow that is what God wanted us to be, we're really sunk. "You're going back to observance," says Paul and that's the key word. There it was, "Do you remember those rules for the servants, rules to be observed?" As soon as you start thinking that and say rules are to be observed in church, as soon as you start to say the Christian life is a matter of doing this and that rule and regulation, you're going right back to the state of infantile superstition.

"God wants sons not servants. God wants people who can rejoice in the relationship and walk with him as free sons, not those who just observe Lent by giving up sweets! There's something much bigger for us in store."

God wants sons not servants

God wants sons not servants. God wants people who can rejoice in the relationship and walk with him as free sons, not those who observe Lent by giving up sweets! There's something much, much bigger for us in store. And so Paul says really you are Christians but you're going back to observing special days. As soon as you have sacred days, you then begin to think of secular days. As soon as you have a sacred month, you begin to think of secular months and I'll tell you what will happen. We observed the beginning of Lent this week – my children and I ate pancakes: we had a real party on pancakes one night. You see what happens because you're going to do without, you have pancakes the night before and have a feast. It happened in the Middle East. I saw Arabs observing Ramadan, the month of fasting. Now they're allowed to eat after sunset but not at all during the day, so they were in a terrible temper all day and at sunset they had a big feast and got indigestion. We just had to go very carefully through Ramadan because of this. Is there any difference between Ramadan and Lent? Paul says, "Don't go back." It's paganism in another form. You go on to Jesus. Remain as sons; remain mature.

Now was Paul really true to Jesus Christ's teaching with this emphasis? Was he really right to be brokenhearted and say, "I've got a fear that all my efforts to help you have been wasted. I really feel you're going right back to where you were"? Yes, he was being true to Jesus and I'll tell you where Jesus said the same thing: Luke chapter 15, verses 11-32.

A certain man had two sons. And the younger of them went away into a far country and then he realized he'd been a fool and so he came back to his father and what did he want to say? "Make me a hired servant." A hired servant in his dad's house. Can you imagine? He didn't even think of his dad's feelings with his own son in the kitchen. "Make me a hired servant. You know I'll work for you; you give me bread. I want a relationship with you that's a servant relationship." Now he had a good reason for saying this. He didn't feel worthy to be a son but he hadn't realized that the father didn't want a hired servant. He wanted a son, and so when the boy got home and said to his father, "Father I've sinned against heaven and in your sight, and am no more worthy to be called your son," he got no further. The father stopped him short. Hired servant, never! The tragedy of it is that the elder son had the same outlook of a hired servant. When the father went out to the elder brother, you notice the elder brother never used the word *father.* His whole conversation reveals that he wanted to be a servant. He said, "Look, I've served you all these years. I've always done what you've said. I've never broken a rule of yours. I've kept them all. And you never gave me a kid." The father said, "All I have is yours. But son, this is your brother."

God doesn't want servants. He doesn't want those who say I've never broken a commandment. He doesn't want people to bargain with him. He doesn't want a contract. He isn't hiring you, wanting you here in church this morning. The father says, "I want sons who'll call me 'dad'. I want a family who'll look on each other as brothers. That's my aim and object. Grow up then. Have done with rules and regulations. Live as sons and heirs. All things are coming to you in Christ." That's God's desire.

So, in closing, I ask once again: what is your relationship with God? Is he your boss or your dad? Are you a servant or a son?

7

Galatians 4:12-31

FAITH OR WORKS?

Paul's argument

Heart – sympathetic feelings (4:12-20)
Brotherhood – how they felt about him
Motherhood – how he felt about them

Head – symbolic facts (4:21-31)
Motherhood – where we come from
Brotherhood – where we get to

My brothers, I beg you, please stand with me. After all, I was willing to identify with you. You've never hurt me before. You know it was because of physical illness that I first came to tell you the good news. My condition must have been a real trial to you, but you never made fun of it, nor were you disgusted with me. Indeed, you gave me a welcome fit for a heavenly messenger or even the Messiah Jesus himself. You were so pleased and proud to have me. Where have all those feelings gone? I recall vividly that you wished it was possible to donate your eyes for transplanting in me. Now you seem to suspect me of being your enemy. Is that because I have been so honest with you?

I know these others are so keen to make a fuss of you; but their motives are not good. They want to have you all to themselves, so that you will make a fuss of them.

Don't get me wrong – special attention is always fine, provided the intentions are right. You are my special concern, even when I am not actually with you. My own children, I feel like a mother struggling with the pains of childbirth until Christ is brought right out in your lives. I just wish I could be with you at this moment so that you could hear the change in my tone of voice. I really am at my wits' end to know what to do about you.

Tell me this – you seem to have such a strong urge to be governed by the law of Moses, but have you really listened to everything it says? Take this one recorded incident:

Abraham was the father of two sons by two women, one a slave-girl and the other free. The slave-girl's boy was the natural result of a physical act; but the child of the free woman only came as the supernatural result of a divine promise. This contrast is intended to picture spiritual realities, for the two sons represent two very different kinds of relationship with God.

One stems from Mount Sinai and its children are born into bondage. Their symbolic mother is the slave-girl Hagar, whose connections were with Arabia, where Mount Sinai stands. She corresponds to the present Jewish capital of Jerusalem, whose leaders and subjects are under oppression. But there is another "Jerusalem" of heavenly origin, represented by the free woman, and she is the mother of all of us who believe. The Bible says of her, "Celebrate, you barren woman who never had a child; burst into cries of joy, you who never knew the pain of labour; for the lonely wife will have a far bigger family than she who has her husband" (Isaiah 54:1).

My brothers, we are like Isaac, for our life was brought into being by a divine promise. As in his day, the child born in the normal course of nature bullied the one born by the power of God's Spirit, so it is today. But look what the Bible says about the outcome of this: "Throw out the slave-girl and her son, for he will never share the father's property with the son of the free woman" (Genesis 21:10). So, brothers, get this quite clear in your minds – we are not the children of a slave-girl but of a free woman.

(Author's translation)

It is a remarkable thing that a letter written 2,000 years ago can be so relevant to our situation today, but I little dreamed when I started this series of studies in Paul's letter to the Galatians how relevant it would prove to be before we reach the end of our studies. Here are some items from the press this week. There are two movements that have now reached the land of Israel which are causing such tension that the government is discussing the two groups. The first is a movement called "Jews for Jesus". I'm sure you know that hundreds, indeed thousands, of young Jews are accepting Jesus as their Messiah. It's one of the most exciting things that's happening. One day we're told a whole Jewish nation will and that'll be one of the greatest days there's ever been when they see that the Messiah they've been waiting for for so long is in fact Jesus. But along with the "Jews for Jesus" movement which began in Chicago and spread to New York and is now right in Israel itself has gone another movement, of which I've only read in the press this week, and which is being discussed by the Cabinet in Israel at the moment. It's called the "Christians for Moses" movement. It seeks to do precisely the opposite of the "Jews for Jesus" movement. It seeks to bring Christians back under the law of Moses. It is being encouraged by the Jewish Defence League as a weapon to use against Christians in Israel. Indeed there is a suggestion before the government of Israel now that a Jew who becomes a Christian has forfeited his right to be a Jew and therefore his right to be a citizen of Israel. This is the situation. I am ashamed and embarrassed to tell you that the movement called "Christians for Moses" has been started by a former Baptist, who is seeking to spread his view that Jesus is a false messiah and that the true way to God is through Moses and through keeping his laws.

It is that battle which Paul had to fight 2,000 years ago and here we are fighting it again today. The letter to the Galatians is still the Magna Carta of Christian liberty. Setting us free from the law which God gave to Moses as a temporary addition to deal with a situation until Jesus Christ came and cured the condition. So we're right back to the fundamental issue: the relationship not just between Jews and Christians or Judaism and Christianity, but also between law and grace, between the way to God that depends on faith, on believing his word, and the way that depends on works, trying to build up a sufficient credit of good deeds in your heavenly account to be acceptable to God.

Paul's argument

Paul fought this battle to the last ditch because he said for Christians to go back to Moses is to go from freedom to bondage, from a state of blessing to a state of curse, from a state in which you will receive everything that God has to a state in which God will have to disinherit you. He's used every argument in the book so far and I don't think I'd like to argue with a man called Paul. He just didn't leave you any ground to stand on. He's used argument after argument. He has just two more arguments to use. In the passage we are studying here, he uses the last two arrows in his quiver. One is a very hot argument and is directed to the hearts of his readers. The other is a cool argument and is directed to their heads and from this I learn a profound lesson. If we are to be integrated people, our heart and our head must say the same thing and point in the same direction. One of the reasons for the modern disintegration of personality in many young people is that their hearts and their heads are going in opposite directions and this tears us apart. On many of the issues of today, eg euthanasia, it is very easy for the heart to rule the head and to run away with the argument. That is not to say there is no place for emotion and feeling but a sound argument is one that can go the same way with head and heart. So Paul uses two last arguments. I'm going to call them the sentimental and the scriptural.

Here are the two arguments which if they go together and point to the same truth seem to me to convince the total personality. So he appeals to their heart with what is admittedly a most sentimental approach. It is one of deep feeling and emotion. But then to keep the whole thing balanced and correct, he switches to a scriptural argument which frankly doesn't move your heart much at all but stretches your brain and causes you to feel and to see that the argument is still the same.

Heart – sympathetic feelings (4:12-20)

Brotherhood – how they felt about him
Let's look first at his argument to the heart. It is an appeal to their memory and through their memory to their feelings. He describes the personal relationship he has had with them and the emotion that has been associated with it in the past. He makes an appeal from his heart to their heart. He says, "My brothers please": he is appealing to their better feelings, to try and get them away from the "Christians for Moses"-

type movement which has already gripped the churches of Galatia.

The basic appeal he makes is a wonderful one: "Please stand with me because I stood with you." It is not a logical argument; it is an emotional one. "Stay with me if only for the reason that I stood with you." Here we have in one sentence the missionary task, the missionary motive, the missionary method: how we are to be to those who are not believers in Jesus Christ. We are to become as they are in order that they may become as we are. There it is in a nutshell: that is love. That's what the heart must do. We must not sit in our ivory palaces of Christian fellowship and say, "Come on in and be like us." The Bible states quite clearly that the first task is to go out and be like them in everything but sin.

That's what Jesus did. Jesus didn't call down from the clouds of heaven and say, "Come on up if you can"; Jesus came and was tempted in every way as we are. He was born of a woman. He came into our life. He knew what it was like. He became as we are. Why? So that we could become as he is and stand where he stands and sit where he sits now. That is our method. Somebody said, "Never board a human soul unless you've come alongside first." The "Cambridge Seven" – C T Studd and six other students who went out to China – grew pigtails as the first step of their missionary preparation. Many others today have discovered that this is the first step in winning someone for Christ: to become like them in everything but sin. Then you can say, "I became as you were. You become as I am. You stand with me. I stood with you." Now that's what Paul had done. He was brought up as a strict Jew with all the traditions, all the scruples of that Jewish background, but he left all that behind and he became as a Gentile. He lived like a Gentile. He ate non-kosher food. He didn't wash his hands before meals. He scrapped all the traditions in order to become like the people he was seeking to win. Now he's saying, "Please stay with me. I came to you. Stay with me." It's a very deep appeal.

But he's got more to say and everything he says tugs deeply at our heartstrings. He then says, "You've never hurt me. Up till now you've never deliberately harmed me. You've done me no wrong." He says this with the subtle hint that they are about to. "I beg you – we've been in a good relationship with you all this time. I've not hurt you. You've not hurt me. Don't spoil it now please!" He then goes back to the beginning of their relationship and tugs even more at their heartstrings. He says, "Do you remember what condition I was in when I first came to preach?"

Here we have one of those little hints of something we can't quite understand because Paul is a little obscure. But he says something like this: "I only came to preach the gospel to you because of physical illness." That's a very strange statement. Those who believe that Christians should never be physically ill need to face this verse where physical illness actually worked out for the spread of the gospel. If Paul had not been physically ill, he would never have brought the gospel to Galatia. Now how could that come about? I can only give you a speculation which I think has good ground for it from the geographical conditions and location of these churches to whom he's writing. They are up in the hills of Pamphylia and we know that Paul came to them across the sea first and then across the coastland which is low lying and swampy and then up into the hills. The low coastline swampy area is packed with malarial mosquitoes. When anybody gets malaria in the swampy coastland, the low lying area, the first thing they do is to go up into the hills to try and get some fresh air. This is the natural and normal thing to do and still happens. Reading between the lines, it looks as if when Paul landed on the coast of Pamphylia that he contracted malaria. It was then that John Mark took fright and left and went back home. If Paul did contract malaria, and if to get a little help he went up into the hills where there was a better climate and fresh air, then this would explain why he says it was because of physical illness that he first came to preach the gospel to them. It brought him up to the hills, to Lystra and Antioch and Derbe and Iconium, the churches in south Galatia.

The point is this: his physical illness was very unpleasant not only for him but also for them. He says, "It was a trial to you." I don't know what it did to him but something affected his public ministry very deeply. Maybe his physical appearance was a bit off-putting or maybe the congregation was so scared he would have another attack in the middle of his sermon that they were all tense. We don't know what it was. The thing is that it was a real trial to them.

What was their reaction to a preacher who was a sick man and embarrassing to the congregation, and a real trial to the people he preached to? Do you know what their reaction was? "You gave me a welcome fit for an angel. If I'd come down from heaven with wings you couldn't have given me a warmer reception." Isn't that wonderful? He said, "Not only did you welcome me as if I was an angel, but you also welcomed me as if I was Jesus himself. I remember that vividly." He's tugging at their heartstrings and he says,

"What's happened to all that. You were so pleased and so proud to have me with you. What's happened? Where's it all gone?" What an emotional appeal!

I shall never forget the story of Thomas Cook, a former principal of Cliff College in Derbyshire. He went to preach at a certain place and stayed the weekend with a family that had a maid. The maid was being fussed around on the Friday so much to get the room ready for him that she was fed up. It was, "Get this ready and make the bed and dust the rooms and all the rest – Thomas Cook is coming!" She went down to the butcher's to get the Sunday joint and poured all her frustration out on the butcher. She said to the butcher with a mocking tone in her voice, "Honestly the way they're carrying on you'd think Jesus was coming!" Thomas Cook came, and one of the results of his coming was that the little maid became a Christian that weekend. So when she went back to the butcher's the next week, the butcher mockingly said, "Did Jesus come?" And she replied, "Yes, he came!"

Paul says, "You welcomed me as if I was an angel from heaven, as if I was Jesus himself." He did not rebuke them for the welcome. There was a time when he had rebuked people in that same area for welcoming him as a god from heaven. Paul would never allow people to think of him as a god. But he didn't rebuke them for treating him as an angel. Why not? Because what is an angel but a messenger of God? And this sick invalid was a messenger of God. In fact, in welcoming Paul they were welcoming Jesus, for this was a man in Christ. Now he says, "What's happened to all those feelings? Where have they gone? Do you think I'm now your enemy? What has spoiled the relationship? The only thing I can think of is that I've told you the truth which is of course a tricky thing for any preacher to do to his congregation. Is it because I've been so honest with you? Is it because I didn't just tell you nice things but told you the tough things too? Is it because I was open and honest that you now regard me as your enemy?"

He then goes back to something else and this may be another clue to his illness. We're not sure what it was but he says, "Do you know you would have plucked out your eyes and given them to me if you could?" I don't know if malaria affects the eyesight or I don't know if Paul was suffering from some eye disease. There are one or two hints in a number of his letters that seem to indicate that he had bad eyesight. For example, at the end of Galatians: "See what large letters I write to you" (6:11). There was a time when he was on trial when he could not make out who was the high priest. He says, "I'm sorry I wasn't able to see who it was."

There are hints that Paul's eyesight was weak. Well whatever it was we won't know till we get to glory, and by then it'll be an academic question. The point is this: he said, "You thought of me so highly then that you would have plucked out your very eyes and given them to me if you could have done to help me to preach the gospel. That's what you would have done!" Does your heart feel all this deeply?

Motherhood – how he felt about them
He has so far regarded them as brothers, with a deep brotherly affection, but now he changes to thinking of them as a mother would think of them. Those who think Paul was a hard intellectual need to read this passage carefully. Here he breathes the feelings of a mother for her children and now he changes from calling them "my brothers" to calling

them "my little children": "I feel like your mother." So Paul is not just all head; there's a heart there too that's feeling for people as a mother does.

What does he say as a mother? He says first of all, "I have a mother's feelings when somebody else is making a fuss of her children." You know how a mother feels when she's brought up a boy and looked after him and cared for him and showered love upon him and suddenly the boy has found a girl and the only woman in his life is this girl and somebody else is pouring love on this boy and the mother just feels a pang. She's bound to: it's her boy. Now here's another woman in his life and taking his love and showering love on him and making a fuss of him. A mother who's poured so much love into a child feels it if the child goes after someone else who makes a fuss of them. Paul says, "These others are so keen to make a fuss of you. I don't mind that. I'm not bitter about that. What I am bitter about is that their motive is wrong. They want to take you away from me. They want to take you away from everybody. They want you all to themselves." It is a possessive love. I want you to imagine a mother whose child is now loved by a very possessive person who wants that person all to themselves and wants to cut off all other relationships. Some of you have been in this situation, I know, and you feel the relationship is wrong. It's not that you're bitter and jealous of someone else loving your child – it's just that it's such a possessive love you can see that it's going to kill love, that it's going to separate them from everyone else. And Paul says that's how I feel about you: "I'm your mother now. My little children; they're making such a fuss of you and you're responding to it but can you see what a jealous exclusive love they have?

Can you see what a possessive love they have? They want you all to themselves ...and that's not good."

To make it quite clear that he's not jealous or bitter himself he says, "Look, it's good to be made a fuss of. There is nothing wrong with having special attention from someone provided the intentions are good." He says, "I want to make a fuss of you. I want to make a lot of you. I want to shower love on you. Not because I want you all to myself but for a very different reason." We don't know how Paul knew about childbirth, whether he'd been present at the birth of a child. But he knew about it and he knew the calm and then the sudden pang that grips. He says, "That's how I feel. I'm going about my daily life here [wherever he was] and suddenly a pang enters my heart as I think about you, and it keeps coming back."

Here is a wonderful picture which is an adult picture but I want you to see it – the mother is straining in childbirth. The pangs are coming with greater frequency and depth. She's trying to bring a child out so that people can see the child and hold the child. Paul is saying, "I'm a mother, and I'm getting these pangs because I'm wanting to bring Christ right out of you." That's a wonderful picture, isn't it? What a heart he had. He said these others are wanting to bring *themselves* out in you. They're wanting you for themselves. "My special concern, the fuss I have made of you, my deep concern for you is not that. I'm wanting to bring *Christ* out, right out in you."

"There are two kinds of pain a Christian will feel for someone else. The first is the pain that brings them to the new birth but the second is the pain that continues until Christ is brought right out in them. The second pain is often much more severe than the first. Christ is not brought out in people without a heart that feels pain."

What are we to learn from this? There are two kinds of pain a Christian will feel for someone else. The first is the pain that brings them to the new birth but the second is the pain that continues until Christ is brought right out in them. The second pain is often much more severe than the first. Christ is not brought out in people without a heart that feels pain and so Paul says, "I'm in childbirth again." The pangs go through my heart. I want to bring Christ right out in you. It's a very tender appeal and he realizes that he can't convey in a letter how he feels. That's the snag with writing, you know. Letters can be misunderstood. Why? Because you can't hear the tone of voice. Paul used a secretary, the Greek word is *amanuensis*, a stenographer. I can imagine Paul striding up and down dictating this letter and the one thing the stenographer could not get down was the tone of voice. You get it from me as I speak. That is why from one point of view a recording is a better medium for God's word than a book because it conveys tone of voice. Paul says, "I just wish I could be with you there now. You could hear my tone of voice change as I plead with you. You would know how I feel." You hear feelings from tone, not from words. He says, "I really am at my wits' end. I don't know what to do with you!" Mothers, have you felt like that about a child? "I'm at my wits' end! I don't know what to do"? Paul is feeling with his heart for his spiritual children. He says, "Brothers, I remind you of how you felt about me. Children, may I remind you about how I feel about you?" What an argument! It must have touched them.

Head – symbolic facts (4:21-31)

Having got all warmed up, let's now cool down as Paul did. Did he think he'd gone too far? Did he realize he'd said enough? Did he consciously think, "I must not appeal to their heart only – I must also appeal to their head?" Whatever the reason, we have here one of those profound unions in Scripture of heart and head, of feeling and thought, of the emotional and the intellectual. If our religion gets too intellectual and too much in the head, it becomes cold. If it gets too much in the heart then it becomes frothy and unstable. But when the heart and the head are partners and feel and think the same way as an integrated person, you can walk in the right way because when your head and heart agree your will must follow. It is when your head and your heart disagree that your will is torn between two choices.

So Paul switches to the head, from a sentimental to a scriptural argument. I find this fascinating because here Paul tells us how to read the Old Testament as Christians. One way of reading the Old Testament is just to read it as history. That is interesting if you're interested in that sort of thing. If you want to know what Abraham did, then read the story. That is one way and frankly I think it's dull and you're wasting your time. I think of some of the Scripture lessons I sat through at school and I realize that treating it only as history was just a waste of our time and how dull it made the Bible. I can draw Paul's missionary journeys in my sleep now. I've done it so often: the first, the second, the third, and so have some of you. If you read the Old Testament simply as history as what happened in the past, then you're wasting your time as it's purely academic.

But Paul says read the Old Testament to see what spiritual reality is being taught by the events, for the simple reason that God has not changed. The God of Abraham and the God of Isaac and the God of Jacob was the God of Jesus and the God of Jesus is our God so the way God dealt with Abraham is the way he's going to deal with me. So I read these events as allegories, for spiritual truth. Allegories are not necessarily myths. *Pilgrim's Progress* is an allegory but it is also a myth because it never actually happened. *Gulliver's Travels* is an allegory but it is also a myth because it didn't happen. C S Lewis' *The Lion, the Witch and the Wardrobe* is an allegory. It's not a children's book; it's an adult book. It's an allegory and it's a myth, as it's not true – it never happened. The Bible is full of allegory but that doesn't make the stories myths. The difference is that they were based on fact not fiction and we are reading real stories. Here is the story that Paul is referring to:

"But Sarah and Abraham had no children. So Sarah took her maid, an Egyptian girl named Hagar and gave her to Abraham to be his second wife. 'Since the LORD has given me no children,' Sarah said, 'you may sleep with my servant

girl and her children shall be mine.' And Abraham agreed.
This took place ten years after Abraham had first arrived in
the land of Canaan. So he slept with Hagar and she conceived
and when she realized she was pregnant, she became very
proud and arrogant toward her mistress Sarah" (Genesis
16:1-4, author's rendering).

Now the thing I want you to notice in that little part of
the story is that God did nothing ... and said nothing. He
didn't tell them to do it; he didn't approve. Some of you have
asked me recently what about the Old Testament saints who
had more than one wife. You tell me where God approved
of that, where he told them to do it. They did it and the
Bible is true to fact and mentions what they did but God is
not mentioned there.

Now, the story continues in Genesis 21:1-12: "Then God
did as he had promised and Sarah became pregnant and gave
Abraham a baby son in his old age at the time God had said
and Abraham named him Isaac which means 'laughter.'
Eight days after he was born Abraham circumcised him as
God required. Abraham was 100 years old at the time. And
Sarah declared, 'God has brought me laughter. All who hear
about this shall rejoice with me for who would have dreamed
that I would ever have a baby, yet I have given Abraham a
child in his old age.' Time went by and the child grew and
was weaned and Abraham gave a party to celebrate the
happy occasion but when Sarah noticed Ishmael, the son
of Abraham and the Egyptian girl Hagar, teasing Isaac, she
turned upon Abraham and demanded, 'Get rid of that slave-
girl and her son. He is not going to share your property with
my son. I won't have it.' This upset Abraham very much,

for after all Ishmael too was his son but God told Abraham, 'Don't be upset over the boy or your slave-girl wife. Do as Sarah says, for Isaac is the son through whom my promise will be fulfilled.'"

Now what does that story mean to you because you are involved in it? Paul is now going to show that that story is about every person. You are either an Isaac or an Ishmael. Let's see what he makes of the story.

Motherhood – where we come from

The first thing that he looks at is the motherhood of the two boys. The important thing is not who your father is but who your mother is. We have seen that in one sense God is the father of all humanity in that we all owe him our existence. He gave us life. But the important question now is: "Who is your mother?" Abraham had two sons and they both took their character and destiny from their mothers, not from their father. That's an important point. A slave-girl can only have a slave-boy, and Ishmael became a slave-boy because his mother was a slave-girl even though his father was a free man.

Looking at the two mothers, we have Hagar the slave-girl and Sarah the free woman. What do these two women represent? What spiritual reality do we see here? Here comes the astounding thing. I will tell you this. I think the next sentence must be the most offensive statement Paul ever made to his fellow Jews. He said, "You are descended from Ishmael." Of course that runs absolutely counter to all Jewish thinking. I'm sure you know that the Arabs are physically descended from Ishmael and the Jews are physically descended from Isaac and this is the ultimate origin of the conflict that we have in the Middle East today. That is the reason why there is still after these 4,000 years the same tension because the Jew and the Arab are physically half-brothers. But the point Paul is making here is this: it is not your *physical* descent that matters in God's sight; it is your *spiritual* descent. He is saying to the Jews, "You may be physically descended from Isaac, but you are spiritually descended from Ishmael. You are slaves, and you've become that way through the law of Moses. Jerusalem, the present capital, is under oppression, not from the Romans, but from the law of Moses. You're born into slavery. I've spoken to enough Israelis to know this to be true. They are born into slavery because they are under the law and that is a bondage the like of which you haven't really known unless you've studied it. So Paul says, "You are spiritually descended from Ishmael. You are under bondage."

I cannot help but apply all this to the Middle East today. Too many evangelical and liberal Christians are held by physical issues, the former supporting Israelis and the latter Palestinians. The fact is that some Palestinians have Sarah as their spiritual ancestor and many Israelis are descended from Hagar. Christians who understand this will be more careful with their support, both financial and political. We are called to "do good to all people, especially to those who belong to the family of believers" (6:10).

Sarah stands for another Jerusalem, not an earthly one, but a heavenly one, not the present one but a future one. The new Jerusalem: "Then I saw a new heaven and a new earth, for the first heaven and the first earth had passed away, and there was no longer any sea. I saw the Holy City, the new Jerusalem, coming down out of heaven from God, prepared as a bride beautifully dressed for her husband" (Revelation 21:1–2). Sarah corresponds to that city. We talk about capital cities as female. Jerusalem on earth corresponds to Hagar the slave-girl. Jerusalem in heaven which is to come down from heaven is the new Jerusalem: the new city corresponds to Sarah.

Paul sees a parallel between the two mothers with their sons and the two major covenants of the Old Testament: the Abrahamic which leads to "children" of freedom and the Mosaic, established on Mount Sinai in Arabia which produces children born in bondage (to the law). He goes on to apply the comparison and contrast to two cities of the same name (Jerusalem), one in heaven "above," who is the "mother" of those who share Abraham's faith; the other on earth below, inhabited by those who share his flesh. He quotes Isaiah 54:1 to underline that the number of the former children of Sarah the free but former "barren" and "desolate" woman is now far in excess of the latter, children of Hagar, the slave.

Which city do you belong to? Every Jew when saying goodbye to another Jew utters this greeting; "Next year in Jerusalem." A Christian could use that. I've got the word *shalom* on my lapel. It is a Jewish word, because I could say to you, "Next year in Jerusalem." The new Jerusalem, not the old one. I don't know which year it'll be, but they say "Next year in Jerusalem," hoping each year that it will be next year and so do I. Next year in Jerusalem: which mother do you belong to? Which capital city do you look to? The earthly one with its laws with its bondage or the new Jerusalem with its freedom? Who is your mother? Hagar or Sarah?

Brotherhood – where we get to

Let us come finally to the sons. Let's consider these two boys not from the angle of motherhood but from brotherhood. Humanly speaking, Ishmael should never have been born. I am not among those who believe that every child is intended by God. I don't think the Bible warrants that. Some children are. Some are not, but let me quickly add that when a child is born, God loves him or her for he loves the world. So no child need ever feel unwanted as far as God is concerned.

That does not mean, however, that God intended every child that is born, for many children are the result of a purely physical act. Some are intended. Some are not. Ishmael was intended but not by God. It was all thought up by Abraham and Sarah between them. They discussed it. Sarah said, "I'm 90 and you're 100. Abraham, if God's promise is to be fulfilled we've got to have a son to pass it on to. How are we going to get a son?" And they talked it over and Sarah said, "Well, Abraham, there's my maid. She's young enough. You'd better lie with her." It was all human ingenuity and the result was Ishmael, a boy born in the course of nature, born as the result of human decision and human act, but not intended or planned by God. He came into the world.

17 years later, that boy Ishmael was present at the weaning ceremony of a younger half-brother called Isaac who was now three years old. They were weaned at three. On that day, the 17-year-old boy who was old enough now to inherit the father's property who'd come of age saw a three-year-old supplant him. The Bible says, "He started bullying him." You've seen that happen between two children, one of whom thinks it's being replaced. Ishmael started bullying little Isaac. Paul says, "Do you know that everyone who is

born of the flesh will be jealous of those who've been born of the Spirit?" There is a permanent tension and antagonism between natural man with his natural religion, his own ingenuity and his own good deeds. There will be a jealousy in that man's heart towards those who not having kept the law and not having good deeds are filled with the joy of the Lord and look forward to heaven.

It's been happening ever since. You see here is the remarkable thing: a respectable good person who has tried to live well all their life and has not done anybody any harm as far as they can see and who's gone to church and has been regular and devoted and so on and suddenly sees a man whose not lived a good life, rejoicing that he's going to heaven, having been born of the Spirit. There's jealousy between the two boys, for one boy is born of the flesh and the other is born of the power of God's Spirit. One is a natural man; the other is a supernatural man. The simple fact is that those two boys will not be able to live together for ever. At a certain stage they must be separated. The inheritance goes to the boy born of the Spirit, not to the boy born of the flesh.

Now do you understand what it's got to do with you? Every single man or woman is either a natural man or woman born as the result of a human act of intercourse struggling in the power of our natural strength to be good with a natural kind of religion. Or else we have been born of the Spirit and the inheritance of our heavenly Father's property will come to us. You're either an Ishmael or an Isaac. There will always be tension between these two. They will live together for a time. They will grow up together. But God has appointed a day when those under slavery to the law will be cursed out and those born of the Spirit will inherit.

That is God's truth and it comes from the law of Moses itself in the story we've read. Who then are the two categories mentioned? Let me say they are not the Jew and the Arab. According to Paul, both are now the spiritual descendants of Ishmael. Nor is the division between Jew and Christian because, praise God, there are Jews and Gentiles who've been born of the Spirit and are descendants of Isaac as there are Jews and Gentiles who are descendants of Ishmael. The real divide right through is between faith and works – grace and law, being born of the Spirit and born of the flesh, the children of God and the children of disobedience. That line runs right through this country and right through our world, and depending on whether you are an Ishmael or an Isaac, your whole eternal destiny is decided.

How then do I become an Isaac? I may be an Arab. I may be a Jew. I may be a Gentile. How do I become an Isaac? The answer is so simple. Receive Jesus. That's how. Believe that he is the Messiah who came to set us free from the law, from sin and from death, and who in his own glorious person became as we are, a son of man that we might become as he is, sons of God.

8

Galatians 5:1-12

DON'T LOSE YOUR FREEDOM

Divine basis (5:1-6)
Lost freedom: "you"
Under law
Beyond grace
Living faith: "we"

Human barrier (5:7-12)
Obstructed progress
Offensive preaching

Conclusion

When Christ set us free, that was real freedom! So hang on to it and don't get tied up again in the chains of slavery. Listen! I, Paul, a Jewish Christian, make this serious statement – if you get circumcised, Christ himself will be of no more value to you. Let me repeat that. I give my solemn assurance to anyone who submits to the initiation ceremony of circumcision, that he has put himself under an obligation to obey every single statute of the Jewish law. The operation will not only cut off part of your body; it will cut you off from Christ! Any of you who tries to get right with God by keeping the commandments will find you have slipped beyond the range of God's undeserved mercy.

We Christians build our hopes on a very different basis. By the help of God's Spirit we wait expectantly for that right standing and state which result from trusting in Jesus the Messiah. Once we are part of him, it doesn't count for anything whether we are circumcised or uncircumcised. The only thing that matters is the kind of believing that is expressed in loving.

You were racing ahead in the Christian life. Who caused an obstruction and stopped you from putting the truth into practice? That kind of plausible persuasion never comes from God, who always calls you to press on. As they say, "It doesn't take much yeast to taint a large lump of dough." Yet somehow the Lord gives me the confidence that you are not going to change your outlook. As for the person who is disturbing you, he will one day have to take his punishment, whatever his position is now.

Regarding myself, brothers, I gather I am supposed to be preaching the need to be circumcised, even after all this time. If that were really true, how can anyone explain the

violent opposition I encounter at the hands of other Jews?
If I was advocating their laws, they wouldn't be so offended
when I speak about the cross. I just wish that those who are
agitating to cut off your foreskins would go the whole hog
and castrate themselves!

(Author's translation)

Freedom is one of the hardest things to obtain but also one of
the easiest things to lose – that's the message of this passage.
Particularly the second statement, how easy it is to lose our
freedom. However, before we can obtain freedom we've got
to decide what it is. The world is crying out for freedom –
you hear this word everywhere you go, but when you ask a
person what they mean by freedom, what they really want to
be when they say they want to be free, you receive a variety
of answers. The most common one is: "I want to be free to
do what I like and do." That's not freedom at all; it is in fact
the worst kind of slavery. Others say, "We want to be free
from need. We want to be free from ignorance; we want
to be free from poverty; we want to be free from disease.
We want freedom of speech, freedom of political action,
freedom from this, that and the other. And most people in
our world want to be free from God – they don't want him
breathing down their necks and telling them what to do and
what not to do.

I want to tell you what I believe real freedom is: it is not
to be free from God; it is not to be free from the restraints of
others. It is not to be free to do what I like. It is to be free from
me – that's real freedom and it's the one freedom none of us

has by nature. It's the one freedom that we sadly discover we have not attained when we've gained all these other things. We discover we are still in chains to a little person called "I." It is freedom from self that Jesus came to bring, in all its forms, not just freedom from sin, for that itself, but also freedom from law, for that produces self-righteousness.

Divine basis (5:1-6)

It is freedom from all that is tied up with me and free at last to be what God wants me to be and to do what God likes me to do – that's real freedom and so Paul begins this section with a crashing statement, "It is for freedom that Christ has set us free," or as I translated it, "When Christ set us free, that was real freedom." I wish the world would stop asking *what* freedom is and ask the question *who* freedom is, because that's the greater question and instead of this big capital "I" spelling freedom, it is the word "Jesus" that spells freedom. It's not *what* freedom is; it is *who* freedom is.

When Christ sets you free, that's real freedom because at last you are free to be good and that's the thing you've never been free to be all your life. You've done bad, you've been free to sin, but you've never been free to be a saint and deep down in your heart you wanted to be. I don't believe I could ever meet a human being who was so degraded, who had sunk so low, that they said, "I've no desire left to be better than I am." Each one of us would wish we had been able to live a better life than we have, whatever our age. It is that freedom that Christ offers, the freedom to be, the freedom to reach that goal and the freedom to be what God intended you to be. When Christ sets you free, that's real freedom, or as the statement could also be translated, "When Christ set you free, he meant you to keep that freedom." The tragedy is, and I emphasize this, that many Christians lose their freedom, having once gained it in Christ. They go back to slavery, to prison, to chains. They go back under a yoke that they're not able to bear. Having tasted freedom, they then go back into slavery and that has been Paul's concern all through his letter to the Galatians.

What the Declaration of Independence is to the United States and what Magna Carta is to the United Kingdom, the letter to the Galatians is to every Christian. This is the final section in the first half of his letter in which he warns us against the danger of legalism. When Christ set you free, he didn't just want you to be free from sin, he wanted you to be free from law, and that's occupied the first four chapters of this letter and these verses in this study, and so he just fires a broadside, big gun after big gun – the statements explode in our minds with devastating illumination.

"Freedom is one of the hardest things to obtain but also one of the easiest things to lose."

Lost freedom: "you"

Here's the first: He says, "Do you realize that if you accept this simple little operation of circumcision, which is over in a few minutes and healed in a few days, you're going to lose your freedom in Jesus Christ? It will put you in this position; it will put you under the law and beyond grace." Now I realize this is a bit of a dead issue because as far as I know no one's going round our church urging any of you to be circumcised – it is not a live issue in this form but it is a very live issue in other forms. If anybody is going around the fellowship saying to be a Christian you must do this or you must do that in addition to trusting in Jesus, they are in fact doing the same thing as was being done in the churches of Galatia.

Anybody that wants to produce rules that Christ has not laid on our hearts through his Spirit, anybody who builds up a list of "You shalls" and "You shall nots," and says, "This is what you must do in order to get to heaven," is doing the same thing. To be under law is sheer slavery; to think about keeping all the commandments all the time – that's bondage. If you go down that path, you're going to be under fear, you're going to be constantly suffering from guilt and you'll build up a gigantic guilt complex and you will have to live with it. I have met Christians who are suffering from all this. How did they build up such a guilt complex when Christ set them free? Because they have developed certain scruples either of their own or from other Christians and they've come back under bondage. The result is they're no longer free as they used to be.

Under law

Now Paul says: You are under law – you can't pick and choose – if you want to get to heaven by keeping the commandments, you have to keep all of them. They are links in a chain: you can't say I've kept six out of ten and that's a pass mark. You've broken the chain: they are pearls on a single necklace and wherever that necklace breaks, the pearls are lost and you've broken the whole necklace. If you're going to keep the commandments, it's all or nothing.

If you put yourself under just one of them, then you've put yourself under all of them. If you are choosing to go the way of the law, then it's all or nothing.

Beyond grace

Furthermore, if you put yourself under the law, you put yourself beyond grace. Now here we're getting a little nearer home. Once you try to be good enough for heaven, you are beyond the reach of heaven's grace. Let's think that through. The most common idea of Christianity that I come across is this, that you get so far by goodness and the rest of the way by grace. That way has God saying, "Do your best and I'll forgive the rest. Make a tremendous effort, you won't get the whole way, but you'll get part of the way and then by my grace I'll forgive the things you don't manage." That is the commonest idea of Christianity in this country, and Paul says these two things don't mix: they are oil and water, chalk and cheese.

Law and grace don't mix. You cannot get part of the way by your own effort and the rest of the way by God's grace. It's either all the way by your own effort, or all the way by God's grace. If you choose the way of effort then you are signing a contract with God, and he will deal with you on a strictly commercial basis. What you achieve will be rewarded, and what you don't achieve will be punished. But if you come to God and say, "God be merciful to me a sinner," it's all of grace – you repent not only of your bad deeds but also of your good deeds. If you were trusting them to get you to heaven, then God says, "You're within the reach of my grace now."

One of the stories that brings this home to me so forcibly

is one told by Watchman Nee in one of his books. He was standing on a shore in China looking out to sea with a friend and they saw a man in difficulties in the water, drowning. He disappeared and came up again, struggling and shouting. Watchman Nee could not swim, but his friend could. He said to his friend, "Go in after him; save him," but his friend stood there and didn't move, and Watchman Nee said, "I can't swim; I can't save him – you go in." His friend still didn't move and the man went down for the third time – then Watchman Nee's friend jumped in, swam out, fished around, pulled him out, brought him to the shore and they brought him round and he was saved. Watchman Nee said "Well, that's wonderful – you've saved him, but why did you not go in when you saw him drowning?" and the friend said, "If I had gone in then, he'd have drowned us both – he was still struggling and he was a strong man and I couldn't have saved him."

This is a marvellous illustration of God looking down from heaven. He sees people struggling to be good, trying to make an effort to be Christian, trying so hard and God says, "I just can't save them while they're struggling. I can't help them while they're in that condition. They're not able to be helped." Then someone gets to the end of their tether and they stop struggling and they say simply, "God, you take over," and God says, "Now I can save you; now I can help you. Now you're within the reach of grace."

The tragedy is that by trying to be Christian, by trying to do good, by trying to reach the standard, we put ourselves beyond the reach of God's grace. This is the gospel: it's not a mixture of trying and trusting; it's not getting so far by your own efforts and then asking forgiveness for the rest.

You start with forgiveness if you're going to get there at all: it's all of grace.

Why? Because you can't have both deserved and undeserved things at the same time. God's grace is undeserved; it's freely given and so there is not one thing that I can do. It is a revelation when somebody repents of their good deeds as a means of salvation. Paul had to do this. He said, "Look at my achievements: 'as for legalistic righteousness, faultless' (Philippians 3:6, NIV); a Pharisee of the Pharisees. I really did try," he said, "Do you know what I think of my goodness now?" Not as bad deeds, [he doesn't give a list of horrible sins] – he says my good deeds. Do you know what I think of them now: "dung, dung, refuse, rubbish," (Philippians 3:8). When a man throws away all his goodness as a base for his hopes for the future and clings simply to Christ and to his cross, then grace can get into his heart.

This may explain why there are so many good people in this country who have shown no signs of God's grace. They are kind, helpful, churchgoing people and yet have no sense of God's grace. That is why you can meet some pretty bad people who've done very little good in their lives but have messed up their own lives and other people's – but when you talk to them, you sense that grace is there. "Maybe it is that we're too good to receive God's grace" – that's what Paul is saying. Now he's saying, "If you go back to the law – if you go back to keeping the commandments – I warn you, Christ will be of no value to you. He will not mix himself up with anybody who is trying to keep the commandments. Christ must stand alone in a person's life."

I must put my whole trust in Christ, not part of it in

my commandment-keeping and part of it in my Christ. I must have it all in him, so if I go back to keeping the commandments and trying to be good, then I'll have to say goodbye to Christ. So in a devastating statement, Paul says, "Circumcision will not only cut off part of your body from you, it'll also cut you off from Jesus." It is possible for a Christian to be cut off from Jesus. We're not now talking about our eternal salvation; we're talking about our life here and now: the freedom we have in Christ. We only have it as long as we are in touch with Christ. If we cut ourselves off from Christ, we shall find ourselves slaves again, and that can happen to any believer right now.

Paul is warning the converts who submitted to this Mosaic requirement that they would be 'alienated from Christ … fallen away from grace' (verse 4, NIV). Allowing this part of the body to be severed would mean separation from Christ himself. He would then become "of no value at all" to them (5:2, NIV). Once again, Paul is claiming that to desert the gospel he preached is to lose the Christ to whom he introduced them.

Living faith: "we"

On the other hand, let's look at the statement we have here about the genuine basis of the Christian life. It is possible that in the studies you've been getting a little tired of me saying these things again and again, but can they be said too often? What is the true basis of being a Christian? To go to church? No. To try and help your neighbour? No. To read your Bible? No. To say your prayers? No. To keep the Ten Commandments? No.

What, then, is the basis of true Christianity? Listen to this and see what a summary it is. The basis of true Christianity is in three persons and three relationships to those three persons. That sounds a bit complicated, so let's look at it. In verses 5 and 6, three persons are mentioned: Father, Son and Spirit. The basis for the Christian life is a relationship with three persons, not just to believe in God. Time and time again people say to me, "I'm not an atheist. I believe in God." I am prepared to accept that they do; most people do believe in God but that doesn't make them Christians. What makes you a Christian is not just to believe in God, but to believe in his Son Jesus Christ and to be helped to do so by his Spirit. It's a full Trinitarian basis, a three-point basis and three points gives you a sure foundation that covers length, breadth and depth that will keep you stable.

Here are three virtues: faith and her two sisters, hope and love. All three are mentioned in these verses. It starts with faith when I put my faith in Jesus the Messiah and say, "You are the Son of God. You're my Saviour; you died for me and you rose again and you're alive now and you're my Messiah." It starts with that kind of faith, but that faith will lead to hope. I wish we could have another word for the word *hope*. I'm afraid it's become such a wishy-washy word in English that when we say *hope* we mean "we're not quite sure": "I hope it'll be fine tomorrow." We feel uncertain about that. "I hope I'll pass my exams" means we're not sure. "I hope I'll get through the driving test." "I hope I'll soon feel better." We've used this word *hope* now to mean something that we're not sure about, but the Bible word *hope* is a Greek word *elpis*, which is translated as *hope* but means something of which you are absolutely sure in the future. If your faith in Jesus is genuine, it will lead the hope

215

and a certainty for the future. If someone asks you, "Are you going to heaven?", you will not say, "I hope so," you'll say, "I know so." If someone says, "Are your sins forgiven?", you won't say, "Well I'll wait till the day of judgment and hope for the best," you can say with assurance, "Yes, they are and I know that on the day when I stand before God, he'll say, 'Acquitted; innocent.'" This is the hope that we wait for, we don't work for.

You could summarize the difference in those two words: are you *working* for it or are you *waiting* for it? Wait on the Lord. "I am waiting," says Paul. We wait because we know we're going to receive it. It's those who are not sure whether they'll receive it who can't wait. Have you noticed that they want it all now to be sure of it, but I'm just as sure of heaven whether I have it today, in 10 years' time or 40 years' time, I'm just as sure of heaven, so I'll wait for it.

Paul says, "We wait in hope for the right standing and state..." – I've summarized the word *righteousness* as *right standing and state*. Do you know that the word *righteousness* in the Bible covers as far as you're concerned two things? First, that God will treat you as a good person, and secondly that God will transform you into a good person. The treating and transforming together make up the word *righteousness*, so when Paul says, "We wait for righteousness," he means he's sure that when he reaches heaven, he'll be treated as a good man, and he's also sure that when he reaches heaven he'll be transformed as a good person. That is the order, thank God, he's put it in... I almost said the wrong way round. We say, "You become a good man and I'll treat you like one. If you become an honest man, then I'll trust you," but God says, "I'll treat you as a good man first and then I'll

216

transform you into one."

"Faith expresses itself in love. There's a kind of believing that is merely intellectual – you've read the books on doctrine; you can go through all the questions and get 10 out of 10, but you don't love. Real faith is when you really put your trust in the Lord, you will love him. It's got to accompany true faith. Love will follow true faith and as you love the Lord, you'll find to your delight you begin to love others too."

That's the glory of justification followed by sanctification. Justification means that as soon as I believe in Jesus, God treats me as a good person and sanctification means that as I go on believing in Jesus, God transforms me into a good person. So we wait for this; we don't work for it. We don't try and earn it; we don't try and deserve it; we wait for it. It's coming and God has promised full righteousness to us, not only of standing but also of state.

The other thing that happens when true faith comes is that not only does hope come in the sense of certainty about the future, but also love comes. The kind of faith that doesn't produce love is not true Christian faith. Faith is the kind of trust in someone that leads you to love that someone, and you cannot believe in Jesus the Messiah in the Christian way without loving Jesus the Messiah.

Faith expresses itself in love. There's a kind of believing that is merely academic and intellectual – you've read the books on doctrine, you've studied theology and you've got all the answers. You can answer a catechism; you can go through all the questions and get 10 out of 10, but you don't love. Real faith, however, is when you really put your trust in the Lord, you will love him. It's got to accompany true faith; it's got to come with it. Love will follow true faith and as you love the Lord, you'll find to your delight you can begin to love others too.

Love flows so that it is the basis of the Christian faith, not a list of my good deeds piling up credit in the bank of heaven. It is my faith in Jesus that gives me a certain hope for the future and expresses itself in love – that's Christianity. Nothing else should carry the label and all our do-gooding and all our church-going should not be called Christianity if it does not spring from faith in Jesus which is confident in hope and expresses itself in love. There we have the true basis and the false basis. God's basis for Christianity and the human basis. God's basis is to believe in him, his Son, his Spirit and have the kind of faith that is accompanied by hope and love. The human version is to do good, go through ceremonies, whatever they are, circumcision, baptism, confirmation or any other rite – none of these is the basis of true Christianity. That is the divine basis.

Human barrier (5:7-12)

We now turn to what Paul says about the human barrier that can stop us reaching our goal. Paul was obviously a keen sportsman, at least a spectator. The Jews on the whole were not sportsmen; they rarely went to the sports. One reason was that Greek sports as you may know were practised in the nude and the Jews had very real hesitations about this and so they did not get caught up in the Greek world of sport.

Obstructed progress

However when Paul is writing to the Galatians, he is speaking to Gentiles who were used to going to the arena and seeing the races and so he often uses a picture from the races to illustrate the Christian life. He says, "Now my dear friends of Galatia, you were racing ahead, you were running so well…" That tells me that the Christian life is not finished with the first step. That may sound rather obvious, but how easy it is to say, "I'm converted, I'm there, I've started so I'm all right." But the Christian life is a race and as far as I know no one ever won a race only by starting. It is one step after another, it is a run, a race. It is going on, so it's not just starting that matters in the Christian life. It is finishing, and from this point of view it is an effort, but an entirely different kind of effort to the one that is trying to gain salvation.

The Christian life is a race, so it isn't just starting – it is finishing – that matters. It's not just one step but many steps. I remember a dear Salvation Army lady giving a testimony and she said, "I've been converted ten times and each time was better than the last," and bless her she meant it! She was using perhaps the wrong language but what she meant was you don't just make one decision in the Christian life, you make one, then another, then another, and another, and another.

You'll make very many decisions through your Christian life – God will call you to deeper and deeper consecration. He will call you to go further and further and to stretch forward and to forget the things that are behind and run the race looking towards Jesus. He is always calling you further like Jesus on the road to Emmaus indicating as though he would go further, and so God doesn't let up in his call. He didn't just call you to be a Christian; he called you to go on. He called you to go the whole way so that when you reach the end of your life you may be able to say, "I have fought the good fight, I have finished the race, I have kept the faith" (2 Timothy 4:7, NIV).

Paul says, "You were racing ahead so well – you were rushing ahead in your Christian life so well that I was able to talk about you and say to others, 'Look at how well those Galatians were running,' but what stopped you? Who caused an obstruction?" "We know what stops a Christian running," Paul says, can I put it simply, "as soon as we stop practising what we believe we stop running."

That's how you stop running. Paul says, "Who caused an obstruction and stopped you from putting the truth into practice?" However plausible the arguments were, however logical they seemed, if someone stopped you from behaving as you believe then you've stopped running. We therefore know what running is: it's listening to God's word and when you see a new truth putting it into practice in your life – that's what running is. Otherwise, you're just sitting in church. But when God says something and we do it, we're running. We've taken another leap forward and the thing that the devil would like to see Christians do more than anything else is to become academics, to become sermon tasters, to become those who enjoy only listening to the word but have no intention of doing anything about it. It is a sobering thought to all of us that if we've gone to church twice on Sunday through the year and just taken one step forward as the result of each time we study the Bible together, there should be 104 improvements in our life every calendar year. 104 assumes two a week but if we listen to God more often than that, are we running or have we, like the Galatians, stopped putting the truth into practice? If we have stopped, then we've separated belief and behaviour. Belief has reverted to the intellectual and behaviour has reverted to the ordinary.

Now Paul says that God never talks like that. There was a remark made in a recent discussion we had on the topic of euthanasia, something like that although the Christian principles are clear, this is such a muddled and evil world that we cannot live by Christian principles in this world today. It sounds plausible, it sounds logical, and it persuades us not to let our beliefs get into our behaviour too much but such calls do not come from God. Where does God expect us to live out Christian principles – if it's only for glory, then why did he give them to us here? It is an agony to have to work them out. It may cost us our job, it may cost us a lot to work them out but anybody who persuades us that you cannot put Christian belief into practice in our situation is doing what was done here and Paul says, "It doesn't take much of this to infect a whole fellowship." A little bit of yeast spreads right through a lump of dough and to the Jew yeast or leaven was always an evil influence: the leaven was malice. Once a year they had to get rid of leavened bread; they had to get all the yeast out of the house. It stood for something that putrefied, that fermented, that changed the whole thing by means of just a little of it. Paul therefore says, "You've heard the proverb – it just needs a little false teaching in a fellowship and it goes through the fellowship like yeast in a lump of dough."

It all sounds rather depressing, doesn't it? So Paul says, "Somehow I just don't believe you're going to let this happen. I don't believe you're going to let this infection spread. I believe that as a fellowship you're going to keep your outlook as it was. I have confidence in the Lord that you're not going to be upset and disturbed, I believe you're going to continue believing in Jesus."

Why did Paul have such confidence? Because he thought he'd written a good letter to them, because they thought that letter would really leave them without a leg to stand on? No. I'm sure he was glad the letter did help but I believe that Paul was confident for one reason that Satan is not as strong as Jesus. Error has pursued the church for 2,000 years, the gospel has been twisted for 2,000 years, and people have changed the basis of Christianity for 2,000 years but I'm not a pessimist, I am confident in the Lord that the true gospel will go on being preached until Jesus stands on the Mount of Olives again. Why am I confident? Because the gospel is of God and though the devil may be able spoil fellowships and though the devil may be able to twist preachers and though the devil may be able to stop Christians from practising the truth, I still believe that Christ will have them back and will get them going again; they'll get back to running.

We've all had times when we have stopped in the race but, praise God, I wouldn't be here today and neither would you, if he hadn't picked us up again and got us going again. He doesn't let you go.

Let's move on. Paul says, "Your progress has been obstructed but I don't believe it'll stop you altogether. I believe the man who is doing it will be punished whatever his position is." Now it was clearly a prominent man in the fellowship doing it and so he says, "I believe he'll be punished for what he's doing."

Offensive preaching

We come now to the last paragraph and it is rather extra-ordinary because it's concerned with Paul's preaching and it's offensive to many people. First of all, there is an extraordinary rumour going around that Paul is actually preaching the need to be circumcised. I don't know how that rumour got started but I do know that rumours are one of the curses of Christianity. One of the things the devil loves to do is spread rumours about what is said or what is done by any Christian so that misunderstanding takes place. Now as a Christian preacher, Paul had circumcised at least one of his converts, I know that, maybe more. The name of the man he had circumcised was a young pale delicate man called Timothy, and Paul had circumcised him. Maybe that had started a rumour, and maybe Paul's enemies were saying, "There you see, even he has doubts about it – he did circumcise someone, he must be preaching it." Now we know why Paul circumcised Timothy: it wasn't to save Timothy; it was for a social reason. Timothy was going to meet a lot of Jews; he was going to stay in their homes – he was going to tell them about Jesus and so Paul thought it wise for Timothy to make a gesture socially towards the Jews and be circumcised. It was exactly the same reason behind the action of C T Studd and the "Cambridge Seven" in growing pigtails, exactly the same reason why Arthur Blessitt wore jeans as he carried a cross around the world, he wasn't brought up to, but for exactly the same reason. That's the only reason Paul ever circumcised anyone for a social reason – on the basic principle that if you're going to win someone for Christ try and be like them first in everything but sin. "I have become all things to all men so that by all

223

possible means I might save some" (1 Corinthians 9:22, NIV). "To the Jews I'm prepared to be like a Jew, to the Gentiles I'm prepared to be like a Gentile, but what I am not prepared to have," says Paul, "is anybody telling the Gentiles they've all got to become Jews to be saved – that's a very different matter."

"I'm glad we're all different. We must not all dress the same, we must not all conform to each other – that's bad in a Christian fellowship because God wants each of us to be a missionary to the kind of people we can reach. There are some people who if I tried to win them, they'd say I was old-fashioned – that I was completely different from them. But, praise God, there's somebody who could go to them who's like them and who can reach them."

That's why I'm so glad we're all different and we must allow for differences. We must not all dress the same, we must not all conform to each other – that's bad in a Christian fellowship because God wants each of us to be a missionary to the kind of people that we can reach. There are people I can't talk to because of my background, because of who I am. There are groups in this town who if I tried to win them, they'd say I was old-fashioned – that I was just completely different from them. But, praise God, there's somebody in this fellowship who could go to that group and who's like them and who could reach them.

But when we start saying to each other, "If you're going to be a Christian, you've got to put on a Sunday tie or you've all got to do this or that," then we're imposing a restriction. Paul said, "If I preach circumcision, do you think I'd get into such trouble from the Jews?" They would stir up the authorities; they would throw him out of town. They would get him imprisoned. They would get him beaten and left for dead. Why? If he was preaching circumcision, the answer of course is he wasn't he was preaching the cross.

The cross is the death of all human effort to save itself. The cross says; "Nothing in my hand I bring, simply to thy cross I cling." The cross says all your circumcision won't get you anywhere. The cross says all your do-gooding won't get you anywhere. The cross says all your church-going won't get you anywhere. The ground at the foot of the cross is level and we all stand there.

It does not matter how good or bad we've been, we stand equally as sinners by the cross and that's terribly offensive. If you say that to a good man he'll be upset. If you say it to someone who has done many good deeds, they'll be upset. Paul says, "I'll tell you what gets people upset: I preach the cross." That is my task today: to say that you'll never become a Christian till you've been to a hill called Calvary and stood at the foot of the cross and said, "He died for me." Do you realize that if I say, "I'm good enough," or if I say, "I never did anybody any harm," what I'm really saying is: "Jesus – you wasted your time dying"? I have noticed this, that the people who talk about Christianity as doing good never talk about the cross; they never talk about the blood of Jesus. They never thank him for dying for them.

I will tell you this too: the people who talk about the

cross and about the blood of Jesus never talk about the good they've done – do you notice that? The two are incompatible and it is the offence to our pride that nothing we can do can save us and the cross not only condemned Jesus to death it also condemns myself to death but praise God that's what sets me free.

What gives me true freedom is that my self was nailed to the cross with Jesus. At last I've come to the realization that whatever bad things other people may see about me they're still not bad enough to be the truth. I know that "in my flesh dwells no good thing" (Romans 7:18) and I'm just rotten through and through; there's nothing in me worth saving.

So God has to begin all over again and make a new life. Paul says, "I'm not advocating circumcision," and then with a rare bold touch that is somewhat offensive to our modern sophisticated, comfortable "churchianity" he says, "I wouldn't preach circumcision; no, but I'll tell you what, I'll preach castration." He's saying almost crudely, "I wish their knives would slip and they'd cut something else off." Now to our sophisticated ears in a nice congregation, this sounds a bit rough, but it's there in the Greek – don't think I'm just playing with the words, this is what it should've been, although it wasn't in most polite English versions until the Good News Bible but this is what Paul is saying.

Now why should he say this? He's not just letting his tongue run away with him, he's saying something very profound and we need to know a little of the background to understand it fully, but he's saying two things.

First of all, in the country of Galatia, the goddess Cybele was worshipped. In the temples of Cybele were male prostitutes and female prostitutes – that was part of their worship. The males, however, were made into eunuchs to avoid babies coming and they did precisely this as part of their religion and what Paul is saying about these people who were demanding this physical operation, "You are no better than the pagan priests around you. It's all part of paganism – it's all part of legalism and there's nothing to choose from this point of view between what they are doing and what your pagan priests are doing."

The second thing that he's saying that is even more profound is that if they did do what he told them they would prevent themselves from ever having any children or of reproducing themselves. Paul is saying it very vividly, "I just wish these people would prevent themselves from reproducing; I just wish they'd stop spreading!" It's the cry of an anguished parent for their children, it's the cry of a pastor for his people when false teaching is getting into the fellowship. It's the cry of someone who is ready to curse those who bring another gospel and we can understand the language.

Conclusion

Let me conclude by telling you the Bedouin parable of the camel. Most Bedouin humorous stories are told about camels; the Middle East's sense of humour centres on them. A camel has been defined as "a horse designed by a committee," and it's an extraordinary animal. That's why Jesus often used humour about camels: he talked about straining a fly out of your coffee and swallowing a camel, hump and all – can you imagine that? Or of a camel trying to be pushed through the eye of a needle: this would cause roars of laughter in the Middle East.

The Bedouin have another story of a camel about a Bedouin Arab who set up his little tent one night in the middle of the Arabian Desert. He crept inside the tent to sleep because the desert nights get very cold when the sun goes down and there are no clouds to keep in the warmth of the earth. That night as he went to bed, the camel was outside the tent and, feeling very cold outside, said, "May I push my nostrils inside the tent and breathe the warm air?" After a debate with himself, the Bedouin allowed the camel to do that. The camel then said, "May I just put my head in to keep warm?" and the Bedouin replied, "All right," then the camel said, "Can I put my neck in?" and the Bedouin again said, "All right," then my front legs and the Bedouin gave in. Then the first hump, and then the second hump until finally the Bedouin finished out in the desert cold and the camel was just beautifully covered with his tent. It's a story they tell that has this message: you go back into slavery by accepting just one little thing, that's all. You slip away from Christ by taking just one little step – circumcision was just a little minor operation, a little surgical act.

Was Paul making a fuss about something little; was he making a mountain out of a molehill? "No," Paul says, "That's just a little thing in itself but see what follows. If you and I go back into slavery after we've been set free from Christ, it will not be through something big happening; it will be through a small step. We were not on our guard and we did not realize the implications and we said, "Just this once or just this," and the camel's nose was in the tent, but that was the just the beginning of the story as I have told you. A chain smoker started with one cigarette, an alcoholic started with one glass, a forest fire started with one cigarette end and the Chinese proverb says a journey of a 1,000 miles begins with one step. Paul is saying, "I beg you don't go back into slavery. This one little thing is all you need do to start the road away from Christ."

We should therefore be on our guard at all times. It is little things that lead us out of our freedom in Jesus. How do we keep that freedom? Very simply, hold onto Christ with one hand and onto the cross with the other. We preach Christ crucified and when he sets you free, that's real freedom, so hold onto Christ. I remember the film *Martin Luther* in which Johann von Staupitz, the superior of the monastery in which Luther was a monk said to Luther, "Martin Luther, if you dispense with the veneration of relics and prayers to the saints and the Virgin Mary and all these other things, what will you put in their place?" and Luther replied, "Christ." We need only Jesus Christ.

9

Galatians 5:13-24

SELF OR SPIRIT?

The principle of liberty (5:13-18)
Self
The law will be unfulfilled
The flesh will be destroyed
Spirit
The flesh is opposed
The law is avoided

The product in life (5:19-24)
The works of the flesh
Sexual
Religious
Emotional
Social
The fruit of the Spirit
Towards God
Towards others
Towards self

Two closing thoughts

So, my brothers, God meant you to be free. On the other hand, don't make this freedom an excuse for indulging your old self. Use it to show your love for others by putting yourselves at their service. For the whole law can be expressed in just one principle, namely "You are to care for your fellow-man as much as you do about yourself" (Leviticus 19:18). But if you snap at each other and pull each other to pieces, watch out that you don't end up exterminating each other altogether!

The approach I'm advocating is to let God's Spirit decide each step you take. Then you just won't try to satisfy the desires of your old self, whose cravings are diametrically opposed to what God's Spirit wants – and vice-versa. The two are incompatible, which is why you find that you can't always do what you really want to. If the Spirit is leading your life, you have nothing to fear from the law.

When the old self is at work, the results are pretty obvious. It may produce promiscuity, dirty-mindedness or indecency. It is behind occultism and drug addiction. It shows up in hatred, quarrelling, jealousy, temper, rivalry, prejudice and envy. It leads to binges, orgies and things like that. I've warned you before, people who go on doing this sort of thing will have no share in God's coming reign.

When God's Spirit is at work, a fruit appears in the character. Each cluster includes loving care, deep happiness and quiet serenity; endless patience, practical kindness and unstinted generosity; steady reliability, gentle humility and firm self-control. No law has ever been passed forbidding such virtues! They have room to grow because those who belong to Christ have nailed their old self to the cross, together with all its passions and appetites.

(Author's translation)

I remember when I began this series I spoke to you about Striding Edge on the mountain of Helvellyn in the Lake District. If you've never been there, that's something worth seeing. It's a very narrow ridge of rock and on either side are two huge hollows called corries which have been hollowed out by gigantic ice balls. They have left this sharp razor-edge of rock with a path along the top. It's dangerous to go along that path, especially in a high wind. If you get afraid of the corrie on one side with its swamps at the bottom, you'll lean over too far the other way and fall down into the corrie on the other side with a great deep pool at the bottom.

Now I use that as a picture of Paul's theme in his letter to the Galatians. He is saying to Christians, "You must stride along a very narrow edge. It will not be easy to keep upright. It will be easy for you to fall into one of two errors. One error is that of legalism. So far we've been looking at that for about six or seven studies. We've now finished with that danger. I know that Paul has dealt with it very thoroughly. It is the danger of imposed virtue. There is really no virtue in a life that has to be made good by laws and punishments: that is not real goodness, and so Paul is saying Christianity is not legalism. You must not go back to rules and regulations. You must not live in fear of penalties. You mustn't fall down that side. Christian liberty is to stay on the mountaintop with your feet standing on the sure foundation of Jesus, breathing the pure air of the Spirit and enjoying the sunshine of God's grace.

But the trouble is that when you talk, as Paul has been talking up till now about the danger of laws and rules and legalism, that people commit the second error and react to legalism by falling over the other side into licence. They say, "Well, if there are no rules, then I'm free to do what I like. Good works don't matter any more. Other people don't matter anymore. I'm free to do exactly what I like." That is not freedom. In fact, it's a worse kind of slavery if legalism brings you into slavery to others. Licence brings you into slavery to yourself and that's worse. True liberty is neither legalism nor licence. It is freedom to let the Spirit of God decide how you live.

The principle of liberty (5:13-18)

So here are the three subjects: *legalism*, my life controlled by society, by laws. *Licence*, my life controlled by self, by lust, sinful desires. *Liberty*, my life controlled by the Spirit in love. Now for the rest of Paul's letter to the Galatians he's going to speak about the second danger, about licence, about slavery to self. He says you have not been set free for yourself, but for others. You've been set free not so much *from* as *for*. It's not just freedom *from* law; it's freedom *for* love. In other words you at last have true freedom, which is to be free from self, able to serve others and able to love God – that's what real freedom is. It is not freedom to *sin* – it is freedom *not* to sin.

Self

Now let's look at what this passage says. It is a brief passage but it is so full of insights. The vital question is this: now that you are free from the law, free from external restraint, who's going to be boss? Who's going to run your life? Self or Spirit? Throughout my translation, I have used the word *self*, particularly the *old self*. Paul used the word *flesh*. Why did I change it? Because in modern English, the word *flesh* has come to have a purely physical meaning so therefore when we say *flesh* today we think purely of our body. However, that is not what Paul was referring to. He is not saying, "All the evil in your life comes from having a body." The Bible never regards the body as evil in itself. That's why in heaven we're going to have bodies. That's why Christ came to redeem our bodies and put them right again. It is not having a physical body that makes us evil.

The word *flesh* refers to all that you are by nature, by heredity, by environment. It means not only your physical side but also your emotional side, your intellectual side and your moral side. It covers how you feel, how you think, how you behave, your motives, your attitudes. All that is included in the word *flesh*. The word *flesh* means what you are naturally.

I'm now going to say something that some of the teachers in the congregation might want to come and discuss with me later. But I believe that we have made a profound error in the theory of education in this country. The error is that self-expression leads to good living. So for the last 15 years or so, our education has been built on self-expression. Then we blame our youngsters for getting the lesson from adults and for expressing themselves and we don't like what they do. But if we've said to them, "Express yourself, let it out, do it, do your own thing. If you've got a feeling inside, then it must become an action" we've told them to express something that the Bible says is not worth expressing. We're going to see that the only thing to do with self is to crucify it, to nail it to a cross, not to express it. So we're living in an age of self-expression, and that assumes that the self is basically good, and that the more you encourage people to express self, the more good will appear. The Bible would say that self is inherently evil and the more self-expression there is, the more evil will appear.

Now I know there's an element of truth in self-expression and it is what you've done yourself. You learn much more quickly than what somebody else has done. But the harm that is done by total self-expression is reaping a harvest that we never thought we'd see in this country.

What does *flesh* mean? If you spell the word flesh backwards and cross off the H, you're left with S E L F. That's what it means: what you are in yourself by nature, your temperament, your outlook, what you do when you're left to yourself, how you behave without any restraints.

Paul says, "Now you've been set free from the restraint of the law, what's going to be expressed in your life? Self-expression or Spirit expression?" Self-expression is slavery again. Spirit expression is freedom. Now he's going to assume for the moment that a person chooses to use or rather abuse their Christian freedom for self-expression, to do what they want, to let "me" come out. They say, "I'm now not bothered about the commandments. I can do what I want to and let myself out."

The law will be unfulfilled

What happens if you let your old self run your life? Two things. First of all, the law will be unfulfilled. In all our studies so far in this letter, we have seen that the law is finished for the Christian. I'm sure you've had some mixed reactions to that constant emphasis. But there are two ways to end a law. One is to abolish it, and the other is to fulfil it. Jesus came to put an end to the law not by abolishing it but by fulfilling it. Can I give you a simple illustration? Everywhere you go in the car today you've got to have eyes in the back of your head. You've got to read so many signs. I counted 16 at one crossroads at the back of Oxford Street. Motorists are supposed to read all these before they move on. Lights, signals and arrows. On the other hand, another possibility of getting rid of all those laws is to put a police inspector in each car. You wouldn't need any signposts then. You'd have someone on board to guide you. Now here are the two alternatives. Both would get the law fulfilled. One does it by external restraint; the other does it by a person guiding from inside. Now ideally wouldn't it be wonderful in this country if every driver was so considerate towards everybody else on the road that there would be no need for the Highway Code? Wouldn't that be marvellous? But we've got to have a Highway Code for the simple reason that the law is not fulfilled in any other way.

Jesus said, "I did not come to abolish the law – every jot and tittle must stand" (Matthew 5:18). As long as heaven and earth are there, the law is there. Jesus Christ came to fulfil that law, to get it done, and the real truth is that the Christian can finish with the law because he can now fulfil it, not because he's abolishing it.

The main purpose of the law – its thrust or summary – can be expressed in one sentence: it's trying to get people to care as much about others as they do about themselves. That's what the law of the land is. You can sum it up in "Love your neighbour as yourself." If each of us cared as much about other people as we do about ourselves, there'd be no need for laws. They would be fulfilled... and could therefore be abolished. Do you see the difference? There is a kind of rebellious anarchy spreading through our society today that wants to abolish the law before it's been fulfilled. But there is no alternative scheme for fulfilling it. Jesus came, however, to get it fulfilled and therefore abolished. That's why if my life is led by the Spirit I'm not under the law. I no longer have anything to fear from the law. I'm being led from within now, so I need no external restraints. This is what is wrong with indulging the old self: it doesn't fulfil the law – it wants to abolish it. It simply wants to be free from rules. It doesn't want to get them done.

The flesh will be destroyed

The second thing about the flesh is that when you let your old self run your life, not only will the law remain unfulfilled but also ultimately flesh is mutually destructive. Paul here descends to the language of animals. I'm intrigued with the number of books that have been published recently in which the title infers that man is an animal. Of course this is the fruit of a hundred years of teaching of the theory of evolution, so that now we've been brainwashed into thinking that we're just naked apes. Of course we're not. We're hairy apes because we have more hair follicles on our skin then any ape ever had. Did you know that? They're just not as thick and as long as the apes' but we've got more hairs than an ape.

Here is the kind of title I am referring to: *The Naked Ape* – it's all about us. *The Human Zoo* – it's all about us. Paul says, "That's legitimate language when you left the old self to run your life." He uses animal language. He says, "You'll bite; you'll snap at each other; you'll tear each other to pieces." The result is you'll have nothing left: if you abolish the law and then let self reign, you'll destroy society. That is what we are seeing happen in our community before our very eyes. If you abolish the law and substitute licence and indulgence of self, you will utterly exterminate society. You make it impossible for people to live together. It can happen in a marriage. I heard it said of a marriage this last week: "They live a cat-and-dog existence." Have you heard that phrase used? Why? Because each partner in the marriage is letting self reign and the result is they snap at each other. They pull each other to bits. Paul says, "Watch out – you'll destroy your society altogether. You'll exterminate each other." I'm afraid you and I know of marriages where husband and wife are just murdering each other slowly. They seem to have the knife at each other the whole time. Paul says, "If you let self reign, not only will the law be unfulfilled so that what it tried to do will not get done but you will also ultimately make it impossible to live with each other."

Let the Spirit reign and you become a voluntary slave of others in their needs… and you are set free from sin for service: that's real freedom! So therefore don't abuse your freedom to let self reign but let the Spirit reign. That's true freedom.

"The Christian life is misunderstood if it's seen as one gigantic step and you're all right. The trouble is we're always looking for this as if we could just find one step to take and then we're there. According to my Bible, the Christian life is a series of steps walking with the Lord, walking in the Spirit, so that every moral decision we make is led by the Spirit. The Christian life is a walk."

Spirit

Having looked at the implications of self running the life, he now turns to the Spirit. He says, "The kind of life I'm trying to paint for you is a life in which each step you take is a step led by God's Spirit." That does not mean that we have to pray about every single action in life. I read a few days ago of a dear lady who took this to extremes: she would pray about what she should wear that day and when she sat at a table she would pray whether to have butter or margarine or jam or Marmite and so on. She prayed about every detail. Now that is going to an extreme which the Bible does not advocate. But it does say this: every step you take – and that means every moral decision you take that has implications for right or wrong or for your relationships with other people – then let the Spirit lead you in that step. That's why the Christian life is always misunderstood if it's seen as one gigantic step and you're all right. The trouble is we're always looking for this as if we could just find one step to take and then we're there. According to my Bible, the Christian life is a series of steps walking with the Lord, walking in the Spirit, so that every moral decision we make is led by the Spirit until like Enoch we take the last step into glory and walk with God and are no longer here on earth. The Christian life is a walk.

The flesh is opposed

If we follow this way, if we let the Spirit guide us in every moral decision, what will happen? The first thing that will happen is that you'll find you can't let the old self run your life at the same time. Here's the great secret. There's no room for two people on the throne of your heart. It will either be self or Spirit. It's like this every morning you get up: it's either self or Spirit. Every moral decision you reach is either self or Spirit. It is never both. If you let the Spirit lead, self can't. If you let the self lead, the Spirit can't. You can never have both. Or if I can put it this way, you can walk either of two roads every day. You can go down the self road and you'll find signposts all the way down: laws. Or you can go down the Spirit road and walking along that road there's freedom. But you can never walk both roads. This is a choice a Christian has to make every day. We talk about getting out of bed on the wrong side. If you do that, you've got out on the self side. This in fact is what we really mean by that phrase. When somebody proves irritable, they cross people, they don't do their best work, you say they got out of bed on the wrong side that morning. They did: they got out on self. So there are two mats by the side of your bed: not his and hers, but self and Spirit. Which one did you step out onto this morning? You can travel either road today: either the self road or the Spirit road. In a service of worship, the self road would be: "Lord, I thank you that I am not like other men. I give tithes of all that I possess and I fast twice in the week. I'm a good boy, I am. Thank you, Lord, for making me so good." That's the self road. But the Spirit road says, "God be merciful to me, a sinner" (Luke 18:9-14). You can't travel both. Now that's the first thing that happens. Why? Because the flesh and the Spirit are mutually incompatible: they never go together. They always go in different directions and you cannot travel both roads. So if I walk in the Spirit, I can't follow the flesh.

But then he puts it the other way round. If I walk in the flesh, I find I can't really do what I really want to do and follow the Spirit. It is a mystery to some people but not to me and I think not to you, that when I become a Christian the tension of my life increases greatly. Psychologically, Christianity is not so good for you: it increases tension, and I've met more Christians with tension then unbelievers without it. In fact, many unbelievers seem more free from tension then some Christians. Of course they are. I'll tell you why: because the unbeliever doesn't even think of following the Spirit. There is simply no tension, no pull in his life. But for the believer there is the tension of Romans 7. "The good I want to do I can't do and the evil I don't want to do I find myself doing" (Romans 7:19). That's the divided civil war that there is in every Christian's heart. I can't promise you release from that tension until you get to glory. The reason is that my old flesh is still hanging around. I still live in my body. I still have the brain that I had when I was an unbeliever. The Spirit pulls one way and the flesh pulls the other: they set their desires against each other.

Every moral decision can be settled with one question. A lady who professed to be a Christian came up to a friend of mine. She was smoking and she said to my friend who is a minister (he wasn't wearing a dog collar but she knew he was a Christian), "Ought I to smoke as a Christian? Very wisely my friend did not say no. He said, "Is it a desire of the flesh or a desire of the Spirit for you?" She just answered, "Thank you." That settles it, and off she went. Now there's your question: in everything you are facing – in every choice you have to make – just stop and say, "Is this a desire of the flesh or a desire of the Spirit?" It can't be both. It's either the something the Spirit wants you to do or it's something that you want to do from your old self. That settles the issue, doesn't it? If you're doing one, you can't do the other.

Here is the real thing. Now that I'm a Christian, I want to do good. I am therefore torn so often because I find myself letting myself down. Don't you feel differently about sin once you're a Christian? Before you thought it was all right. You said, "Everybody does it." Now you feel so ashamed and embarrassed that you want to kick yourself. You feel, "That's not the real me. I've let myself down." And you have. The real you really wants to follow the Spirit and that's why when the flesh gets a hold at any point you can't do what you really want to do and follow the Spirit. It's one or the other.

The law is avoided

The other thing that happens when the Spirit is leading you is that you have nothing to fear from the law. If you're driving properly along a road, you've nothing to fear from the police car behind. Similarly, when you're being led by the Spirit, you've nothing to fear from the law of God. Not one thing. So the flesh is subdued and the law is superseded when the Spirit is leading you.

The product in life (5:19-24)

Now let's come to the second part. We have been talking about the basic principle in a Christian's life – whether self or Spirit is going to lead. But how do you know which is leading you? How can you test whether self did that or the Spirit did that? The answer is very simple: you look at the product. If the principle is right, the product will be right. If you're walking in true liberty, then true life appears. This is the best test.

The works of the flesh

Now let's assume that a Christian is going to let the old self run his or her life. What kind of thing appears? What kind of thing happens when the flesh is indulged? Well certain *works* appear. That word is very interesting. It implies a mechanical process of production. It implies things that you can produce instantly. It implies a kind of impersonal factory churning out things: *the works of the flesh*. The contrast is between the word *works* and the word *fruit*. Which would you rather have: works or fruit? The words themselves are the difference between a factory and an orchard, between a rubbish dump and a garden. Let's look at the works of the flesh. There are four groups here: sexual works, religious works, emotional works and social works. It's perhaps like reading the Sunday papers. Let's look at what will appear when the old self is allowed freedom.

244

Sexual

It's a sad comment on what we've done with God's creation that the very word sex makes us uncomfortable, and yet God made male and female. It was the first aspect of life to go wrong when Adam and Eve got out of God's will. Here is something that God meant to be very precious and lovely, one of the major features of our life and society.

But look what the old self does to sex. Paul uses three words: the first is *promiscuity*. God has said quite clearly that there is one context for sexual physical expression, and that is when two people have decided to live together as long as they shall both live. That's what God intended it for. The word here means to take this physical act out of that context and use it anywhere. The results are unhappiness, insecurity, neuroticism, and so many of the problems of our age and young people will, if they're honest, tell you of the problems this is causing. Self on the throne says, "I can enjoy myself anywhere, anyhow." The Spirit does not say that.

The second word is *dirty-mindedness* which I think is fairly well illustrated by Andy Warhol's works. It comes out in entertainment and literature. It comes out in the fact that you can hardly name a decent comedian today. There is a ministry in helping people to relax and laugh but there's hardly a comedian who can get by now without sexual innuendos.

The third word is *indecency* which means to have reached the state where you do not mind shocking public opinion. You don't mind what you do in front of others. You have moved beyond the position where you are shocked by something offensive. In fact, it's a word that means really you enjoy shocking other people.

Religious

The second group of things comes under the religious heading. Here I've translated them as *occultism* and *drug addiction*. The first word is literally *idolatry*. But behind the idols were demons, and what really is wrong with idolatry is not that idols are not gods but that behind the idols are evil spirits who grip a person once they begin to worship a block of wood or stone. In the same way, nowadays people in our country don't bow down to blocks of wood or stone but they do get involved in spiritism, in horoscopes, in black magic, in white magic, in all kinds of other things, or even just superstition: think of "touch wood," "cross your heart," "a black cat crossing your path." And that's really the word that should be applied today. Occultism.

The second word that Paul used is an interesting word: *pharmakeia*, from which comes our word *pharmacy*. It means "drugs." Did you think drug addiction was something new? Did you think it only started recently? Read your history, and you'll see that occultism and drug-taking are often partners: they go together. They did in the ancient world, because people started by taking trips, trying to get through to some religious experience, trying to get through to eternity, reality or something, taking a trip into the supernatural. Occultism and drugs go together. So the Bible does mention drug addiction, *pharmakeia*, the wrong use of drugs to have religious experiences. Do you think those works of the flesh have disappeared? They're bigger than ever.

Emotional

What a list here: *hatred*: the opposite of love; *quarrelling*, being argumentative; *jealousy*, that burning destructive jealousy that is over-possessive. I've seen husbands and wives who are over-possessive of their partners and parents over-possessive of their children. Jealousy can burn someone up. *Temper.* Paul here literally uses a word that means "boiling over." What's your boiling point? *Rivalry*: personal ambition, determined to do others down and get ahead. There's a lot of that in the business world. *Prejudice*: the word literally means "to stand apart from others." It means, "I'm white and you're black." "I'm rich and you're poor." "I'm educated and you're not." *Envy.* You know what that did to Cain and Abel and many other people. It's a pretty horrible list, isn't it? But if you let self run your life, that is what will appear.

Social

The fourth list is more in the social area: it is when people can't have a good time without over-indulgence. My younger daughter went to a schoolgirls' party and came home saying she had drunk punch. It seems any party for young people over about the age of 14 is going to have bottles to it. It is in such situations that the restraints come off, the wrong kind of spirit is in control and things happen that cause a lifetime of regret. Paul is saying when self is on the throne, you can't even have a party without plenty of booze. You can't have a good time without stepping over the line. That's the flesh. That's self on the throne.

Now look at the end of verse 21: he says, "Do you realize what this will cost you? Do you realize that any of these things is enough to keep a man from sharing the coming reign of God?" Now I want to ask you a very difficult question. It is this verse that says those who go on doing these things will not share in God's reign. Now, is that verse addressed to unbelievers or believers? I believe it's addressed to Christians. I know that any of these things can drag an unbeliever to hell but Paul says to the Galatians, "I warn you as I've warned you before." He's speaking to Christians. What does it mean? Does that mean that Christians could lose their salvation and be lost eternally if they go on doing these things, if they go on in their former life after they're a Christian? Yes, I'm afraid it does. This is just one of eighty such passages which contain a solemn warning to believers that they can forfeit their future in Christ and cease to be the heirs of what they would have inherited with him (see my book: "Once Saved, Always Saved?"). In other words, sin matters just as much in believers as it does in unbelievers. In fact, it is even more serious (read 2 Peter 2:20–22 asking why such backsliding believers are "worse off"). "It is a fearful thing to fall into the hands of the living God" was said to Christians (Hebrews 10:31).

The fruit of the Spirit

Now let's turn to something lovely. This is like walking from a rubbish dump into an orchard and seeing fruit trees. Fruit doesn't appear overnight, however. You can produce the works of the flesh overnight: one bad night and you've got the lot. But the fruit of the Spirit is different: the fruit grows in the character as somebody walks in the Spirit. A mark of somebody who is walking in the Spirit is that the fruit begins to appear: just a bud at first, maybe just a flower then the bud. Then you see it growing, swelling and ripening.

Let's look at the fruit of the Spirit. This is the picture of character. Note the word fruit is singular: one fruit, nine flavours. There is a fruit in the Mediterranean, *Mysterio Deliciosus*, which has many different flavours. You take a bite and you think it's one thing, and you take another bite and it tastes of another flavour. How lovely to have a fruit with many different flavours! Well, this fruit grows. I've brought out the singular in my translation by saying "a fruit grows in the character."

In each fruit you'll find nine lovely things. We can divide them up into those that refer to our relationship with God, those that refer to our relationship with others, and those that refer to our relationship with ourselves.

Towards God

Loving care: love has this element not just of emotion or thought but of caring. If you love God, you care for him: you are concerned about his glory. Love is caring. So *loving care*. Secondly, *deep happiness or joy*. Some people find their happiness in things: I would call that pleasure. Some people find their happiness in people, which is a bit better. But others find it in the Lord which is best of all. Thirdly, *quiet serenity or peace*. I'm told that three out of every four people in England are taking pills of some sort. The most widely used are called significantly tranquillizers. Bed shops not only sell beds that are comfortable or beds that will tip up or those that bend at the touch of a button but also beds with soft music being played inside the pillow and just about every kind of thing you can think of to try and tranquillize people. The fruit of the Spirit is quiet serenity. If I've lost my serenity, the first question I should ask is this: "Who's been on the throne today – self or Spirit?"

"Do you know who are the only two men (apart from Jesus) in the New Testament who are called 'good'? Both had the same name: Joseph. Joseph surnamed Barnabas and Joseph of Arimathea. Each was generous. Barnabas sold a field and brought it and laid the proceeds at the feet of the apostles. Joseph of Arimathea had a lovely plot in a cemetery for himself and he gave it to Jesus."

Towards others

The second group of flavours is concerned with my relationship with others. *Endless patience*: the word is literally "long tempered." A word that's died out of the English language for some reason, although *short-tempered* hasn't! It means to be able to put up with that awkward, difficult, irritable, irritating person. It means to be able to go on being patient with them. Putting up with others. *Practical kindness*. This means taking the trouble, making a special effort to do something for other people, especially for those who are unlovely; loving others in their need. Being kind can be time-consuming and demanding and it seems out of place in today's competitive world. It includes being sympathetic, stopping and listening to others, being willing to enter into their world.

Unstinted generosity. Paul uses the word *goodness.* Do you know who are the only two men (apart from Jesus) in the whole of the New Testament who are called "good"? They both had the same name: Joseph. Joseph surnamed Barnabas and Joseph of Arimathea. What was there about these two men? Each was generous. Barnabas sold a field and brought it and laid the proceeds at the feet of the apostles. Joseph of Arimathea had a lovely plot in a cemetery for himself and he gave it to Jesus. Further, they both were generous in mind even when others had narrow minds. Joseph of Arimathea was alone in the council in saying, "I believe Jesus is innocent." Joseph Barnabas went to Antioch where there were some professing Christians who were criticized by others, but Barnabas had a generous mind: when he "saw the evidence of the grace of God, he was glad" (Acts 11:23, NIV).

Towards self

Steady reliability, thank God for people with this fruit: the church would not survive without them. Those who are always there. Those we've asked to do a thing who will do it whether they get noticed or thanked or not. Secondly, *gentle humility.* Those who don't push themselves forward. Those who just get on with the job quietly and humbly. And *firm self-control*, those who've got a grip on themselves. That last word means a man who can say no to himself.

Two closing thoughts

First, Paul says there is no known case in history of any law ever being passed forbidding these virtues. He says this to show that the fruit of the Spirit is just beyond the scope of the law altogether. Can you imagine somebody trying to pass a law that says no more loving kindness in this land? You must never be patient, never be humble with anybody ever again. Can you imagine that? No, you can't. When you're in the realm of living in the Spirit, the law just has nothing to say. You don't need it. It's finished with.

Secondly, if you're going to grow a fruit you've got to prune: you've got to cut something out. That's true of an orchard. If you have one, if you've got a fruit tree, you'd better get the secateurs out and get busy and cut out the diseased and the dead wood: cut it back, cut it out. What is the Christian to cut out to make the fruit of the Spirit grow? Paul says if this fruit is to grow then you'll need to crucify self. Self-crucifixion is the only secret. Not self-expression – that's slavery.

The day you became a Christian, you came to the cross. You said not only, "Jesus, you died for me," you also took yourself and you nailed yourself to that cross. But that crucifixion does not kill immediately.

Here is the explanation as to why my old self which has been crucified with Christ still bothers me. Why did they have soldiers around the foot of the cross? Why did they keep a guard at the crucifixion having nailed Jesus to the block of wood; why did they not go home and leave him there to die? Because his friends could have pulled the nails out.

A man was crucified on Hampstead Heath a few years ago – did you read about it? A gang of thugs took a young boy and they literally nailed him to a tree on Hampstead Heath. But fortunately he was found within a few hours and they pulled the nails out and they saved his life. You can do that after you've crucified someone. So the soldiers stayed at the foot of the cross. "Those who belong to Christ Jesus have crucified the old self with its passions and desires" (verse 24).

But the trouble is he's not dead yet. Hanging on that cross of Jesus, he says, "Let me down for just a few hours – you can put me back next Sunday. Just let me down for a little while. The agony is awful." Do you know, it is agony to crucify yourself. It's a very painful process. Your self cries out to be let off the cross for just a bit and you'll regret it – there will come a time when you want to put self back on the cross again.

But Paul is saying, "Just let self stay there. Let self stay there until he's dead. You have crucified him. Let him die." When you cut self out, this is what it means to follow Christ and take up the cross daily: to commit self-crucifixion daily and say, "Not self today; Spirit today." "Not self tomorrow; Spirit tomorrow." "Not self on Tuesday; Spirit on Tuesday." Each day it's going to be that way, and as you do that, the fruit will grow.

I can sum up this message in one question. You've got to be controlled by someone: is it to be *society* through the law – which is legalism – or *self* through desire – which is licence – or *the Spirit* through love – which is liberty?

10

Galatians 5:25 – 6:5

KEEP IN STEP WITH EACH OTHER

Walking step by step
Walking in step

The three duties of the Christian life
Loving God
Loving your neighbour
Loving other Christians
The importance of the church

Getting out of step (5:26)
Pride
Getting ahead of others
Rivalry
Envy

Keeping in step (6:1-5)
Someone slips
Someone is overloaded
Someone is not being responsible

If God's Spirit is leading our lives, let the same Spirit keep us in step with each other. We get out of step when our hollow pride wants a reputation of being ahead, regards others as rivals and is envious of their progress.

Brothers, if anyone slips up and is caught doing wrong, those of you who are spiritually mature should get him on his feet again. But handle him gently and humbly, keeping an eye on yourself, for sudden temptation could just as easily hit you.

When the strain is too much, help to carry each other's burdens; this is simply carrying out Christ's instructions. If anyone thinks he is too important to stoop to this, he really isn't worth anything and only fools himself.

Let everyone weigh up his contribution, to see whether he is doing enough. Then he can take pride in his own work, without making odious comparisons with what others are doing. For each must shoulder his own load of responsibility.

(Author's translation)

The theme of Galatians is freedom. But what kind of freedom? This little letter is the Magna Carta of Christian liberty. But what kind of liberty? In the first half of this letter Paul is saying that Christian freedom is freedom from law, from external control, from rules and regulations which are slavery and bondage, which can bring us under the fear of penalty. A Christian is free from the law or legalism but that's only part of Christian freedom. Moreover, many who are not Christians would love that kind of freedom. The anarchists would love to get rid of all authority and control, to have no laws or rules, and let everybody do what they like but that is not true freedom. In Paul's day, it was called *antinomianism*, a long word which means quite simply "anti-lawism." We now call it *anarchy* and we know that anarchy does not leave people free but leaves them in bondage to fear. So the second part of this little letter is concerned with the other side of the coin: true freedom is not only to be free from law but also to be free from self: that is real freedom. Those who think that to be free is to do what I like confuse that with slavery to self, which is the worst kind of slavery. We call it license because it is not liberty.

It is in this second section that we read this short passage where Paul has been saying you must not be governed by the law from outside you or from self inside you, but by the Spirit above you: that is true liberty. He puts it in the form of a picture of the Christian life as a walk in which you don't just take one step and then you're all right, you're going to ride the escalator to glory, but in which you walk with God to glory.

Walking step by step

The Christian life consists of step after step after step. Who is going to decide which step you take? The law should not decide it. Self should not decide it, or as Paul calls the old self, *flesh* must not decide it. Let the Spirit teach you how to walk. Let him direct your path step by step. In our last study, we looked at the aspect of a Christian's walk that is private: the Christian's personal walk. The decisions he takes by himself. He can either walk after the flesh and as a result produce that horrible list of the works of the flesh, which we considered in our last study, or he can walk in the Spirit and he will produce a lovely fruit in his character: love, joy, peace, in relation to God; patience, kindness, generosity in relation to others; and faithfulness or reliability, meekness and self-control in relationship to himself. All that was from verses 16 to 24 in which he described a Christian's personal walk in the Spirit.

Now in verse 25 he says for the second time "walk in the Spirit." At least that's how it is in most English versions. You could be forgiven if you use a traditional version for assuming that Paul is repeating himself: verse 16: "walk in the Spirit," and then more about the works of the flesh and the fruit of the Spirit. Verse 25: "walk in the Spirit." Is he repeating himself? No. Unfortunately, our traditional English versions fail to bring out the fact that Paul uses two words for *walk*.

The way in which we walk says a lot about us. Lord Baden-Powell confessed freely in his autobiography that he first noticed the lady who was going to become Lady Baden-Powell by her walk; he said that hers was the walk of a woman of character. He wanted to get to know her and he did. The British medical missionary Sir Wilfred Grenfell confessed exactly the same. On board the liner that took him to Labrador, Canada, he noticed a lady and he said, "The way she walks tells me that she is a wonderful lady." He later married her and she became Lady Grenfell. And the Lord Jesus looks from heaven to see how his bride walks.

"The Christian life consists of step after step. Who is going to decide which step you take? The law should not decide it. Self should not decide it, or as Paul calls the old self, *flesh* must not decide it. Let the Spirit teach you how to walk. Let him direct your path step by step."

Walking in step

The two words for *walk* that Paul uses in verses 16 and verse 25 are different. In verse 16, it's the word used of a man who goes for a walk by himself. It's the word used for my individual progress. It's the word used for my personal, private walk with God. But in verse 25 the Greek word translated *walk* is the word *march*. It means "to walk in step with someone else, to walk by their side." If you go for a walk with someone, you will find you need to adjust your stride to the other person. When I was first courting my wife, I discovered that we didn't have the same length of stride. It was one of the many adjustments we needed to make in our married life. We had to learn to walk together and settle down into a stride: she lengthened hers and I shortened mine. We went for walks together in the Lincolnshire countryside.

There is one aspect of the Christian life which is concerned with walking in step with the Lord, but now Paul is concerned with the other aspect: learning to walk in step with other Christians. The church is an army and an army is useless if it cannot march. If you're going to learn to march, you've got to learn to keep in step, to line up with each other, to march together. You learn that the hard way on the parade ground in the square-bashing of the first few weeks in the army, Only then can you go out together to battle.

The church must move like a mighty army. It must never be a kind of conglomeration of highly individualistic believers each with their own private walk with the Lord heading off in a multitude of different directions. The army that is needed to deal with Satan today is an army that can march together in step with one another. Christians who are united and who've adjusted to each other can as a fellowship face the enemy and advance together.

So Paul says, "If we live by the Spirit – if we've found new life in the Spirit – if we've got the Spirit in us, then let us ask the same Spirit to teach us how to march." May I give a personal story at this point? I was thrown in at the deep end in the Royal Air Force. I hadn't done National Service; I was in agriculture at the time. So when I went into the Air Force, I found myself a commissioned officer unable to salute or march. On the first parade at which I had to march out in front of some 2,000 boy entrants and salute the man who I thought was the commanding officer, it wasn't; it turned out to be the warrant officer who was three ranks below me! I remember it – it was an absolute nightmare! I'm afraid I'll make a confession now, I bribed a sergeant major with cigarettes to come into my office. With drawn curtains, he paraded me round and round that office and made me learn to march so that I could go out on that parade ground with somewhat less embarrassment and fear.

Paul is saying, "Let the Holy Spirit deal with you in such

a way that you'll be able to parade with other Christians. Let him teach you how to keep in step. Let him teach you to be part of an army. You're on duty now. You're on active service. You've got a battle to fight but it's not just a personal battle with the flesh. It's also a corporate battle with the devil. So if you know the Spirit's life, then let us keep in step by the same Spirit. Let's learn to march together." That's the setting.

Just a few more words and then we'll turn to our passage. Why is this so important? It is important to Jesus who summed up the entire Old Testament law in two principles: "Love God with all your heart and soul and mind and strength and love your neighbour as yourself" and then he said, "I've got a new commandment you've never heard before. It's new for my disciples." You won't find it anywhere in the Old Testament. On the last night of his life, Jesus said to his 12 disciples, "I want you to love one another."

The three duties of the Christian life

Loving God

Here, then, are the three duties of the Christian life: to love God, to love your neighbour – and Jesus defined your neighbour in the parable of the good Samaritan as anybody in need – and to love your fellow Christian. I will be frank and say that the third is the hardest of the three without a shadow of doubt. It is much the hardest. I'm sure you have found it as hard to love me as sometimes the Lord tempts me in the other way. It is the hardest thing of all. Why? Well it's comparatively easy to love God because frankly he's such a lovable person. The more you know him, the more you love him. And he doesn't let you down, nor play dirty tricks on you or prove untrustworthy. The more you know him, the more you love him. So that from that point of view, it's easy to love God. The only hard part is that it takes faith and you've got to, as it were, imagine him from his word and it's not easy to love someone you haven't seen. But the more you know of him, the more you love him.

Loving your neighbour

It's also comparatively easy to love your neighbour because you don't have to live with him. I mean by that if you read the parable of the good Samaritan he did a fine work, he put the man on his own donkey and took him to an inn. He paid sufficient money to keep him there until he returned and said he'd pay more if he needed it. He then went back home to his wife. He'd done his deed. Having met the need, he was out of the relationship. In a sense, it is relatively easy to meet other people's needs. When a need arises, there is something in us that wants to help others. If there's a natural disaster, our heart says we will help. If we meet someone in need, there is something in us that wants to meet the need.

"You can develop a kind of like-dislike relationship with your fellow Christians. You know in your heart you can't get away from them. But you also find that if you get too close to them, you can infuriate each other. It is this fact of being in a family: you haven't joined a club when you join a church – you've joined a family. You can leave a club; you can resign your membership. But you can't resign from a family."

Loving other Christians

There are some neighbours, however, that are not always easy to help. The lady who went out of a church muttering, "I'd like to see the vicar love my neighbour," was expressing some of the hesitations we have. But when it comes to loving your fellow Christian here is something else: you do not choose your fellow Christians. When you join a church, you don't choose the members of that church. God has set you within a family. They are all your brothers and sisters. You're going to live with them in heaven but the problem is not that – the problem is to live with them on earth! After all, in heaven we're all going to be perfect and we shall just find it as easy to love each other there as we do to love God. That is something to look forward to. But the fact is that on earth, because we are not entirely sanctified, because we have things that make life difficult for others, it is difficult to love each other. You can develop a kind of like-dislike relationship with your fellow Christians. You know in your heart that you can't get away from them. But you also find that if you get too close to them, you can infuriate each other. It is this fact of being in a family: you haven't joined a club when you join a church – you've joined a family. You can leave a club; you can resign your membership. But you can't resign from a family. My three children are brothers and sisters and they have to accept that relationship. At times they may get on; at times they may not, but they cannot disown the relationship. They've got to learn to be brothers and sisters in a family. Neither can you walk out on a family. If you do, you're treating the family as a club which you joined for your own convenience. We are brothers and sisters.

This is why on the mission field the most difficult problem for every missionary is relationships with other missionaries. You need to pray about this. At home the most difficult problem is relationships with Christians. It is much easier to have a private devotional walk with God and go about trying to help your neighbour than trying to live with that lot. But God wants a family.

The importance of the church

What Jesus said after he'd given us the new commandment to love one another – and that covered all his disciples – he didn't say you can go off into a house group with that three or into a fellowship group with those three – all 12 of you are to love each other. That will be the proof to the whole world that you're my disciples. If they can look at your fellowship and say, "Look at those people: different ages, different temperaments, different outlooks, different backgrounds, different tastes, and they still love one another! That's amazing! They're not in cliques or little groups; they're a family. They've learnt to be together as a family, to live as brothers and sisters and to walk together in the Lord." That's the proof. It does not prove anything to the world that you love God. They don't believe in God. It does not prove anything that you love your neighbour because they also help their neighbours. But when you can cross all these frontiers and love one another, there's something they can't understand happening and they know that the supernatural power of God is at work. That is why Satan puts this high on his list of priorities. He has undone more Christian work by setting Christians out of step with each other than through any other method he knows. If he can divide a fellowship, he knows he will bring its impact on the community to nothing. So that's why it's important to keep in step.

Now having introduced you to the subject we can look at the few verses. I've divided them into two sections. Verse 26 and then verses 1 to 5 of chapter 6. Verse 26 deals with three ways in which people can get out of step as Christians. Verses 1 to 5 deal with three ways in which we are to help each other to get in step and to keep in step. The negative then the positive. Three don'ts and three dos.

Getting out of step (5:26)

We'll look at the three don'ts. As the proud mother said as she watched a passing-out parade, "Look at my Jonny, he's the only one in step." Her heart was bursting with pride. We are considering here what happens with people who can keep in step only if you leave them alone: the rhythm is spoiled. Just as in an orchestra, it only needs one instrumentalist who is out of tune and out of time to ruin all the music. Just one Christian in a fellowship who is out of step can spoil the harmony very quickly. If it is a handful of Christians, then that church will begin to be distracted from the work of serving the Lord. That church will become introspective, spending time and energy trying to patch up something that shouldn't have arisen in the first place. Given a church like this, it's the end of that church's testimony.

Pride

Now what lies behind getting out of step? Paul says very bluntly and simply that the main cause is *pride*. That is the theme that runs throughout the section we're looking at. And *pride* is just another word for self. It is the deadliest of all the seven deadly sins. Pride is the one sin that the Bible says God hates and abominates. How does pride get in and what does it do? It's intriguing that Christianity and Judaism, the two biblical religions, were the first religions of the world to condemn pride and to uphold humility as a virtue. Humility was regarded as a vice in the ancient world and a sign of weakness. But Christianity lifted humility to the role of a virtue.

There are three ways in which pride shows itself in a fellowship. First, those who want to get ahead of the others and to walk ahead because they want a reputation for being super Christians. Secondly, those who stay in line but are just so irritating and so provocative that people walking alongside pull away from them and so leave a gap in the ranks. And thirdly, those who get envious of others and who in fact pull behind because they are unwilling to be shown up as having fewer gifts than others. Whichever way, the line that was marching steadily ahead to meet the enemy now breaks. One person has gone ahead, another has made people pull aside and another is lagging behind. They are no longer walking in step. Pride lies behind all three ways.

Getting ahead of others

The first is pretty obvious. We hear a lot about inferiority complexes but what about superiority complexes? They're pretty damaging. Although the people who suffer from them don't feel they're suffering and that's why we don't hear so much about them! But it's possible to develop a superiority complex and step out ahead of others. If you can't do this with spiritual things, you can with natural gifts. You may have gifts of music, organization, speaking, leadership, all sorts of things. You can actually take the natural gifts that God gave you and for which you should have no pride because they were given to you. They were a gift literally and you can use them to try and stride out ahead of others and say, "I'm better than them." But if you cannot do it with natural gifts, you can do it with spiritual gifts, like singing in the Spirit. If you can do it with natural oratory, you can do it with prophecy. You can get to the point where you can boast that you have got spiritual gifts. "I'm ahead of the others in the fellowship. I want to forge ahead and I'm going to forge ahead" and you'll leave others behind and leave them out of step. You can do it with holiness. You can even do it with penitence. Do you remember that little poem:

> *Once in a saintly passion*
> *I cried in desperate grief.*
> *"O Lord, my heart is black with guile,*
> *Of sinners I am chief."*

Then stooped my guardian angel
And whispered from behind,
"Vanity, my little man
You're nothing of the kind."

You can even do it with humility. You can be proud of your modesty. I even copied a sentence out of an autobiography: "My life has always been characterized by that humility which is the mark of truly great men." I don't know if the author was saying that tongue in cheek. But pride can take strange forms and it can even take a spiritual form. We can stride ahead of others convinced that we are more spiritual and mature than they are instead of saying, "Look I'm going to stay with them and help them along with me."

Rivalry

Secondly, there are those whose pride takes the form of provocation in the aspect of rivalry regarding the people alongside not as colleagues but as potential competitors. The spirit of competition should never enter into a Christian fellowship. In the selection of officers, elders, or deacons, in any division of the fellowship for service of fellowship there should never be any rivalry. Because what does rivalry do? It pricks those alongside. They get the message: "Oh so I'm not a colleague now, am I? I'm a competitor. All right then, I'll show you. If you're challenging me, I'll show you." This then produces a break in the line sideways: there is provocation. Paul uses the word "pricking." We would say *needling*: treating people as competitors, not colleagues.

"An inferiority complex says, 'You're better than me and I resent it.' It's pride that says, 'They've got a gift of prayer in the prayer meeting. I'm going to keep my mouth shut in case anybody thinks I'm not praying a very good prayer.' That's pride. That's a tragedy when gifts are held back."

Envy

Thirdly, pride can take the form of envy. Someone has put it like this: "A superiority complex says, 'I'm better than you and I'll prove it.' An inferiority complex says, 'You're better than me and I resent it.' It is this kind of pride. It's the kind of pride that says, "So and so can do it better than I can, so you won't catch me doing it or people will compare us. They've got a gift of prayer in the prayer meeting. I'm going to keep my mouth shut in case anybody thinks I'm not praying a very good prayer." That is a form of pride. It's inverted pride that envies another and buries the single talent because somebody else has five or ten. I tell you, that's a tragedy when it happens. Gifts are going to be held back and that person will soon be lagging behind the fellowship and the fellowship will notice they're not keeping up and wonder why – and the reason is envy in spiritual things. "Don't get out of step with pride," says Paul. The pride that will take you on ahead or the pride that makes you lag behind or the pride that pushes people away – just let pride be broken and keep in step.

Keeping in step (6:1-5)

We turn now from the negative to the positive. How do you keep in step? Paul says, "If you're going to keep in step, you will need to help each other to do so." What happens on a battlefield if a man is wounded? For my bedtime reading I'm currently reading Winston Churchill's dispatches from the Indian frontier. It is fascinating reading. What a command of English he had! Again and again he describes how a wounded comrade is picked up by his fellow officers even at risk to their own lives and they carry him along to keep him going, to get him back. There is an immediate closing of the ranks to help the weak. Or if a man is struggling under his burden and carrying part of a heavy gun – they had to carry their equipment the hard way in those campaigns – what happens if a man staggers? Do they leave him there? No. Somebody else runs forward and helps him to carry his load.

Someone slips

Paul takes this picture from army life and he says, "You do this." He outlines three situations when extra help is needed from Christians. Number one, somebody can slip. There are plenty of spiritual banana skins around. The devil seems to love bananas because he leaves such a lot of skins right in the path of Christians. We're marching along together in step and suddenly someone slips. This will happen in every Christian fellowship. We are not safe until we get to glory and at any time any of us can be overwhelmed with temptation and we can fall. We can slip and we can be caught doing wrong. What should you do? Should you spread the word around rapidly and gossip and say, "Have you heard about so and so?" Never. Should you ostracize that person and cut yourself off from them? Never. Do you realize that their slipping and falling has left a gap in the ranks and a point at which the enemy can get through? What do you do? The spiritually mature in the fellowship should go and get that man back on his feet again. Pick him up, get him in step again, get him back into the ranks again. It's vital to the line and it's vital to the battle. Don't leave him there and talk about him. Get him back into step and get him back into line. Get him back on his feet. But do it without any pride.

If you think you're better than the man who slipped up, then remember that the banana skin could be under your foot next. Remember that it could suddenly hit you and "there but for the grace of God" it would have been you. Do it without pride. You can restore an erring brother with pride or you can restore him without pride but gently and humbly. The outstanding example is surely our Lord with the woman taken in adultery, with the self-righteous younger men so full of pointing fingers and Jesus just said, "Go and sin no more" (John 8:4, KJV). He gently and humbly put that woman back on her feet again. He was the one who didn't need to worry about himself in that sense for he'd never fallen although he was tempted.

"Some of God's people get over-burdened. The pressures of life get them down. What should you do about it? It doesn't say pray for them. I think that is our immediate reaction: 'So and so is under strain, so pray for them.' But Paul says, 'Carry some of their load.' That's much more practical and more necessary. What a joy it is when that happens in a Christian fellowship!"

Someone is overloaded

The second situation that Paul mentions here is where somebody is overloaded. Life is not getting any easier. I began my ministry 25 years ago and trying to recall then and trying to be objective about it, I just do not remember anything like the present tide of counselling that is needed for people under strain. I don't recall it. Life is now becoming full of tension. It is speeding up and the pressures on us are growing and Christians are going down under the strain everywhere. I just don't remember that 25 years ago. I remember spiritual problems coming and moral problems but I don't recall the kind of psychological problems of strain and stress that is a growing burden nowadays. To be a Christian today is to be under great strain because our world is as it is and because the church is as it is.

Some of God's people get over-burdened and over-strained. The pressures of life get them down. The fellowship should notice that. What should you do about it? It doesn't say pray for them. I think that is our immediate reaction: "So and so is under strain, so pray for them." Do you know what Paul says? "Carry some of their load" (verse 2). That's much more practical and much more necessary. That's what's going to relieve it. If somebody's carrying too much, take some of it from them and give it to someone else. Spread the load; share it. Don't just pray for them. Carry one another's burdens. This is Christ's law. These are his instructions. If you notice a Christian under strain, some others of you are to go to them and say, "Can I help you? Can I take anything from your shoulders? Can I share the load?" What a joy it is when that happens in a Christian fellowship! The result is that the breakdown doesn't come because somebody helped carry the burden before it all got too much.

Here again if anyone notices pride creeping in – if anyone is too proud to carry someone else's load – then he thinks he's a somebody but in reality he's a nobody. Pride can stop us stooping to help someone else in their job. But pride can also stop us from being helped. That isn't in the Bible but I'm putting a little bit of my own thoughts here if you don't mind. Pride spoils this mutual help. You can be too proud to ask for help, too proud to admit that you've got too much on your plate, too proud to let someone else share your burden. Do you see how pride spoils it all?

Someone is not being responsible

Finally the last picture is a rather different one. A man who's boasting of how well he's doing in Christian service may not be doing enough. Paul then quotes a proverb from the army: "Every man must shoulder his own pack." Again, to go back to Churchill's dispatches, he describes how when they had to carry heavy guns over the mountain ranges they would take the guns to pieces and they would spread the load among everybody. Everybody was carrying as much as they possibly could. They got over the mountain range and won the battle. I'm not glorifying physical war at this stage. I'm using it as the Bible does, as an illustration to say that if we're going to get over the mountains, if we're going to win and overcome the enemy, then the only way we'll get there is if every member of the fellowship is carrying their full load.

In the King James Authorized Version, the same word is used in both these last two cases (verses 2 and 5): *burden*: "Bear one another's burdens" and "every man shall bear his own burden," but Paul used different words. The first word is a Greek word, *baros*, which means "an overwhelming, crushing load that is too much to bear." But the word *burden* in the second case means "kit bag." Do you realize that if any member of a Christian fellowship is not carrying their kit bag somebody else has got to carry it? We've got to move the equipment to the right place. What we need is fellowships of Christians in which every member is fully responsible, and then they can take legitimate pride in their work. That is the right kind of pride. Not comparing what he's done with others, because he may not be doing all he should. But saying, "Lord, at the end of the day I believe I've done what I should have done." And if you can say that, your heart will swell with pride when he says, "Well done, good and faithful servant. You carried your share. You took your full responsibility. You carried your load. You took it on."

What a picture we've had of a church in this study! Wouldn't you like a church like that to go to? A church in which nobody is proud or trying to push ahead; one in which nobody provokes or needles anybody else, a church in which nobody has resentment or envy of another. A church in which everybody lifts up a person as soon as they fall, a church in which people naturally carry each other's burdens and a church in which every member is on active service. What a church! Shall I tell you where the church is so that you can all rush off and join it? I'll tell you where it is: it is wherever Christians walk in the Spirit.

The opposite is true too: a church that's got pride, irritation and envy in it is walking in the flesh: a church in which people keep slipping and don't get lifted up, a church in which there are over-strained people and a church in which many members just sit and don't take any responsibility: that's a church in which people are walking in the flesh. So we've caught a glimpse of what we ought to be. God forgive us we're not what we ought to be, but praise God he can make us what we ought to be.

11

Galatians 6:6-10

SOWING AND REAPING

Odds and ends?

Our instructor (6:6)
Teacher and Scripture
Pupil and support

Our character (6:7-8)

Our neighbour (6:9-10)

A person who is being taught to understand God's Word should give his teacher a share in the material things in life.

Don't be under any illusion – no one can turn their nose up at God and get away with it. It is a universal law that a man must reap exactly what he has been sowing. If he cultivates his old self, he will harvest a character that has gone rotten. If he cultivates God's Spirit, that Spirit will produce life of a lasting quality.

So let us never get fed up with doing good. One day there will be a grand harvest, if we don't give up. So whenever we get the chance, let's give as much help as we can to everybody, and especially to our immediate family of fellow-believers.

(Author's translation)

Odds and ends?

We're now drawing to the last part of Paul's letter to the Galatians which seems at first sight to be made up of all those odds and ends that come at the end of letters. After you've covered the main ground, you tend to put in everything else that you want to say. But there are no odds and ends to God: one of the proofs to me of the inspiration of God's word is that it's often the little odds and ends, the small asides and the little things that are just squeezed in between important paragraphs that have something profound to say.

This section seems at first sight to be simply odds and ends or, if you like, separate pearls of wisdom. Is there a string that ties all these pearls together? Yes – there is a theme running through all these odds and ends: it is the theme of sowing and reaping. As soon as you realize that, everything Paul writes in this section hangs together.

First of all, he writes about those who sow the word. That is what I do as a preacher. I haven't really changed jobs since I stopped being a farmer and became a preacher. I'm now sowing in soul, rather than soil, but I'm still sowing. A preacher is a man who goes out to sow. The seed he sows is God's word.

In the second case, he talks about those who are sowing habits and this is something each one of us does. We sow habits and we are going to reap a character as a result. The third kind of sowing he mentions are those who travel through this world sowing good and generous deeds in other people's lives. Sometimes that's very discouraging: there are not always immediate results. People are not always appreciative or thankful and it's so easy to give up. But again, Paul says, "If you're sowing something, there will be a harvest. So you don't need to give up." That is the theme of this section.

Our instructor (6:6)

Verse 6 is, to say the least, an embarrassing verse for a preacher to have to expound. At the end of last week's sermon, somebody asked me why didn't I include verse 6: "Are you going to leave that out?" I replied, "No." But that's the great advantage to preachers of expounding the whole word of God. We've got to say things we'd never choose to preach on. Let's look at verse 6. Some people think it goes better with verses 1 to 5, which refer to the mutual carrying of burdens within the Christian fellowship, and they say this is another example of that aspect. The preacher or teacher who is spending time teaching God's words to others should have the material burdens of his life carried by those who benefit from his teaching. So in a sense it does link with verses 1 to 5. But it also links with verses 6 to 10 in that it is an example of sowing and reaping.

Paul makes a rather blunt, and to some embarrassing, statement that a man who sows spiritual things will reap material things. Let's look at this carefully and see what Paul is actually saying.

Teacher and Scripture

First of all, there is the principle that all of us need teachers to help us understand God's word. That is why when Jesus ascended on high and led captives in his train, he gave different gifts to men (Ephesians 4:8). Among those gifts he included the gift of teacher. This gift is given to help the whole body of Christ understand what God has said in his word.

Do you remember the poignant question the Ethiopian eunuch asked when Philip found him in his chariot reading the prophet Isaiah? Philip asked him, "Do you understand what you are reading?" The poignant question of the Ethiopian eunuch was: "How can I unless someone explains it to me?" (Acts 8:31, NIV). It is a principle of God's dealings with us that he has spoken and that he sends teachers to explain to us and help us understand what God has said.

There are two dangers that I think we need to avoid in this matter of understanding God's word. One is to treat any teacher as a pope. I mean by that to say because Mr So and So says that's in the Bible or that's what the Bible means, then that settles it. I hope that all of you have heard me say often enough that I do not expect you to accept everything I say as in the Bible simply because I've said it. I want you to do what the Berean Christians did in Acts 17 with Paul himself, after he had argued with them from the Scriptures, they went to their own homes, took down their Bibles and searched the Scriptures for themselves to see whether these things were so (Acts 17:11, KJV). I hope you do that when I've tried to open up a passage to you. I hope you go home and say, "I'm not just taking Mr Pawson's word for it. I'm going to read it for myself and see if what he said was there is there." And if it isn't there, you can safely scrap what I've said. You can do what some do from time to time and write me a letter and say, "You shouldn't have said it because it's not there." That's helpful. You might get a letter back from me as well! But then we're free to discuss together the things of the Lord. That is one mistake we make as teachers. We accept one teacher as a pope, as an infallible guide and there is no such teacher on earth. Indeed, the preacher, no less than the hearers, is on his way towards holiness and sanctification. He has not arrived. He is not already perfect and can therefore let his own thinking and feelings affect his preaching and teaching.

The other error, which is equally common, is to make yourself your own pope. This error is saying, "All I need is the Bible and the Holy Spirit. I don't need to learn from human teachers." That error goes right against the New Testament teaching about teachers and yet Christians are prone to do this, especially when they have reached a certain stage of understanding. It's very easy to say, "Now I know enough to be my own teacher. I don't need any commentaries. I don't need any preachers. I am able by myself to interpret infallibly the word of God." I've said this before and I mean it tongue in cheek, I admire the Roman

Catholics for limiting themselves to one pope, because I think we Protestants produce many popes: teachers who are regarded as infallible and individual Christians who think they know enough about the word of God to do without any teacher.

So those are the two dangers we need to avoid: avoiding the extremes of regarding a teacher as infallible or regarding myself as sufficiently infallible not to need a teacher. God has given teachers to open up the word of God to people. It's part of his plan.

Pupil and support

The second part of verse 6 is the part that can be embarrassing to us preachers. We move from the teacher whose job it is to give the Scripture to people to the principle that the pupils' response is to give material support to the teacher. I can say straightaway there is no need for me to underline this in my present situation. However, since I believe there are many situations in which men labour long and lovingly to help people understand the word of God but are inadequately supported in a material way, I feel I can expound this for the sake of some of my brethren who have the gift and ministry of teaching for whom the second part of this verse is not applied by those who benefit from their teaching.

Here, I think we should break down the false dual morality that is often laid down between those who are described as clergy and those who are described as laity, or if you like, between those in full-time Christian service and those who earn a living as "butchers, bakers and candlestick makers" and so on. It is often thought – even if it is not said – but I dare say that perhaps many of you have this feeling as I'm talking now – that a person in full-time Christian service ought somehow to be above such matters as wages or salaries. Such thinking is that it's all right for a company director to receive a salary; it's all right for a factory worker to have a wage or a salesman or a shopkeeper but to talk of ministers and missionaries in the same kind of language is somehow a little unholy. This produces a false dichotomy among God's people. It's interesting that again and again in the Scriptures those who are in full-time Christian service as a missionary or engaged in ministry are commented on by the phrase "The labourer is worthy of his hire" (eg Luke 10:7; 1 Timothy 5:17f). It is no more moral or immoral for me to be on a wage as it is for any of you to be on a wage. We must break down this kind of thinking that says of a full-time Christian worker they must be without a wage and live "by faith." Everybody's got to live by faith whether they have a wage or not. Let's stop using this phrase "living by faith" if we mean by that "living without a wage." Let's say everybody's got to live by faith whatever their work, secular or missionary. Let's see the whole of the people of God in the same kind of way and in the same kind of thinking. That is why the New Testament talks on at least eight occasions about paid teaching or evangelistic ministers. Some sections of the Christian church have felt that the New Testament does not have paid ministers but the principle is utterly clear. Look up Luke 10:7; 1 Corinthians 9:11; 2 Corinthians 11:7; Philippians 4:10; 1 Thessalonians 2:6, 9; 1 Timothy 5:17f. These all speak of a person in full-time Christian service being worthy of hire, worthy of receiving wages.

Now having said that, let me say that once again there are two dangers. The first danger is for preachers and the second danger is for congregations. The danger for preachers is to see their role simply as a professional job that he is in just for the money. As soon as a man finds that in his heart, he must stop taking the money for his own spiritual good. That's the danger on the preacher's side – that it becomes no more than a job. He's just doing it as a job because he gets wages. That's a very subtle thing. But then if you're doing your job just to get wages you are equally immoral. Do you see the difference? Unless you are doing your job for the Lord Jesus and I'm doing my job for the Lord Jesus, our motives are wrong. We are wrong if we're doing it with one eye on the clock and the other on the wage packet. That is not the Christian way. Therefore what I'm trying to say is that as a minister, as a pastor and teacher, I am paid a wage and I have a job. But I must do it for the glory of God and so must you, whatever your job. Let's treat each other in the same way and not have these higher groups of people who "live by faith." If the Lord tells you to live without a wage, then you must live without a wage. If the Lord tells you to live with a wage, then you're living with a wage. Both ways you're being faithful to the Lord's leading.

The other danger is in the congregation. If you realize, as you ought to, that I'm in a job and that you pay me for the job, you must not therefore expect me to teach what you want to hear. That's the danger when it's put on the level of a job that "whoever pays the piper calls the tune" and that cannot be done in a congregation. A teacher must teach the word of God and be free to do so. That is why Paul does not talk about it as a payment but as a partnership – a sharing. Each of us is sharing what we have to give with the other. I'm able to share because you've set me apart from a normal occupation. I'm able to share the fruits of the hours that are spent studying God's word and preparing the meal for you so that you, having spent a busy week earning your money, can come and put that offering in and receive the benefits of the teaching. That is what God intended.

Our character (6:7-8)

The second way in which we sow and reap is not concerned with what we sow in our instructor but with what we sow in our character. Here Paul starts with a blunt statement: "Don't fool yourself – you can't fool God." I suppose the worst kind of deception is to deceive yourself. Most of us do it at some time or another. Perhaps all of us have a different view of ourselves from the one that corresponds to reality. "Don't deceive yourself. Don't fool yourself. Don't be under any illusion," says Paul. No one can fool God. Literally he says in the Greek: "No man can turn his nose up at God," meaning no one can sneer at God. No one can say to God, "You've got nothing on me. I can get away with it." No one can despise God in this way. He is referring in particular to the terrible delusion that many men and women are under and that is that they've got away with it. A man has fooled himself if he thinks he's fooled God into getting away with wrongdoing. You can't fool God. As someone has said, "God doesn't send his bills in every Friday." But his accounts must be settled and because we get away with things for a time that doesn't mean we've got away with things and we can sneer at and be contemptuous towards God. Don't fool yourself.

What every man sows that he will also reap. It's a universal law. It's written into nature. What have you been

285

sowing in your garden in the last few weeks? What will you be sowing in the next few weeks? Then I will tell you exactly what you will reap, what you will get later this year. It may be many months before you get it, but I can tell you exactly what you'll get if you tell me exactly what you've done in your garden. We've been sowing some nettles and one or two other things like that. I know what we'll get later in the year unless we do something radical about it but whatever you've been sowing in your garden that you will reap. We forget that what applies to nature also applies to human nature because we are part of God's creation. Do not fool yourselves: what a man sows he will reap. The bills must be paid and the accounts must be settled.

I want to help you now realize something important: forgiveness does not wipe out the consequences of our wrongdoing; it only removes the penalty. This is very important, because there are those who wrongly feel even after they've become a Christian that now forgiveness is available they can do whatever they like and they'll never have to pay. But they will, for this law – what a man sows that will he reap – applies to a Christian as much as to anybody else. Paul is writing to Christians here and telling them the law applies to them. It is true that if a Christian sins, then the penalty of that sin – broken fellowship with God – can be removed and it can be restored by forgiveness. But the consequence of that sin cannot be. That remains. This is the law of God in nature and human nature.

Here is an illustration to explain the difference between penalty and consequence. A small boy climbs into someone else's garden and pinches some half-ripe apples and eats them. He is discovered. The penalty for that is that he gets spanked. The consequence is that he gets tummy ache. The two pains in different parts of his anatomy are totally different in nature. One of them can be removed by forgiveness but the other cannot. However much the owner of the garden forgives the boy, he can't remove the tummy ache. Do you see the difference? The penalty may have gone but the consequence has not. And it's very important to realize that the law of harvest applies to every human nature including Christian human nature.

Let me give you some other examples. King David was a man after God's own heart: a good man, a man of faith, humility and courage. But after King David fell, he paid the consequence for the rest of his ministry, for the rest of his reign, for the rest of his life. The sword never left his land until he died and God said, "That's going to be the consequence of this."

God forgave him and out of his sin came the wonderful psalm of confession, Psalm 51 "Have mercy upon me, O God" (Psalm 51:1, KJV). But although the penalty was removed, the consequences remained for the rest of his life.

Let me take another simple example, a sin that we don't always count as a sin, one that we don't take too seriously: gluttony. A hotel proprietor used to tell me that he had conferences of clergymen and church people at his hotel and he always used to ask the organizer, "Is it going to be a high-church conference or a low-church conference?" The organizer would say, "What difference does that make to the hotel?" and he replied, "A lot of difference to the catering, because the high-church people drink and the low-church people eat!" Now you can make of that what you like.

Billy Graham's definition of gluttony is "digging your

287

grave with your knife and fork." Overeating is a sin according to the Bible. This sin is therefore bound to carry the penalty of reduced enjoyment of fellowship with God. The penalty is removed as soon as it is confessed, but the consequences of gluttony and overweight don't vanish with your forgiveness. You will have a bad digestive system or many other things that will come later in life as a result.

"If I sow to the Spirit, I am building up a life of lasting quality. Written into the life of the Spirit is durability and eternity. If I sow to the Spirit, other things being equal, the longer I will live and the more quality of life I will enjoy – true life in the Spirit."

This is what Paul is saying here. Whatever a man sows, whether he is an unbeliever or a believer, that he will reap. He therefore now applies this directly. If you sow to your old self, you are bound to reap a character that is rotten – if you indulge your pride, your lust, your greed, your gluttony, your envy, whatever, every time you do this you are sowing something that will reap a harvest. I remember as a boy a great children's talk about a boy who stole a melon from his father's melon patch. After he'd eaten it, he got worried about the penalty and so he got the skin and the pips lying all around his feet. He then dug a little hole next to the garden path and buried them. And he went in and he thought that's it. He waited for a few days and his father never noticed that the ripest melon had gone, so he thought he had got away with it. It was only some weeks later that his father came in to tea and sat down and said, "You know, I've just seen a rather funny thing. There's a melon plant coming up next to the garden path." Looking around the table, he saw a boy with a red face, who got the message. Paul says, "If you indulge your old self, even though forgiveness removes the penalty, there will still be consequences to face." When the prodigal son got back home, forgiveness removed the penalty – which was estrangement from his father – but it did not remove the consequence that he'd lost all his money, for all that was the father's now belonged to the elder brother. It is a solemn warning and necessary reminder to us that whatever a man sows that will he reap.

"Do not be deceived: God cannot be mocked. A man reaps what he sows. The one who sows to please his sinful nature ["the flesh"], from that nature will reap destruction [eternal ruin]; the one who sows to please the Spirit, from the Spirit will reap eternal life" (verses 7-8, NIV). Let us heed this solemn reminder. The consequences of both good and bad sowing lie in the future. The "reaping" takes place in eternity.

If I sow to the Spirit, what kind of harvest am I building up for the future? A life of lasting quality. That's the nearest I can get to communicating "eternal life." It's not just a life of quantity; it's also a life of quality. It's a life of a particular character. Written into the life of the flesh in this world is decay and corruption. And written into the life of the Spirit is durability and eternity. Therefore, the more I sow to the flesh, other things being equal, the shorter I will live and, other things being equal, the less the quality of my life. If I sow to the Spirit, other things being equal, the longer I will live and the more quality of life I will enjoy: true life in the Spirit.

Our neighbour (6:9-10)

The third way in which we sow is to sow good deeds to others. One of the hardest lessons in Christianity is to learn where good deeds fit in to the Christian life. If I begin here with a little saying, this might help: "A Christian is someone who does good deeds. But a person who does good deeds is not necessarily a Christian." Do you understand what I'm saying? Let me explain. The whole of the letter to the Galatians so far has been making it clear that I am not saved by good deeds. Nobody ever arrived in heaven by good deeds. Nobody ever became a Christian by following through the Scout law of doing a good deed every day. Nobody ever managed it because nobody ever has become good enough. But here's the other side of the coin. I am not saved *by* good deeds but I am saved *for* good deeds. Little badges were given out in our Sunday school when I was a boy. The words on the badge were "Saved to serve." Do you remember that? Saved to serve: to do good deeds, not being saved *by* them but saved *for* them. Not to do good deeds *in order* to reach heaven, but to do them *because* I'm going there. That's the place of good deeds in the Christian life.

Paul therefore says, "Don't get fed up with doing good deeds." Do you know it's the easiest thing in the world? If you try and live like our Lord doing good, I will guarantee that very quickly you will become discouraged and weary and be tempted to grow slack and flag. Why? Because this is not a world in which it pays to do good or to be good. It's not a world in which somebody going around doing good will be universally popular. Above all, it's not a world in which doing good brings immediate results. I would say that one of the curses of our present way of life is the word *instant*: instant coffee, instant this, instant that. We want to live in a world in which you press a button and something immediately comes out of the slot. That's our mentality. It's got to be quick and immediate. We've got to see immediate results or we get so easily discouraged. We live in an instant world but God's world is not an instant world. I've been a farmer and you can't have instant crops. In fact, farming is a very healthy life because it keeps you geared to God's speed. You can't hurry up God's nature very much. You can hurry it a little with fertilizers and other things, but a farmer has to learn to be patient, because nature has its own speed. It is our present artificial technological age that wants instant results, and because of this we don't adapt easily to God's spiritual world. We want things to happen by tomorrow at the latest.

All of us have had this temptation. Didn't you within six months of becoming a Christian want to be a missionary in China? Straightaway! You wanted to be up and off. You wanted to go out and witness, and you wanted to go out on a Saturday afternoon and come home in the evening rejoicing, bringing your sheaves with you. You went out and there weren't such instant results. Do you know, I know missionaries in Arabia who have been preaching the gospel for 40 years and they haven't seen their first convert yet? But they do it in the toughest mission field in the world in the sure belief that they're sowing a seed that is bound to have a harvest and that there must be some secret believers in that Muslim world in whose hearts there's been germination.

And they've done it for 40 years without a convert. I don't think I could keep it up like that. We want instant results but there won't be instant results.

Paul therefore says: When you go out into the world doing good, sow the seed of good deeds in your neighbour but don't expect instant results. Don't expect them to say, "For that I'm going to come to your church next Sunday." Don't expect it. When you invite your neighbour to come along to church, don't expect them to come the first time. But continue to sow the seed. There is a time for casting your bread on waters and believing that after many days the tide will bring it back again (Ecclesiastes 11:1). So don't let's become weary of doing good because there's going to be a harvest. There's got to be if God is God and nature is nature and human nature is human nature. Sow the seed of goodness and there's bound to be a harvest.

I like to think that Jesus was content to let someone else reap where he'd sown. For three years he went about doing good and the result was he was left alone. Not even his disciples stayed. But seven weeks later there were 3,000! Do you think that had nothing to do with Jesus going about doing good? Have you ever thought why Peter in his second sermon or in the sermon he preached to Cornelius could say you know how Jesus of Nazareth went about doing good and the harvest that was reaped was the result of Jesus' sowing? Jesus did that, although he didn't see it before he died. In the same way, I believe that a congregation like this scattered through this community, going about doing good, may not produce immediate results, but Paul says, "Don't give up." One day there's going to be a harvest if we don't give up. So let's go on doing good.

Let's continue to do good ... to whom? Well finally, there is a circumference of a Christian's good deeds and a centre. A large circle and an immediate circle. And we must be careful to keep them in balance. Number one, the circumference of our good deeds is the world in which God loves everybody. I've jotted down what John Wesley said in one of his sermons to his converts: "Do all the good you can, by all the means you can, in all the ways you can, in all the places you can, at all the times you can, to all the people you can, as long as ever you can." That's a great seven-point sermon for Christians. That's enough to be going on with for most Christians. That's the circumference of our help.

Now let's zoom in, let's focus. A Christian has a duty to help anybody in the world in need – anybody at all. But as Christians, we have a particular duty and responsibility to help our own family. The Bible is strong on this: a man or a woman who neglects their own family to help others is doing something wrong. Let me quote to you one text in the New Testament which you may not know but which is pretty strong: "If anyone does not provide for his relatives, and especially for his immediate family, he has denied the faith and is worse than an unbeliever" (1 Timothy 5:8, NIV). Charity begins at home but it must not end there. For the Christian home, family is this family of brothers and sisters in Jesus Christ. We have a special duty to our brothers and sisters to do good to them. Why? Firstly, because the world may not do good to them, and secondly because they are my brothers and sisters and my first duty is to my relatives. Thirdly, because the Lord says so and that's good enough for me.

Here is the circumference. How far out do we go to the

world? Where do we start? With the church. Learn to do good to your spiritual brothers and sisters and then you'll be able to go out and do good to others.

This is the message of this passage – it's down to earth, practical, sober – but we need this too. Let us sow that we may reap: in our instructor, our character and our neighbour. We can be certain that whatever we sow we will reap. God says so.

12

Galatians 6:11-18

CIRCUMCISION OR THE CROSS?

Paul's scribble (6:11)

Circumcision – religion (6:12-13)
Social distinction
Outward respectability
Human merit

Cross – re-creation (6:14-16)
Personal detachment
Inward righteousness
Divine mercy
"Even to the Israel of God"

Paul's scars (6:17-18)

Look what sprawling letters I use in my own handwriting! It is those who are concerned about outward appearances and like to show off who are pressurizing you into being circumcised. Their real object is to avoid the unpopularity associated with the cross of the Messiah. Even though they observe circumcision, they don't seem to bother about the rest of the Jewish law. They only want to get you circumcised so that they can brag about the number of converts to their ritual.

Never let me boast about anything or anybody – except the cross of Jesus the Messiah, our Lord. Through that execution I am dead to society and society is dead to me. Our standing in Christ is neither helped by being circumcised nor hindered by remaining uncircumcised. What really matters is being made into a new person inside. All who live by the simple principle will receive the undisturbed harmony and undeserved help of God, whether Gentile or Jew.

From now on, let no one interfere with my work again. I have the marks I want on my body; I am branded with scars gained in the service of Jesus.

May the generous love of Jesus, our divine Master and anointed Saviour, fill your inmost being, my brothers. So be it.

(Author's translation)

Paul's scribble (6:11)

Paul starts this short section by saying, "Just look at my handwriting. Have you ever seen such a mess? Great big sprawling letters all over the paper." Why would Paul say that? Why were his letters big and sprawling? Why does he mention it? Why does God include this in his word?

We're going to have to dig a little here, and I freely admit

I'm going beyond the letter of Scripture. I'm speculating but I'm going to share with you some of the thoughts that have been shared with me by a member of my congregation who belongs to the medical profession. I think the first question that we've got to ask is what is he referring to when he says, "Look how big, how sprawling, how spidery my writing is"? Some people have thought that this remark refers simply to this very last paragraph and that Paul, who normally used a secretary (called an *amanuensis* in those days not a stenographer), used to sign a letter off himself to avoid forgeries. Thessalonica was one church that had received a letter with the name of Paul at its beginning but it was a forgery and it misled the church. After that, Paul used to adopt the habit of signing off in his own hand and letting a secretary write it.

But is that what it is being referred to here? If so, it is a strange place to say it at the beginning of the paragraph before he's used this spidery writing. Literally, he says, "Look at these spidery letters that I have used to write to you." It seems clear that the whole letter is written in these large letters. Greek could be written in large spidery one-inch high letters, and it looks as if that is what he's referring to. Well now why? Why was Paul's handwriting so bad? Why was it so distinctive, so childish, for these large one-inch high letters was the first alphabet children learned to write? They were taught to write like this. Some have thought it was because Paul was not educated in the Greek language but then if he didn't know it very well, he could just as well make his mistakes in small letters as in large ones. Some have wondered if his writing hand had been injured. But there is one possible reason which not only fits the context but also explains a number of other stray remarks in Paul's letters – and it is that Paul suffered from partial blindness.

Now there are basically two sorts of blindness that Paul may have suffered from. We know that he did suffer from one kind. First, there is the blindness that attacks the back of the eye, the retina where the image strikes. When Paul was on the Damascus road he saw a light that was brighter than the midday sun, and he was looking straight at it. Every time there is an eclipse of the sun some adults and children suffer from temporary or even permanent blindness through looking directly into the sunlight. A light lighter than the sun would burn the macular region of the retina at the back of the eye and destroy it either temporarily or permanently. That's what would have happened to Paul on the day of his conversion, and the back of the eye would be burned. If there is a recovery from that, it is always slow and gradual, showing that the fact that Ananias, sent by God to minister to Paul three days after his conversion, was the minister of a miraculous power and healing which totally and permanently healed the retina of Paul's eye. That condition would not return because when God heals, the recovery is complete.

Secondly, there is also the blindness that affects the front of the eye, the cornea. There is in the Middle East a very common disease which infects children and then shows symptoms in adult life which particularly affected Jews for some reason, called trachoma. This disease aggravated the front of the eye, the cornea, the eyelids, the eye lashes and produced scars under the eyelid which rubbed on the cornea and disfigured it horribly, causing it to go white and opaque so that the physical appearance was off-putting to other people. It destroyed near sight for reading and writing and it destroyed far sight so that you could not see at long distances, but with large letters you could write and read. It is a disease that would be aggravated by a hot climate and by dusty roads. It's like having something permanently in your eye. If you've ever had something in your eye, you know exactly what it feels like. Can you imagine your eyes permanently full of things like that with the scars rubbing on the front? Now this would explain a number of things that puzzle us otherwise. For example, it explains the fact that Paul wrote to the Galatians saying, "I recall vividly that you wished it was possible to donate your eyes for transplanting in me" (4:15). It explains why Paul at his trial did not recognize the high priest at the other side of the courtroom and said, "I didn't know it was the high priest when I said that" (Acts 23:5). It would explain a great number of things and the actual physical sensation of this disease would also be perfectly described by the phrase "thorn in the flesh" (2 Corinthians 12:7), because that's precisely what it would feel like.

Now if that is what Paul was suffering from – if that was his thorn in the flesh which was nothing to do with the blindness of his conversion which was at the back of the eye but with a very common condition in the Middle East at the front of the eye – then his writing would be big and spidery. It would be the only writing he could do. It would also explain a great deal of some of the features of his writings and help us understand just what lay behind God's word to him, "My grace is sufficient for you" (2 Corinthians 12:9) and how much the men went through to go on his missionary journeys, exposing their eyes to the dusty roads.

Think too of the labour involved in writing a letter to the Galatians as long as this if he had to do it that way. Why then did he mention it? Why did he draw attention to the fact? They could see they were large letters. I think the answer is seen in the context, as often is the case. In verse 10, he wrote, "Do good to everyone, but have a special concern for the household of faith." An example of this labour is his letter and he's saying, "Look at my letter. Look at what this has cost me to write. Look at the labour of love behind it. I have a special concern for you, the household of faith. It's taken me a lot to write this long letter to you in my own handwriting. I could have had it typed [or the equivalent in those days]; I could have had it done by a secretary. But I've written this to you. I'm concerned about you. I have a special concern for the household of faith." Or look at verse 12, where he says there are people who are concerned about showing off, who are concerned with outward appearances. "Look at my handwriting. You can see straightaway that I'm not concerned about appearances. I'm concerned about realities. If I wanted this letter to look right I wouldn't have written it in my handwriting. I'd have got someone else to write it up properly and neatly. But I'm not concerned about outward appearances. I'm concerned about you."

But probably there is a simple explanation as to why Paul suddenly said this, and it is the fact that he had come to the end of his paper before he realized. With large, spidery writing, the scroll was being unwound over the edge of his table and suddenly he realized he'd got about six inches left. They didn't use writing pads in those days – they used a long scroll and then rolled it up and sealed it. As he is writing away, peering down at the paper perhaps with big scrawling letters, struggling to get down on paper the burden of his heart, he suddenly realized he's only got a little bit left. "Oh my, look what sprawling letters I've been using. I've come to the end of my paper. I'll have to summarize. I'll have to say in my last paragraph what it's all about."

If that is so, it explains the concentrated teaching of the last few verses. He's suddenly going to take them right back to the big issue. He's mentioned many subjects but now he goes right back to the one that started it all. Among the Gentile converts of the churches of Galatia, false teachers were saying to those new converts, "You've got to become a Jew if you want to be a full Christian. And if you want to be a Jew, you'll have to be circumcised." They were saying, "Jesus was a Jew, and he wants you to be the same. If you want to follow Jesus he was circumcised, so you must be as well. If you really want to belong to the true people of God, then you need to be circumcised as well as converted."

Now some people think that because of his choleric temperament Paul loved to "take a sledge hammer to crack a peanut" and that on this little issue he writes a whole letter and bangs away at the point and brings argument after argument from Scripture and experience to hammer home this point. But Paul knew what he was doing. If I may change the metaphor, this question of circumcision was just the tip of an iceberg. It was the point at which a whole issue surfaced and the issue was whether they were going to have religion or Christianity. That's the issue today too. It's not an issue that is out of date even though it no longer takes the form of circumcision. The real battle is between religion and Christianity – not between Christianity and non-religion. Religion is still the worst enemy of true Christianity, whether it is the religion of Judaism which Paul knew as a young man or whether it's the religion of "churchianity" which is the most common religion in this country. The great enemy of Christianity is religion, and so Paul, realizing he's got to the end of his letter, takes his pen for the last few little sprawling letters and says, "I'll go right to the heart of it. Religion or Christianity? Circumcision or the cross? Which is it going to be?" and that is what we're going to consider now.

Circumcision – religion (6:12-13)

Let's look at religion as it appears in circumcision. Man is a religious animal. You can take his religion away from him but he'll invent a new one in its place. Man has got to be religious. He knows he's not the biggest thing in the universe. He knows there are powers greater than himself. Human beings want a religion to relate to those powers, and the number of religions they have invented for themselves is legion. Religion has certain objectives, motives and characteristics. Paul had been brought up on religion. He'd had a religious background. He was brought up on Judaism and that was a religion, and he'd come to the point where he realized that religion was worthless rubbish – that's his own term for it: "worthless rubbish" (Philippians 3:8). Religion gets you nowhere. The tragedy is we always think it does, and in this country, as I've said, the religion is "churchianity". Hundreds and thousands of people in this country are putting their trust in religion – "churchianity" – and it gets them nowhere – it's worthless rubbish. Paul came to view circumcision in that light, although it had been a profound religious ceremony in his own life, undertaken by his own parents in utter sincerity, but he said it's worthless.

What is religion concerned about? Paul strips off the veneer of the religion of these false teachers and he says they're really concerned about three things: social distinction, outward respectability and human merit. You will find that these three characteristics appear in all religions.

Social distinction

First of all, social distinction. I can sum it up in one phrase: "the done thing." People take part in religion because it's the done thing. I honestly believe that the majority of infant christenings in this country are undertaken solely because it is the done thing. "My parents 'did' me and my grandparents 'did' them and my great-grandparents 'had it done' for them so 'I'll "have it done" for mine.'" It's the done thing. Why do many people still get married in church, even though they don't know God and they don't love him? Because it's the done thing. It is somehow still more respectable than in a registry office. Why do 98% of the people who die in Britain get a member of the clergy to bury them? Because it's the done thing. We suffer in this country from having had religion established in our midst and so it becomes the done thing.

We used to have a little joke between us three chaplains in the Royal Air Force at our station. There was the Roman Catholic chaplain, the Church of England chaplain and the OD (other denominations) chaplain, the odd-bods chaplain, who was me. When new men came to the station, they had their various religions in the top right-hand corner of their arrival card and we parcelled them out between us. The Anglican chaplain had first pick and he got most and then the RC chaplain had his pick and the rest were shunted over to me and I got the lot: atheist, agnostic, everything – I got what the other two chaplains wouldn't take. Although it was a job between us, the higher in rank, the more the C of E chaplain got his pick. We would joke about it, but I'm afraid it is true: where religion is established – the higher you go in society – the more established it gets. Social distinction begins to play a part in religion. People go to church because it's the done thing. Where will you go to meet the right people? I remember that in the colony in which I was stationed overseas it was announced in the officers' mess in the middle of the week whether Her Majesty's governor of the colony would be at church the next Sunday morning or not. Attendance at church reflected the announcement only too severely.

Paul strips all that away and he says religion is concerned with social distinction, with the done thing. It's concerned with conforming; it's doing what everybody else is doing. It's concerned with social acceptance, and Paul makes it abundantly clear that the cross is not socially acceptable, and it never will be. In society you may talk about the church and you'll be socially acceptable but talk about the cross and you will not. You may talk about your minister or your vicar and you'll be socially acceptable but talk about your Saviour and you will not be. The cross and cocktails don't mix. Paul says this is the first mark of religion: it is concerned with social distinction, and religious people don't like opposition or persecution. That's why I would predict that if Christians in this country were persecuted, the religious people would leave the churches. It would tell us straightaway who was religious and who was under the cross.

Outward respectability

The second mark of human religion is that it's concerned with outward respectability, not with how we look to God – because he looks on the heart – but with how we look to each other. It is concerned with having the right outward form and ceremony. It means that we're more concerned about what Sunday clothes we're going to wear to church than what the state of our heart is. It means we become obsessed with outward ritual and what's worn and how it's done and whether our walking around the church is dignified or not. We become obsessed with outward appearance. That's religion, and so where there is religion, outward form and ceremony develop. Paul strips that away too and he says that he can prove that these teachers are not bothered about the real requirements of the law even though they say circumcision is a legal requirement. Once they've got someone circumcised, they don't bother with the rest of the law. It's outward respectability. Once you've been "done", you're all right. Again I say that the tragedy is that the majority of people in Britain today have been through religious ceremonies. They are outwardly respectable – they've been christened, confirmed, they'll be married and buried with religious rites and ceremonies but they don't know Jesus Christ the Saviour, they only know religion.

Human merit

The third feature of religion that Paul mentions here is the worst feature: the fact that it's based on human merit. You can always say at the end of it, "We have achieved this or that. We've had so many conversions, we've had so many baptisms, we've had so many confirmations, we've got so many people." This is about counting heads and building up merit, about establishing before God a basis of human achievement. Paul again strips it away and says these circumcisers are only doing it so they can brag about a successful mission. Do you know that finds us all out at a deep level? The New Testament never talks about a successful church – have you ever noticed that? As far as I know, the word *success* never occurs in God's word. It just isn't anything that would have occurred to the New Testament church. They were too busy preaching the cross to be bothered with religion.

Those are three facets of human religion. I'm going to say two more things now about our contemporary situation. They hurt and yet they are true. I'm going to use a term for lack of a better one, which may offend. I don't intend it to be offensive but it's for lack of a better one. It has long been known that in this country what used to be called the working class has little time for church. The working class constitutes 65% of the population. Why? Shall I tell you? Because I think they are discerning and have seen too much religion and too little Christianity in the churches. They have seen too much social distinction; they have seen too much outward respectability, too much human merit. If they had seen the cross, I believe this would not have occurred.

The other large group in our country that the church is in danger of losing is the young generation. A generation is growing up that has no time for outward respectability, no time for social distinction. A new generation sees right through this and doesn't want it. I tell you it is that generation who are fascinated by Jesus Christ but they have no time for the church at all.

We've got to face these facts. Here are two huge groups. The working people of Britain and the young people of Britain and they've seen too much religion in the church, and they haven't seen enough Christianity. So they've rejected the church. We are now seeing these two groups again starting to become interested in Jesus Christ. They'll say. "Talk to me about Christ but don't mention the church." What is the answer to this? Is it to reject the church? No! I believe that way lies the danger of "throwing the baby out with the bath water." The answer is for the Christian cross to be put at its rightful place in the church again. Not as a symbol on a wall. Not as a crucifix on an altar but in the hearts of the worshipping people. When people see Christianity, not religion, in church, I believe they will come. I believe that it doesn't matter what a person's age or background or income group may be, where there's real Christianity I believe they'll come. Because true Christianity satisfies this deep need that otherwise searches after religion.

Cross – re-creation (6:14-16)

The danger would be that the young generation in rejecting the respectability which they would call hypocrisy, in rejecting the social climbing, in rejecting all that suburban Christianity has been associated with, in rejecting all that – the danger is they then have nothing to put in its place. If I turn religion down, if I say that religion is worthless rubbish, what goes in its place? The answer's absolutely simple and fundamental: the cross. There is no substitute for the cross. The cross, not as a religious symbol, not as an ornament, not as a charm to be worn round your neck (I'm not happy about that development today) but to wear *in the heart* the cross as a spiritual experience and reality, for the cross means not religion but re-creation: new life.

I want you to get the flavour of this next sentence (verse 14). Paul says, "I won't boast about anybody or anything. I'm not going to boast about my converts, how many churches I've started, how successful my mission is. I'm only going to boast about one thing. I'm proud to be associated with the cross." Now can you imagine that … can you imagine the impact of that? You can't really, because you've never seen a real cross and you've never seen anybody hanging on one. So you can't really imagine what Paul is saying. And since we abolished capital punishment in this country we can't even talk about that, but supposing I said, "I boast in the electric chair. I boast in the guillotine. I boast in the hangman's rope." You'd think I was crazy, but Paul says, "I boast in the cross" and that's what it meant in his situation. "I'm boasting about an instrument of torture and execution: that's what I'll boast about. That's what I'm proud of. God forbid that I should glory except in the cross of Jesus Christ." What a thing to boast about! And do you know we're a bit ashamed about the cross, so we boast about anything else: we'll boast about our church, the congregation, the collection, anything but to boast about, be proud of, the cross. I'll tell you why we don't boast about the cross – because other people don't see it as anything to be proud about. The world sees it as something to be embarrassed about, but Paul says, "I'm going to boast about the cross."

"Christ didn't die to make us respectable; he died to make us good. He died to change our hearts. The outward ceremony doesn't matter. What really matters is whether I'm being made a new person inside. You can test all your devotional practice with this. Is it changing the inside of you or is it just the outside that has been affected?"

Personal detachment

Paul then points out the three features of any religion that is based on the cross, not on religiosity. First, it will mean a personal detachment from the world. I came across a very interesting thing about the Greek language at this point. There is a very subtle play on words, which I didn't know until I studied this. There is a Greek word *stauroo* which means "to crucify", but it also means "to erect a fence." And the reason that the word means both those things is that you actually crucify and build a fence the same way. You stick a post into the ground vertically and you put another one and nail it to it horizontally. You make a cross that way and you make a fence that way. Paul is saying "I am fenced off from the world by the cross and the world is fenced off from me. When I came to the cross and came to the other side of the cross between me and the world, the cross stands as a fence – a barricade – I'm cut off." You see religion is concerned with social popularity and acceptance. The cross is concerned with being crucified to the world and the world crucified to you.

A teenage girl came to Charles Haddon Spurgeon and said, "I've been converted. I've become a Christian. How much of the world should I give up?" He replied, "Don't you worry about that my dear – the world will give you up." And that's what happened. Not only is the world dead to me but I am dead to the world. Believe me, the world writes you off when you're a Christian. You'd better put your social ambitions in the dustbin because the world has written you off. You are now a fanatic, you are now one of those funny people who takes Christianity seriously. You're a social misfit now. You're a bit of an embarrassment. You can't laugh at the jokes. You can't fit in. You're a social misfit. The world has written you off. The world is dead to you and you're dead to the world. Society no longer holds the attractions for you that it once did. The things you used to enjoy you don't enjoy any more. The cross fenced you off.

Real religion in God's sight – the religion that's based on the cross – is not concerned with social popularity or acceptance or the done thing; it has a personal detachment from all that. It seeks only to please God. That is why you are dead to the world and the world is dead to you.

Inward righteousness

Secondly, as against outward respectability, the religion of the cross is concerned with inward human righteousness. Respectability counts for nothing in God's sight. It's righteousness that he wants – and that's something inside. Paul is saying, "It doesn't matter what outward ceremony you've been through – whether you're circumcised or not, it doesn't matter. What matters is whether you are being changed inside." That's the rule of thumb for the Christian. That's the test of every service: not have I been to church and sung the songs and hymns and been through the routine, but have I been changed inside – has it touched my heart? That's the real principle of the religion of the cross. Christ didn't die to make us respectable; he died to make us good. He died to change the inside of a man. He died to change his heart. He died to create a new being within that person. That's what matters. The outward ceremony doesn't matter. What really matters is whether I'm being made a new person inside. You can test all your devotional practice with this. Is it changing the inside of you or is it just the outside that has been affected?

Divine mercy

Thirdly, the religion of the cross is based not on human merit but on divine mercy. Human merit seeks to build up a bank account in God's sight. Divine mercy is for those who are in debt, with debts so deep that they can never possibly be repaid. Divine mercy is for those who come to the cross. The cross separates me from the world, so social ambition will go. I've been cut off. I'm dead to society. The cross will make me a new person inside. That will show outside but it's the inside that gets changed first at the cross.

The cross brings me the mercy of God and therefore the peace of God. The two things always go together. Mercy and peace. That's why you can't have peace through religion. I've lived in a very religious land in Arabia. I've seen how devoted and pious good Muslims can be: how they'll pull out their prayer mat and go down and pray to Allah, how they'll save up all their life to make a pilgrimage to Mecca, how they'll fast for a whole month during Ramadan during the daylight hours and not touch any food. They do it with utter sincerity. But there are two things missing from their religion: mercy and peace. If you ask them, "Do you know that your sins are forgiven?" they answer, "No; I don't know." There is no peace for human merit because you never know if you've got enough balance in your account. You never know if you've worked hard enough. You don't know if you're good enough. There's no peace there. But divine mercy brings peace. "Mercy and peace be to all who live by this rule" (verse 16). What rule? The rule that what matters is whether you get changed inside at the cross.

"Even to the Israel of God"

Then Paul makes a daring little addition in verse 16: "Peace and mercy to all who follow this rule, even to the Israel of God" (NIV). This is the ultimate proof text of those who believe the "replacement/fulfilment" claim that the church is God's "new Israel." Elsewhere some Old Testament *descriptions* of Israel are applied to the church in the New Testament (compare 1 Peter 2:5 with Exodus 19:6). Here the *name* of Israel is apparently transferred, giving final confirmation of the succession. To call Gentile believers "the Israel of God"' is in harmony with his teaching that those who "belong to Christ are Abraham's seed" (3:29, NIV).

However, this conclusion can be challenged, in three ways. First, this is the *only* place in the whole New Testament where the name of the nation is used in this way. Though this succession may be deduced from other Scriptures, this is the only clear statement to that effect. It is never sound exegesis to build such an important principle on a solitary verse.

Secondly, the verse is obviously a personal greeting at the end of a letter and not in the earlier didactic (teaching) part of the epistle. In 6:11-18, Paul has taken over from his amanuensis (secretary) and is writing with "large letters," probably because of defective eyesight (4:15, as discussed above). There is no new teaching here but a sharp summary of what he has already said. It is the cross and the new creation it has made possible that are all-important now: "Neither circumcision nor uncircumcision means anything" (6:15, NIV). Undoubtedly, "those who follow this rule" (or "principle" NLT) refers to the irrelevance of circumcision. That is, those who have been so convinced by Paul's teaching and resisted that of his Judaizing opponents.

Thirdly, there is a valid alternative translation of this verse, with rather different implications. The sentence contains two phrases: "those who follow this rule" and "the Israel of God." Do both expressions refer to the same people or are two groups in mind? The answer and the sentence itself hinge on the conjunction in the middle, the Greek word *kai*. It can be translated "even," which means both phrases relate to one group, but 99 times out of 100 it means "and", inferring two groups.

Paul would then be pronouncing a blessing on those for whom circumcision is a matter of indifference *and*, by implication, those to whom it is a matter of importance. Who could this second group be? Obviously, his Judaizing opponents, whom he calls "the circumcision party" (2:12, NIV). It is vital to remember that they were believers, part of the church in Jerusalem. Paul is sure their teaching

313

is mistaken and misleading but he is not writing them off as unbelievers or advocating that they should be excommunicated from the church. They simply had not yet grasped the truth of Gentile admission as Peter had (Acts 10:9-23) and of which Peter had to be bluntly reminded by Paul (Galatians 2:11-16).

This group had every entitlement to be called "the Israel of God," according to Paul's own teaching (Romans 9:6; 11:5). So he includes them in his greeting. It is also possible that Paul has adapted his usual greeting ("grace and peace," Romans 1:7; 1 Corinthians 1:3; 2 Corinthians 1:2) for the occasion to "peace and mercy" – peace for the believers who accept his position on circumcision and mercy for the believers who don't.

Since there is legitimate doubt about the translation, neither interpretation should be ruled out.

Paul's scars (6:17-18)

Paul has now reached the last half inch of his paper and as he writes with his big scrawling writing he notices scars on the back of his hands and on his arms. He puts his hand up and feels his face – there are scars there too. His back is painful. There are scars there as well. Do you know his body was just covered with scars? Wondering how to finish off the letter, he says, "These circumcisers want to scar your bodies to show that you belong to Jesus. Well, I've got all the scars. These are all the marks you need. These are the brands of a slave of Jesus not to be circumcised. I've got these scars and I got them in the service of Jesus. They want to circumcise you because they want to avoid the persecution of the cross. But I've had the persecution of the cross." And truly he had. The backs of his hands would have been scarred as he shielded his face when he was pelted with stones and left for dead. They threw stones at him until they thought they'd killed him and he lay there outside one of the churches in Galatia to whom he was writing. He says, "I've got in my body the scars." He'd been flogged five times. He'd been shipwrecked and pelted with stones. He'd had the Roman rods across his back. He'd had whips beaten against his flesh. His body was scarred from top to bottom. So Paul says, "Look, I've had enough. I've reached the end of my paper ... I've reached the end of my tether. Let nobody interfere with me any more. I've had enough. I've got the marks. Don't interfere with my mission any more. Let no one take away my converts and drag them back into religion. They've left the Gentile religion – don't drag them into the Jewish one. Leave them at the cross. Let no one interfere with my mission. The only marks I want are the ones I've already got. They're the marks gained in the service of Jesus."

How did Paul do it? How did he manage to go through all that and remain sane? We see here the courage of the man, a man struggling with partial blindness and certainly struggling with the scars and the wounds he'd gained in the service of Jesus. Now he was facing this misleading of his own converts. How did he do it? I know: he's told us. He told us when he mentioned his thorn in the flesh. God said to him, "My grace is enough." And so having begun the letter to the Galatians with the words "Grace be to you," he finishes it off with the same amazing word, *grace*. I've paraphrased it as "generous love" because it's a word you can't really translate. It's a word you can't get the full feel of it. It means "God's undeserved favour; his generous love; the love that he pours out on you; his love freely given." *Grace* is one of the most precious words in the Christian vocabulary, and God's grace is found in the person of our Lord Jesus Christ. It is an inward experience. It is experienced in your inmost being and it is a shared experience in the family, "my brothers". "The grace of the Lord Jesus Christ be in your inmost being, my brothers." Amen. So be it: no doubts; no uncertainties. The one thing that you can be absolutely sure about in our world is that at the cross the grace of the Lord Jesus Christ is yours.

EBOOKS

Most books by David Pawson are also available
as ebooks from:

amazon.com and amazon.co.uk Kindle stores.

**For details of foreign language editions
and a full listing of
David Pawson Teaching Catalogue in MP3/DVD
or to purchase David Pawson books in the** UK
please visit:
www.davidpawson.com

Email: info@davidpawsonministry.com

Chinese language books by David Pawson
www.bolbookstore.com
and
www.elimbookstore.com.tw

Printed in Great Britain
by Amazon